BURKE AND PAINE

*On Revolution
and the Rights of Man*

BURKE AND PAINE

On Revolution
and the Rights of Man

ROBERT B. DISHMAN
UNIVERSITY OF NEW HAMPSHIRE

Charles Scribner's Sons
NEW YORK

Printed in the United States of America
SBN684–41227–6
Library of Congress Catalog Card Number 76–126935

Contents

BURKE AND PAINE

*On Revolution
and the Rights of Man*

Editor's Preface

The controversy over the French Revolution in which Edmund
Burke and Thomas Paine played such leading roles may well be, as
Thomas W. Copeland suggests, "the most crucial ideological debate
ever carried on in English." [1] It is certainly the most celebrated.
Both Burke's *Reflections on the Revolution in France* and Paine's
reply in *The Rights of Man* had enormous influence in their day.
Unfortunately, their influence was restricted largely to the audience
which each author had in mind, and, as James T. Boulton has
pointed out, their audiences were quite distinct.[2] Burke addressed
himself through his anonymous "young gentleman" in France to
the "men of light and leading" in England who shared his veneration for the British constitution, such as it then stood. As events
were to prove, they included almost all of the more substantial of
his countrymen except the radicals in his own party and the Non-
conformists who opposed the church establishment. For awhile, at
least, he had little desire to reach the masses in either country; rather,
his appeal was to their "proper chieftains," [3] the "active men in the
state" whom he regarded as "true samples of the mass," [4] i.e. "the
great peers, the leading landed gentlemen, the opulent merchants
and manufacturers, the substantial yeomanry," whom he called "the

natural strength of the kingdom." [5] This is shown not only in the objects of his praise and abuse but in the style of his rhetoric. Even if he had wished to reach a mass audience, his literary allusions, many of them in Latin, and his rich, at times overrich, imagery would have doomed the effort.

Paine, on the other hand, directed his *Rights of Man* to the humbler ranks of men from which he himself had risen. Even if he had been better educated or had merely read more widely, it is doubtful whether his thought or his style would have been much different. He was above all a practical man with an uncommon gift for expressing simple truths, as he saw them, in words which other practical men could understand and accept. This was at once his strength and his weakness as a polemicist. He was able to reach "the farmer, the manufacturer, the merchant, the tradesman, and down through all the occupations of life to the common laborer," [6] who he implied were his intended audience. He had very little appeal to the English ruling classes whose acquiescence, barring revolution, had to be gained if his ideas were not to be proscribed, as indeed they were. Perhaps this was only to have been expected. Though he was not as extreme in his views as many of the French radicals, his influence was much more feared than theirs in the Britain of George III. Still, one suspects that Paine was rejected by the English establishment almost as much for snobbish as for substantive reasons. Paine was no gentleman, and he certainly did not write like one. His language was plain and not always grammatical, his allusions commonplace, and his humor crude and at times uncouth. Though he was as much the conscious artist as Burke, Paine was also much more prone to let his personality intrude itself into his writing. The qualities which endeared him to the English masses were no doubt seen in quite a different light by their "proper chieftains." To most of them, as to Burke, his boldness must have seemed mere brashness, his optimism, foolish presumption, and his pride, sheer vanity.

The fact is that the controversy between Burke and Paine was not truly a debate. Each appealed to a different set of judges who he believed would share—or could be induced to share—his own views and values. Perhaps the emotions which they did so much to arouse in England and France were too strong for any impartial body of judges to be found. If so, that is no longer the case. Most of the "active men of the state" no longer seem so passionate in their feelings for or against the established order. Their sons and daughters, perhaps, but not they. To many of all ages even the issues over which Burke and Paine contended no longer seem relevant; yet this, I suggest, is simply not true. "A certain *quantum* of power must always exist in the community, in some hands, and under some appellation," [7] Burke once observed, and its precise location is as crucial now as it has ever been. So are the questions of how quickly the state is to respond to the need for change, by what criteria, whether of theory or experience, insofar as they are separable, and at what costs to the present and future generations, insofar as they are calculable. These issues are not only timely but timeless, and they will always be the central concern of those who are serious in their study or practice of politics.

All that is needed to restore the Burke-Paine controversy to its original vigor is to free it, as much as possible, from the more transient events to which both men were responding. That task has been undertaken in the present volume. Both the *Reflections* and *The Rights of Man* have been abridged to delete passages which now seem unduly repetitious, irrelevant, or ephemeral. Readers who are familiar with both works in the original hardly need to be told that many such passages are to be found. In Part I of *The Rights of Man* Paine even threw together some observations, as he put it, into a "Miscellaneous Chapter," which he sought to excuse by saying that "Mr. Burke's book is *all* Miscellany." [8] In each work the text has also been rearranged so as to bring ideas and issues into closer confrontation. Though each in its own way is a classic of rhetoric, their organization is likely to strike the reader as careless, if not haphazard. In his *Reflections* Burke is especially vulnerable to this criticism. With some justice Paine could speak of the "disorderly cast" of Burke's genius, which was "a genius at random, and not a genius constituted." Instead of "proceeding with an orderly arrangement" to attack the French Revolution, as he intended, "he has stormed it with a mob of ideas tumbling over and destroying one another. . . . I have now to follow Mr. Burke through a pathless wilderness of rhapsodies, and a sort of descant upon governments, in which he asserts whatever he pleases, on the presumption of its being believed, without offering either evidence or reasons for so doing. . . . As Mr. Burke sometimes speaks of England, sometimes of France, and sometimes of the world, and of government in general, it is difficult to answer his book without apparently meeting him on the same ground." [9] Though the indictment is overdrawn, it is not wholly unjust, and it is no defense, at least it is not a complete defense, to say with Boulton that this "feeling of a grand disorder" about which Paine and others have complained was deliberate and "not the result of careless extravagance on Burke's part." [10] Burke himself soon realized that the length of his book and its apparent disorder kept it from reaching the very audience which was most susceptible to the new revolutionary doctrines, and he gave his consent to two abridgments, in one of which the text was rearranged. In this way not only was the price of the book reduced to enable it to compete more effectively with *The Rights of Man,* the text was purged of those passages which Paine's followers would find most offensive.

Whatever else might be said of it, the present rearrangement at least avoids all such distortion and concealment. Every effort has been made to present the arguments of both men fully and fairly. Though their original works have been abridged and rearranged, nothing essential to their case has been omitted. On the contrary, their argument is more fully developed here than in the original texts, because excerpts have been added, where appropriate, from their other works. The shorter excerpts have been appended as footnotes, together with a few short quotations taken from sections of the two basic works not included in the abridged texts. The longer excerpts have been incorporated as integral parts of the rearranged text, but they are clearly identified. Since *The Rights of Man* is more nearly self-contained than the *Reflections,* it was necessary to draw upon only two of Paine's other works to develop his argument more fully—his *Letter to the Addressers on the Late Proclamation* (1792) and his *Dissertation on First Principles* (1795).

Burke's *Reflections* presented a much more difficult challenge, because the book, as he originally conceived it, was never finished. His "original purpose," he explained late in the book after it had "grown to great length," was to "take a view of the principles of the National Assembly" and to compare them with the "great and fundamental establishments" of the British constitution—the "monarchy, aristocracy, and democracy, as practically they exist." This is confirmed much earlier in the book after he explained why he and all other right-thinking Englishmen intended to "cleave closely" to their establishments and not quarrel with them. "We are resolved to keep an established church, an established monarchy, an established aristocracy, an established democracy, each in the degree it exists, and in no greater. I shall show you presently," he promised the reader, "how much of each of those we possess." [11] Burke made good his promise to show the degree to which the church, the monarchy, and the aristocracy were established in the British constitution, but he had little if anything to say about the democratic part of the establishment. This was most unfortunate because the omission made Burke appear not merely conservative but reactionary, which on balance was not the case. Until the French Revolution became an obsession with him, Burke had staunchly and passionately defended the rights not only of his English and Irish compatriots and their American "brethren" overseas but of the Indian masses as well. It was only after he became convinced that the rights of man, in the abstract, threatened to undermine the other parts of the British establishment that his voice, once so readily raised in support of popular rights, became muted. For Burke's defense of the democratic element of the British constitution, therefore, it is necessary to turn to his earlier works, and this has been done. The section on "The Commons and their Representation" has been drawn largely from his *Address to the Electors of Bristol* (1774) and his speeches in Parliament on the *Duration of Parliaments* (1780), the *Plan for Economical Reform* (1780), and *Reform of Representation of the Commons in Parliament* (1782). Selections have also been included from two of Burke's other writings which deal directly with the Revolution. Part of the discussion of "An Aristocracy of Wealth and Talent" and of "Majorities and Minorities" and all of the section on "Rights and Duties" have been taken from *An Appeal from the New to the Old Whigs* (1791). Similarly, part of the discussion of "Resistance and Revolution" has been taken from Burke's long private letter to Charles-Jean-François Depont in November, 1789. The inclusion of these writings is especially appropriate. Depont was, of course, the "very young gentleman at Paris" to whom Burke addressed his *Reflections*. The *Appeal* was in part a reply to Part I of *The Rights of Man,* and it provoked a partial reply from Paine in Part II of his work.

Inevitably something of value has been lost in the process of abridging and rearranging the original texts. The reader will look in vain for Paine's often dramatic narrative tracing the origins of the Revolution and describing the storming of the Bastille and the "expedition to Versailles" to take the royal family into custody. Nor will he find Burke's detailed criticisms of the more transient features of the new French regime—its subdivision into seemingly "separate" and "incoherent republics," its contradictory scheme for providing representation in the legislature, the reorganization of its executive and judicial powers, the reconstruction and "debauchery" of its army, and its unorthodox system of finances. Yet it must be recognized that their accounts of both historical and contemporary events was partial in both senses.

•

For a more complete and objective understanding of the Revolution, the reader is advised to turn to one of the standard histories of the period. Georges Lefebvre's *The French Revolution from Its Origins to 1793* (New York: Columbia University Press, 1962) would provide a good introduction. But even with this more intimate knowledge about the French Revolution, the reader is not in a position to assess the impact which Burke and Paine had on their contemporaries unless he reads their books in their entirety. Fortunately, both Burke's *Reflections* and Paine's *The Rights of Man* are available, unabridged, in a number of inexpensive editions still in print. At least two paperback editions carry the full text of both works. In this volume I have used Philip S. Foner's *The Complete Writings of Thomas Paine* (New York: Citadel Press, 1945–46, 2 volumes) as the source for *The Rights of Man* and all but a few of Paine's other writings. Burke's works are much more widely scattered. Even his public writings have never been compiled into a single comprehensive and authoritative edition. Of the many editions issued to date, the most recent was published in 1906, and it includes only the better known of Burke's speeches in and out of Parliament. The rest must still be gleaned from such contemporary sources as Hansard's *Parliamentary History*. In the absence of any standard edition of Burke's works, I have had to use a number of sources for the text of his voluminous writings on the American and French revolutions. Most of the quotations from the less accessible of Burke's public papers have been taken from the Bohn Edition of *The Works of Edmund Burke*, 8 volumes (London: George Bell & Sons, 1900–01). Two more carefully edited and recently published sources were used for the text of Burke's best known public addresses on America and France: *Burke: Selected Writings and Speeches on America* (1964) and *Burke: Reflections on the Revolution in France* (1955), both edited by Professor Thomas H. D. Mahoney and published by Bobbs-Merrill in the Library of Liberal Arts. Fortunately, most of Burke's private letters and papers have been recently compiled by a team of Burkean scholars headed by Professor Thomas W. Copeland and published by Cambridge University and the University of Chicago under the title, *The Correspondence of Edmund Burke*, eight volumes to date (1968–1969). I am indebted to the publishers for permission to include the excerpt from Burke's private letter to Depont in the section on "Resistance and Revolution." I am also grateful to Professors Max and Fredelle Maynard of the University of New Hampshire, to Dr. David G. Nicholls of the University of the West Indies (St. Augustine, Trinidad), and to Mr. Joel Benjamin of the University of Guyana for their careful reading of the text and their helpful suggestions. Any errors of fact or judgment which remain are, of course, my own.

NOTES ON FOOTNOTES

Two types of footnotes are used in Part I, "The Consecrated State of Edmund Burke." Those which appear at the bottom of the page where the reference occurs, designated either by an asterisk (*) or a dagger (†), have been drawn from Burke's own writings. Some are taken from the *Reflections* itself, either from Burke's own footnotes to the original text or from passages in the original text not included in this abridgment. Most, however, are short quotations, excerpted from Burke's other writings, which illustrate, extend, or, in a few instances, qualify the argument in the *Reflections*. The source, in each case, is clearly indicated: e.g., the Library of Liberal Arts edition of the *Reflections on the Revolution in France* (New York: Bobbs-Merrill, 1955) and Bohn's Standard Library edition of *Burke's Works* (London: George Bell & Sons, 1900–01).

The numbered footnotes are by the editor; they will be found on pages 283–93. The English translation of the quotations by Cicero and Horace has been taken from the Loeb Classical Library.

Two types of footnotes also are used in Part II "Thomas Paine on the Rights of Man." Those which appear at the bottom of the page where the reference occurs, designated either by an asterisk (*) or a dagger (†), have been drawn from Paine's own writings. Some are taken from *The Rights of Man* itself, either from Paine's own footnotes to the original text identified only by the author's name in brackets or from passages in the original text not included in this abridgement. Most, however, are short quotations excerpted from Paine's other writings, which illustrate, extend, or, in a few instances, qualify the argument in *The Rights of Man*. The source in each case is *The Complete Writings of Thomas Paine,* ed. Philip S. Foner (New York: Citadel Press, 1945).

The numbered footnotes are by the editor; they will be found on pages 295–309.

Although abridged and rearranged, both basic texts and their accompanying footnotes follow the original. Only the spelling and, less consistently, the punctuation have been revised as an aid to the modern American reader.

Robert B. Dishman

Durham, New Hampshire
July, 1970

PRELUDE
TO THE GREAT
DEBATE

Prelude
to the Great
Debate

"It is an age of revolution," Thomas Paine once said of his time, "in which every thing may be looked for." [1] So it was—and so it continues to be—thanks in no small part to the two great revolutions in which Paine took part, the first in America, the other in France. No one has ever doubted that the revolution in France was a cataclysmic event in Western history. To Edmund Burke, the British statesman, the "transactions" across the Channel precipitated "a great crisis, not of the affairs of France alone, but of all Europe, perhaps of more than Europe." [2] As he foresaw, the "armed doctrine" of the Revolution soon spread throughout Europe and beyond, and no *ancien régime* has felt secure ever since. Even more than its Marxist offspring, the French Revolution in its proletarian phase is still the prototype for ideological revolutions against social injustice. Nor did the generation of Americans which fought for their independence ever doubt that they were making a revolution. Certainly Tom Paine did not. "The independence of America, considered merely as a separation from England, would have been a matter but of little importance, had it not been accompanied by a revolution in the principles and practice of governments," he wrote. "She made a stand, not for herself only, but for the world,

and looked beyond the advantages herself could receive." [3] Today
many Americans seem almost embarrassed at the suggestion that
even now, almost two centuries after the event, the American Revolution has not yet run its course. Yet, as Arnold J. Toynbee has
pointed out, this is indeed the case. The American Revolution has
become world wide and the Old World as well as the New is "swarm-
ing with its progeny." [4] Whether Americans like it or not, their
Revolution is still the prototype for nationalist revolts against foreign domination—in Vietnam no less than in Hungary. The shot
fired in 1775 has indeed been heard 'round the world.

REVOLUTION AND COUNTER-REVOLUTION

In the Anglo-American political tradition two men, above all
others, Paine and Burke, are associated with revolution and counter-
revolution. [5] Though they were later to quarrel over the French
Revolution, they were not far apart on the issue of American independence. Nor is this surprising, though both men, in a sense, were
English, one by birth, the other by adoption. Paine had found in
America opportunities for advancement which were almost completely lacking in his native England. His father was a staymaker of
such modest means that young Tom had to leave school at thirteen.
For the next twelve years he practiced his father's trade, but he was
too restless and ambitious to be content with making corsets for
the rest of his life. While sixteen or seventeen, he served aboard a
privateer, but he soon found that a seaman's lot was even less to
his liking. Eight years later he left a shop of his own to enter the
excise service as a tax collector. Eventually, this interlude proved
also to be a blind alley. He was dismissed after three years, and
while waiting to be reinstated, he tried his hand at teaching school.
His second stint as excise officer lasted six years, and when it ended,
he was worse off financially than he had been before. Excisemen in
those days were paid only fifty pounds a year, and if they travelled,
as Paine did, they also had the expense of keeping a horse. In 1772,
after four years' service, he had to sell all his household furniture,
stock in trade, and other property to satisfy his creditors. In these
straitened circumstances he wrote an appeal to Parliament to raise
salaries in the excise service. "No argument can satisfy the feelings
of hunger or abate the edge of appetite. Nothing tends to a greater
corruption of manners and principles than a too great distress of
circumstances. . . . He who never was an hungered may argue finely

on the subjection of his appetite; and he who never was distressed, may harangue as beautifully on the power of principle. But poverty, like grief, has an incurable deafness, which never hears; the oration loses all its edge; and 'To be, or not to be' becomes the only question." [6] It was an able brief which revealed Paine's sympathy for the underdog and his talent for advocacy, but it seemed to have had little effect save perhaps to have attracted him to the unfavorable attention of his superiors. In any event, within two years he was once again dismissed from the service, so he decided to quit England for America.

PAINE IN AMERICA

This seems not to have been a difficult decision for Paine to make. He saw little hope of advancing himself as a teacher and no prospect at all of regaining his position with the government. Nor was he burdened with family responsibilities though he was thirty-seven at the time. He and his wife had just separated amicably after three years of a childless and apparently Platonic marriage. In America he hoped at first to be able to establish an academy of the kind at which he had taught in London. Still, he might never have left England but for a meeting with Benjamin Franklin, then in London as agent for Pennsylvania. Franklin took a liking to Paine and gave him an introduction to his son-in-law in Philadelphia. Paine was "very well recommended" to him, Franklin wrote, as "an ingenious, worthy young man," who would make a "very capable" clerk or assistant tutor in a school, or assistant surveyor. In October, 1774, Paine sailed for America, and after a nine-week voyage in which he nearly died of typhus, he arrived in Philadelphia. Franklin's letter was all that he needed to find a job more suited to his talents than corsetmaker, tax collector, or clerk. For a few weeks during his convalescence he was engaged as a tutor, but he soon became a free-lance journalist and editor. In his very first article, he turned his back on the Old World in favor of the New. Soon he became embroiled in the great moral, political, and social issues of the day. Slavery and the slave trade were the first to stir his wrath. It was wicked enough, he argued, for nations to enslave the prisoners they took in war. "But to go to nations with whom there is no war, who have no way provoked, without farther design of conquest, purely to catch inoffensive people, like wild beasts, for slaves, is an height of outrage against humanity and justice, that seems left by heathen nations to be practised by pretended Christians. How

shameful are all attempts to color and excuse it!" [7] Although other
Christian nations were no less guilty, Paine was particularly harsh
with Britain for her leading part in the slave trade and for her treatment of the Indians, both east and west. "When I reflect on these,"
he wrote in October, 1775, "I hesitate not for a moment to believe
that the Almighty will finally separate America from Britain. Call
it independence or what you will, if it is the cause of God and humanity, it will go on." [8]

Separation from Britain came sooner than Paine foresaw, and in
no small measure because of his efforts. In January, 1776, scorning
any attempt at reconciliation, he sounded a call to arms in his famous tract *Common Sense*. Although it was not the first such call,
it was unquestionably the most forthright and effective. By Paine's
own account, which was not always reliable where his vanity was
concerned, 150,000 copies were sold in America alone—"the greatest
sale that any performance ever had since the use of letters—exclusive
of the great run it had in England and Ireland." [9] Unlike those on
both sides of the Atlantic who believed that America's quarrel was
only with Parliament, Paine laid much of the blame on the King, as
though he ruled without ministers. Not content to castigate George
III as the "royal brute of Great Britain," and a "hardened, sullen-
tempered Pharaoh," he paid his disrespect to the "so-much boasted
Constitution" in which Englishmen took so much pride. Granting
that "it was noble for the dark and slavish times in which it was
erected," it was based, he insisted, on "two ancient tyrannies"—
monarchy and aristocracy—"compounded with some new republican
materials"—an elective House of Commons "on whose virtue depends the freedom of England." In this mixed system, he declared,
the "overbearing part" was the Crown. "Why is the Constitution
sickly, but because monarchy hath poisoned the Republic; the
Crown has engrossed the Commons." That individuals were no
doubt safer in England than in some other countries he conceded,
"but the will of the king is as much the law of the land in Britain
as in France, with this difference, that instead of proceeding directly
from his mouth, it is handed to the people under the formidable
shape of an act of Parliament." [10]

Even more effective than Paine's invective, one suspects, was
his naked appeal to national self-interest. To the argument that
America had flourished—and would continue to flourish—under
British rule, he replied that nothing could be more fallacious. "We
may as well assert that because a child has thrived upon milk, that it
is never to have meat, or that the first twenty years of our lives is

to become a precedent for the next twenty." To the suggestion that Britain was the mother country and entitled to the respect due a parent, he scoffed, "Then the more shame upon her conduct. Even brutes do not devour their young, nor savages make war upon their families." Besides, he pointed out, "Europe, and not England, is the parent country of America. This new world hath been the asylum for the persecuted lovers of civil and religious liberty from *every part* of Europe. Hither have they fled, not from the tender embraces of the mother, but from the cruelty of the monster." To those—like his patron Benjamin Franklin, though his name was not mentioned —who once dreamed of a British Commonwealth in which America would be a full partner, Paine asserted that not a single advantage would be gained and that only "injuries and disadvantages . . . without number" would result. "It is the true interest of America to steer clear of European contentions, which she never can do, while, by her dependence on Britain, she is made the make-weight in the scale of British politics." Those who favored conciliation, he claimed, fell into four categories: "interested men, who are not to be trusted, weak men who *cannot* see, prejudiced men who will not see, and a certain set of moderate men" who by thinking better of the European world than it deserves will be "the cause of more calamities to this continent than all the other three." To these "men of passive tempers" Paine insisted that anything short of separation and independence "is mere patchwork, that it can afford no lasting felicity, that it is leaving the sword to our children, and shrinking back at a time when a little more, a little further, would have rendered this continent the glory of the earth." His conclusion was that "everything that is right or reasonable pleads for separation. The blood of the slain, the weeping voice of nature cries, 'TIS TIME TO DEPART." [11]

Paine was to make an even greater contribution to American independence before it was finally gained. Unlike the *philosophes* who were then undermining the *ancien régime* in France, the author who called himself "Common Sense" had little use at first for speculative theories. Instead, from the start, he plunged boldly and bodily into the revolutionary movement. Early in the war he served in the Pennsylvania militia, then as General Nathaniel Greene's aide-de-camp, and finally as an official observer with Washington's army. Next he turned his attention to diplomatic affairs. From August, 1777, until January, 1779, he was secretary to Congress' Committee for Foreign Affairs, from which post he was able to follow closely the negotiations which resulted in the alliance with France. But

Paine's greatest fame was won not as a soldier or diplomat but as a propagandist. Throughout the war, not only in the early years, the American cause suffered serious setbacks, and each time Paine was ready with his facile pen to bolster morale. In all, he wrote sixteen tracts bearing the title *Crisis,* each signed by the name he had made famous, "Common Sense." The tone was set in the opening words of the first number, written soon after Washington's defeat at Long Island. "These are the times that try men's souls. The summer soldier and the sunshine patriot will, in this crisis, shrink from the service of their country; but he that stands it *now* deserves the love and thanks of man and woman. Tyranny, like hell, is not easily conquered; yet we have this consolation with us, that the harder the conflict, the more glorious the triumph. What we obtain too cheap, we esteem too lightly; it is dearness only that gives every thing its value." [12] It was a theme which he was to repeat time and again. "Those who expect to reap the blessings of freedom, must, like men, undergo the fatigues of supporting it. . . . It is not a field of a few acres of ground, but a cause, that we are defending, and whether we defeat the enemy in one battle, or by degrees, the consequences will be the same." [13]

These were bold, even brash words, but in the war of words the enemy was clearly bested, both at home and abroad. For Sir William Howe, the British commander-in-chief whom he called "the tool of a miserable tyrant," Paine had only cold contempt. "Let me ask, sir, what great exploits have you performed? . . . I know of no one action of yours that can be styled masterly." Instead, his movements, "in and out, backward and forward, round and round," reminded Paine of "the labors of a puppy pursuing his tail; the end is still at the same distance, and all the turnings round must be done over again." And for his part in circulating counterfeit Continental bills in New York, Howe deserved the same fate that forgers met in England, death on the gibbet. "America is anxious to bestow her funeral favors upon you." [14] Paine was no more respectful of the British army. "England was never famous by land; her officers have generally been suspected of cowardice, have more of the air of a dancing master than a soldier." Nevertheless, it has been Britain's folly, he said, "to suppose herself more powerful than she really is," when, in fact, for more than a century she had had to rely in every war upon German mercenary troops. "In all the wars which you have formerly been concerned in," he told Lord Howe, Sir William's brother, "you had only armies to contend with; in this case you have both an army and a country to combat with. . . . Were you to garrison the places you might march over, in order to secure their subjection, (for remember you can do it by no other means,) your army would be like a stream of water running to nothing. By the time you extended from New York to Virginia, you would be reduced to a string of drops not capable of hanging together; while we, by retreating from state to state, like a river turning back upon itself, would acquire strength in the same proportion as you lost it, and in the end be capable of overwhelming you. . . . [T]he more surface you spread over, the thinner you will be, and the easier wiped away." [15]

Toward those Americans who did not share his zeal for independence, Paine was at first inclined to be tolerant. "I am not for declaring war with every man that appears not so warm as myself: difference of constitution, temper, habit of speaking, and many other things, will go a great way in fixing the outward character of a man, yet simple honesty may remain at bottom." [16] But as the military situation worsened, his views hardened toward those who were lukewarm or indifferent to the American cause. The time had come, he decided, for Americans to declare themselves. "A person, to use a trite phrase, must be a Whig or a Tory in a lump. . . . He cannot be a Whig in *this* stage, and a Tory in *that*. If he says he is against the united independence of the continent, he is to all intents and purposes against her in all the rest; because *this last* comprehends the whole." There was a simple "touchstone," he said, "to try men by: *He that is not a supporter of the independent States of America in the same degree that his religious and political principles would suffer him to support the government of any other country, of which he called himself a subject, is, in the American sense of the word* A TORY; *and the instant that he endeavors to bring his toryism into practice, he becomes* A TRAITOR." Some Tories professed to be against independence from "*some kind of principle*," though Paine doubted whether this were in fact the case; most of them, he was sure, were opposed because of "*avarice, down-right villainy, and lust of personal power.*" [17] The only cure for Toryism of the latter cast, he insisted, was to test it and to tax it.

The test which he proposed was to require every citizen to foreswear all allegiance to the Crown. Those who refused to do so, he argued, would stand exposed as enemies of American independence and taxed accordingly. If they were unwilling to support the Revolution with the "*best services*" within their power to provide, they deserved to have their property taxed heavily to indemnify the patriots for their losses.[18] In most states the Tories were treated even more harshly than Paine had proposed. Those who would not take the oath were usually fined and deprived of the right to vote and hold office, and, in some states, even denied access to the courts to protect their rights. In many states the larger Tory estates were confiscated outright. In a few states, doctors, lawyers, and teachers were not allowed to practice their profession. Nor was it safe for Tories to complain publicly about their treatment except, of course, in those areas under effective British control, because in every state except Georgia, South Carolina and perhaps New York, they were greatly outnumbered by those who were either ardent patriots or largely indifferent. Eventually some 75,000 to 80,000 Tories were driven into an exile from which very few returned. In almost every state they comprised much of the social establishment if not the ruling elite—i.e., many, if not most, of the largest landowners, the leading merchants (except perhaps in Boston, Philadelphia, and Charleston), the wealthiest planters (except in Virginia and perhaps North Carolina), the most eminent lawyers and doctors, the Anglican clergy, and, of course, the royal officials. To this limited extent the American war of independence was a social as well as a political revolution.[19]

Paine addressed himself also to his former countrymen, the people of England. "I know what England is, and what America is," he declared, "and from the compound of knowledge, am better enabled to judge of the issue than what the king or any of his ministers can be." The plain truth, as he saw it, was that "America is above your reach. She is at least your equal in the world, and her independence neither rests upon your consent, nor can it be prevented by your arms." Why is it, he asked, you have not conquered us? His answer was "Either the means in your power are insufficient, or the measures ill-planned; either the execution has been bad, or the thing attempted impracticable; or, to speak more emphatically, either you are not able or heaven is not willing." Even if this were not the case, what advantages, he asked, would be gained by conquering America? Certainly none, he said, to the merchants and manufacturers who were the "great bulwark" of the nation. "War never can be the interest of a trading nation, any more than quarreling can be profitable to a man in business. But to make war with those who trade with us, is like setting a bull-dog upon a customer at the shop-door." [20] So far, he pointed out, England had been spared the miseries of war. "You knew not what it was to be alarmed at midnight with an armed enemy in the streets. You were strangers to the distressing scene of a family in flight, and to the thousand restless cares and tender sorrows that incessantly arose. To see women and children wandering in the severity of winter, with the broken remains of a well furnished house, and seeking shelter in every crib and hut, were matters that you had no conception of. You knew not what it was to stand by and see your goods chopped for fuel, and your beds ripped to pieces to make packages for plunder. . . . Yet these are but the fainter sufferings of war, when compared with carnage and slaughter, the miseries of a military hospital, or a town in flames." But England was no longer safe from attack. A combined French-Spanish fleet was now prepared to challenge the British navy in its own waters, and Captain John Paul Jones had been so bold as to raid the English and Irish coasts. Clearly it was now possible for invasion to be turned against the invaders and for America's miseries to become England's. This was a prospect at which every Englishman ought to tremble, because it would be "far more dreadful there than in America." If invasion comes, "you will have neither their extended wilderness to fly to, their cause to comfort you, nor their hope to rest upon." Paine's message was clear, if not entirely credible. "Your present king and ministry will be the ruin of you; and you had better risk a revolution and call a Congress, than be thus led on from madness to despair, and from despair to ruin. America has set you the example, and you may follow it and be free." [21]

Paine addressed himself to Parliament in quite a different vein. Though he had only contempt for the king and the House of Lords, he respected the House of Commons as the only republican part of the British constitution. Nevertheless, Parliament was not without blame for the problems which beset both England and America. The war had originated, Paine maintained, over the "pretence" that Parliament had a "legislative right over America." That claim was clearly asserted in the Declaratory Act of 1766 which affirmed Parliament's "full power and authority to make laws and statutes of sufficient force and validity to bind the colonies and people of America . . . in all cases whatsoever." If "being *bound in that manner* is not slavery," Paine declared, "then is there not such a thing as slavery upon earth. Even the expression is impious; for so unlimited a power can belong only to God." [22] If Parliament expected to vindicate its claim to such sweeping authority by supporting the Crown in its war against America, it was likely to be disappointed. In the event America were to be conquered, the Crown alone would triumph because both the Army and the defeated colonies would be subject to its control, not that of Parliament. So, at least, the king and his ministers might argue, Paine suggested, and the result would be a "new and interesting opposition between the Parliament and the Crown." [23] This was a very shrewd thrust aimed at the Whig minority in Parliament. To their credit, as Paine was well aware, the Whigs had shown their friendship for America by opposing the harsher policies of the Crown, yet even they held two "erroneous notions." One was the opinion that "America would relish measures under *their* administration, which she would not from the present cabinet." Early in the dispute, this belief may have had "some degree of foundation," but now, he said, it served only to prolong the war. The other was the assumption, shared by many Whigs, that America's independence was still an open question, "whereas the only question that can come under their determination is whether they will accede to it or not." [24]

BURKE ON AMERICA

The best-known member of the Whig Opposition in Parliament, at least in America, was Edmund Burke. Though born in Ireland and educated at Trinity College in Dublin, Burke had come to London as a young man to seek his fortune. After studying law to please his father, he found writing much more to his liking and set out on a literary and journalistic career which soon thrust him into the politics of the day. His interest in America seems to have been first aroused by his collaboration with his relative William Burke on a two-volume work published in 1757 under the title *An Account of the European Settlements in America.* The book was well received, and went through a number of editions. Within a year he became an editor of the *Annual Register,* a review of national and international affairs in which the American colonies played an increasingly conspicuous role. Though he was to hold the position for the next thirty years, it brought him neither fame nor fortune. Indeed, he made it a point later in his career to conceal his association with the review, so lowly esteemed were the journalists of the day. Soon, however, his great talent and engaging manner brought him to the favorable attention of some of the leading literary, artistic, and political figures of the day. In 1764 he was one of the first to join Dr. Samuel Johnson's famous Literary Club whose members included Sir Joshua Reynolds, Oliver Goldsmith, David Garrick, Richard Brinsley Sheridan, and James Boswell. In 1765 he began a long association with the Marquess of Rockingham, leader of one of the factions or "connections" which then comprised the Whig party, though it was hardly a party in the modern sense. From that moment

Burke's political career prospered. He first served Rockingham as his private secretary during the first of the several brief periods when the Rockingham Whigs controlled the British government. Within six months he was made a member of Parliament from Wendover. Already, as Burke was later to remark, Britain's relations with America had become "the most important and delicate object of parliamentary attention." [25]

It was only during the first Rockingham ministry (1765–66) that Burke was in a position to influence British policy toward America. Thereafter, throughout almost all of his long parliamentary career, he was a member of the Opposition. Toward the end of the war, to be sure, the Rockingham Whigs regained power briefly, but by that time America had for all practical purposes won its independence. Prior to 1764, British imperial policy, as Burke saw it, had been one of "wise and salutary neglect," [26] though "neglect" is hardly the term to describe the various mercantile measures which restricted the colonies' economic development. Not only were American merchants barred from buying goods brought in foreign ships, planters were not allowed to sell their cotton, tobacco, sugar, rice and indigo in the lucrative Dutch, German, Scandinavian, and Russian markets because this trade was reserved for English merchants. Restrictions were also placed on the woolens, hats, and finished iron products which the colonies were allowed to manufacture. Not that mercantilism was entirely one-sided in the advantages which it conferred; American shipbuilders and shipowners prospered under the policy. As long as the colonies were allowed to control their own finances, they were ready to accept the restrictions on their trade, especially those which were not rigorously enforced. At least there was no serious and concerted opposition to British rule until after the costly Seven Years' War (1756–63). Throughout the war the colonial governments had employed their own militia against France and her Indian allies and taxed themselves toward its support. Nevertheless, the Grenville ministry which took office in 1764 was determined to make the American colonies contribute more directly and regularly in support of the Crown. First, by the Sugar Act (1764) it clamped down on the collection of the import duty on molasses which the colonists had been largely able to evade through smuggling. Next by the Quartering Act (1765) it required each colony to house and supply all British troops within its borders. Finally, in the Stamp Act of 1765, it required virtually every document from legal papers of every description to newspapers, almanacs, and college diplomas to be affixed by a revenue

stamp. The Sugar Act, standing alone, might not have aroused much
controversy, because having previously accepted the imposition of
customs duties, the colonists were in no position to challenge their
collection. The Quartering Act was resented because the only apparent need for British troops, as opposed to the militia, was to
put down smuggling, but at least it was not openly resisted except
in New York. Not so, however, the Stamp Act. From the start it
aroused widespread and effective opposition on the ground, among
others, that the colonies had been taxed without their consent, i.e.,
without representation in Parliament. Before the act could take
effect, nine colonies sent delegates to a national congress to take concerted action in protesting the tax. In Massachusetts and elsewhere,
agents were forcibly prevented from selling the stamps, and many
were intimidated into resigning. In Boston a mob wrecked the
homes of the stamp distributor, the comptroller of the customs, and
even the lieutenant governor.

Burke reacted to these events with a tolerance which he tended
to reserve for Americans. As a patriotic Englishman, though one who
was never allowed to forget his Irish origins, he deplored "the insolence of the mutinous spirits in America." As a loyal member of
Parliament he was distressed that one of its laws, even one not to his
liking, should meet with such "universal disobedience and open
resistance." Yet as a zealous party man, he was much more critical
of the Tory ministers whose policies had aroused so much discontent
in America and distress to the "whole trading interest of the empire."
The spirit of that interest, he declared, was pervasive, "always qual-
ifying and often controlling every general idea of constitution and
government." Those who rely upon "the mere abstract principles of
government or even upon those of our own ancient constitution, will
be often misled." The "great object" for which the colonies were
founded was a system of trade which was at once extensive, intricate,
and "wholly new to the world." Policies dealing with that trade were
most likely to be sound, therefore, when they are "drawn from its
actual circumstances," not from the arguments of "the most respectable authorities, ancient or modern" or "the clearest maxims drawn
from the experiences of other states and empires." To regulate trade
with America was a difficult task because "a multitude of restraints
very alien from the spirit of liberty" had to be imposed upon a
people "of a high and free spirit." There could be no doubt as to
England's *right* to impose "all manner of restraints"; the only question, he insisted, was whether it was wise or expedient to do so.

"People must be governed in a manner agreeable to their temper and disposition, and men of free character and spirit must be ruled with at least some condescension to this spirit and character," indeed, "by every indulgence that can by any means be reconciled to our interest." [27]

The "indulgence" which Burke and his party granted to America in 1766 was to repeal the Stamp Act. They were prepared to go even farther. Since there was no practicable way for the colonies to be represented actually in Parliament, they should be allowed, as before, to tax themselves through their own legislative assemblies. To Burke, no idea was more "contemptible" than to try to get any revenue from Americans "but by their free and most cheerful consent." Parliament, to be sure, would retain its own taxing power, but it would never be used in the first instance or as a source of revenue. (In all its deliberations concerning America, the Rockingham ministry was guided by two ideas, Burke was later to say—"to take trade as the primary end and revenue but as a very subordinate consideration.") [28] But with this concession to the liberty of America came also an insistence on its subordination. The American colonies were part of a great empire, "composed of a vast mass of heterogeneous governments, all more or less free and popular in their forms." At the head of this empire sat the British Parliament, "as from the throne of heaven." Her "superintendence" was needed, Burke later explained, because individually, the colonial governments could "neither preserve mutual peace, nor hope for mutual justice, nor effectually afford mutual assistance." As long as they were "equal to the common ends of their institution," they need have no fear that Parliament would intrude. But he was no less sure, as the events in America had already shown, that it would be necessary, on occasion, for Parliament to "coerce the negligent, to restrain the violent, and to aid the weak and deficient by the overruling plenitude of her power." [29] It was in this view of the needs of empire that the Rockingham government enacted the Declaratory Act to which Tom Paine had taken such strong exception. This, then, was how Burke and his party sought to reconcile the liberty of America with its subordination: Parliament, "in her imperial character," would have unlimited power to "bind the colonies and people of America . . . in all cases whatsoever," but for reasons of expediency, equity, and lenity, in Burke's words, she would not use that power to tax the colonies as a source of revenue. Whether all this could be reconciled in "legal speculation," Burke professed not to care. "It is reconciled in policy, and politics ought to be adjusted not to human reasonings but to human nature, of which the reason is but a part, and by no means the greatest part." [30]

If this policy had prevailed America might have continued to accept subordination under British rule, but it was not to be. The Rockingham ministry fell after slightly more than a year in office, and the governments which followed were less willing to make allowance for human nature. One of the first acts of the Chatham ministry was to restore some of the revenue from America which had been lost by the repeal of the Stamp Act. Under the Townshend Acts (1767) new import duties were imposed on tea, glass, paper, and painters' colors, strict measures were taken for their enforcement, and the revenue was used to pay the salaries of royal officials and to support the British army in America. Customs duties were, of course, no innovation in America, but never before had so many imports been taxed or their collection so tightly enforced. The resistance was as determined, if not as widespread, as it had been against the Stamp Act, especially in Massachusetts. In that "obnoxious colony," as Burke was later to call it, four of the new customs commissioners were forced to flee to a British man-of-war for protection. There, too, the General Court as the legislature was, and still is, styled was ordered dissolved for denying Parliament's right to tax the colonies without their consent and urging the other legislatures to do likewise. At its prompting, too, another boycott was organized along the entire seaboard against the importation of British goods, and, as before, it proved more effective than either violence or remonstrance. Burke, as usual, saw more clearly than anyone, unless it was the ailing Chatham, that Britain and America had reached an impasse in their relations. "The Americans," he told the House in 1769, "have made a discovery, or think they have made one, that we mean to oppress them: we have made a discovery, or think we have made one, that they intend to rise in rebellion against us. . . . [W]e know not how to advance; they know not how to retreat. . . . Some party must give way." [31]

The North ministry, which took office in 1770, began its administration on a conciliatory note. It repealed all of the Townshend duties except one; the tea duty, though reduced, was retained as a symbol of Parliament's right to tax the colonies with or without their consent. In America the response for the most part was favorable. Even though the duty on tea remained, it was largely evaded through widespread and systematic smuggling. Except for such sporadic incidents as the Boston Massacre in 1770 and the seizure of the British sloop *Gaspée* two years later, popular unrest appeared to subside. Once again, however, the insensitivity of a British government plunged the colonies into turmoil. The East India Company, which Burke was later to call "a state in the disguise of a merchant," [32] had been brought to the verge of bankruptcy, in part because of the American boycott. With Parliament's approval the company was authorized to ship its tea directly to America and thus avoid the duty which previously it had been required to pay in England. In this way the East India tea could be sold in America through merchants favored by the company at a lower price, despite the Townshend tax, than Dutch tea could be smuggled into the country. Instead of rejoicing at the prospect of cheaper tea, the colonies saw the measure as a sinister attempt by the Crown to get them to pay the Townshend duty and, in doing so, to recognize Parliament's authority to tax them to raise revenue. By one ill-considered act the North ministry succeeded, where all others had failed, in stirring many of the wealthy seaboard merchants to make common cause with the radicals. Their strategy was to keep the East India tea from reaching the market, because once there, it was sure to be bought because of its lower price. In most ports the company's ships were simply forced to return without discharging their cargo, but in Boston the ships were actually boarded and the tea chests dumped into the harbor. The British government was quick to retaliate. The port of Boston was closed to all shipping until the tea was paid for, the provincial government was replaced by one more responsive to the Crown, the Quartering Act was stiffened, and the rebels were warned that they might be tried for treason in England before a special commission.[33] Within a year the American colonies were in open revolt.

These developments were distressing to Burke, all the more because of two changes in his own circumstances. From virtually the day he took his seat in the House of Commons, he had made a name for himself as a brilliant orator and as a loyal and effective party man. Though his personal finances were often at loose ends, he served his party as its organizer. As Ernest Barker has pointed out, "he suggested policies, drafted petitions, arranged for meetings, looked after elections, arranged everything, and goaded everybody." [34] It is not surprising, then, that in 1770 he was asked by the New York legislative assembly to be its London agent or lobbyist in Parliament. It is somewhat surprising that he not only accepted the position but held it until Britain and America were at war. Even by the loose parliamentary standards of the day, the arrangement must have appeared somewhat irregular, though he was not the only member to hold such a position. Yet, as Thomas W. Copeland suggests, Burke had his reasons, and they were not in any sense venal. As a member of Parliament, he received no salary at all for his services, and as a person of modest, indeed straitened, means, he was in need of a regular income from some source, and this his agency provided—£500 a year to which £140 was ultimately added for expenses. His views toward America, moreover, had been fixed long before 1770; only his enemies, for which he never lacked, could believe that he was being bribed to support the colonial cause. Finally, his party would remain out of power for many years— though this, to be sure, neither Burke nor the New York Assembly could have foreseen—so he was in no position to influence colonial policy directly.[35] In any event, Burke proved to be as independent-minded as a lobbyist as he was a legislator. In 1774, for example, he warned his New York employers that their "only *true friends*" in England would insist on "the proper subordination of America, as a fundamental incontrovertible Maxim, in the Government of this Empire." At the same time he assured them that their subordination was in no way "derogatory to the real essential Rights of mankind which tend to their peace and prosperity, and without the Enjoyment of which no honest Man can wish the dependence of One country upon another." It was most unfortunate, he thought, that the advice of "Temperate Men"—meaning himself and his friends —had been "little attended to" on his side of the Atlantic "and rather less on the other." [36]

Burke's sympathy for America also played a part in his shift in parliamentary constituencies in 1774. During his first eight years in the House he had been a member from Wendover, a pocket borough controlled by Lord Verney. In that seat Burke had no need to nurse his constituency except at election time, and even then his campaign expenses were borne by his patron. But Verney suffered severe financial losses, so Burke was obliged to find another seat. Rather than impose on a far richer patron—the Marquess of Rockingham —to find him another "safe" constituency, he accepted an invitation to stand as a Whig candidate from Bristol. In that thriving seaport, which Burke called "the second city in the kingdom," he had to undergo the rigors of a genuinely popular election for the first and only time in his long parliamentary career. As before, however, his election expenses, necessarily heavy, had to be borne by others— this time by a group of well-to-do merchants who had been attracted to Burke by his sound Whig principles. With their support, he was elected to the House largely on the strength of his reputation as a parliamentary orator and a friend of America. To his new constituents, friendship for America meant continued opposition to the policies of the Crown which had seriously hurt their trade with America. But this arrangement, apparently so advantageous on both sides, was not to continue past a single term.[37] The electors of Bristol grew tired of a member who made such a point of asserting his independence even to the point of paying only a rare visit to the city. "You choose a member, indeed"; he had told them even before taking his seat, "but when you have chosen him he is not a member of Bristol, but he is a member of *Parliament. . . .* Your representative owes you, not his industry only, but his judgment, and he betrays, instead of serving you, if he sacrifices it to your opinion." [38] In the end, though, Burke may have been hurt as much for continuing to support America after the war broke out. By that time Bristol, like most of England, had rallied 'round the flag, and Burke and his party had become unpopular.

On his return to Parliament late in 1774, Burke continued his efforts to stop the drift toward war. Never was he more eloquent in debate or more wise and farseeing in his judgment than in his first *Speech on Conciliation with America* on March 22, 1775. Though he had in no way abandoned his belief in Parliament's "supreme authority," he put to one side the whole controversy over its legal right to tax. "The question with me is not whether you have a right to render your people miserable, but whether it is not your interest to make them happy. It is not what a lawyer tells me I *may* do, but what humanity, reason, and justice tell me I ought to do." Nor was he willing to rely on "mere general theories of government" or on "abstract theories of right." ("I am not here going into the distinctions of rights nor attempting to mark their boundaries," he had told Parliament the year before in his *Speech on American Taxation*. "I do not enter into these metaphysical distinctions; I hate the very sound of them.") Americans must be governed according to their "true nature" and their "peculiar circumstances." One of their circumstances, he reminded the House, was the "three thousand miles of ocean" which separate them from England. "In large bodies, the circulation of power must be less vigorous at the extremities. Nature has said it. . . . The sultan gets as much obedience as he can. He governs with a loose rein, that he may govern at all." The predominant trait of the Americans' character, he declared, was a "fierce spirit of liberty" which was stronger, probably, "than in any other people of the earth." It was not a spirit, he said, which could be reconciled with an exercise of power in England, however lawful. No matter how excessive that spirit may appear in England the question was not whether it deserved praise or blame, but "what, in the name of God, shall we do with it?" [39]

Short of "giving up the colonies," which to Burke was unacceptable, there were but three ways to deal with the Americans' "stubborn spirit," he declared: "to change that spirit, as inconvenient, by removing the causes; to prosecute it, as criminal; or to comply with it as necessary." The first of these plans, he believed, was all but impossible. "The temper and character which prevail in our colonies are, I am afraid, unalterable by any human art. We cannot, I fear, falsify the pedigree of this fierce people and persuade them that they are not sprung from a nation in whose veins the blood of freedom circulates." Nor was it any more feasible to prosecute that spirit as criminal. Britain was not dealing with "the irregular conduct of scattered individuals or even bands of men within the state" but with "civil dissensions" which were agitating an entire continent. "I do not know the method of drawing up an indictment against an whole people." But even if this could be done, "I really think that for wise men this is not judicious, for sober men not decent, for minds tinctured with humanity not mild and merciful." His preference, he made clear, was for "prudent management" rather than "force," since he considered force to be a "feeble instrument" for governing a people as numerous, active, and spirited as Americans. In the first place, force is not always effective, and if it fails, "you are without resource, for . . . no further hope of conciliation is left. Power and authority are sometimes bought by kindness, but they can never be begged as alms by an impoverished and defeated violence." Even if successful, force tends to be self-defeating— "the thing you fought for is not the thing which you recover, but depreciated, sunk, wasted, and consumed in the process." Only a *"whole America"* would content him, he declared. "I do not choose to consume its strength along with our own, because in all parts it is the British strength that I consume." And he added, "I do not choose wholly to break the American spirit, because it is the spirit that has made the country." [40]

No way was open, he concluded, but the third—"to comply with the American spirit as necessary or, if you please, to submit to it as a necessary evil." What he proposed, in essence, was to extend to America the same constitutional rights and privileges which England had already granted to Ireland and Wales to their mutual benefit. One of these rights, he conceded, posed a difficult problem. Though

Americans had as strong a claim as the Irish and Welsh to be represented in Parliament by members of their own choice, they were too far removed for this to be practicable. But they *were* represented actually in their own colonial assemblies, and it was these bodies whose "legal competency" he urged Parliament to recognize in laying taxes "for the support of their government in peace and for public aids in time of war." [41] Here he was repeating a plea he had previously made in his *Speech on American Taxation*: "leave America, if she has taxable matter in her, to tax herself. . . . Be content to bind America by laws of trade; you have always done it." [42] And what, he asked, would prevent the colonies from challenging Parliament's supremacy in other matters once they were conceded the right to tax? Their disinclination "as Englishmen," he answered, to push any "speculative principle," whether of government or of freedom, to its logical conclusion. "Man acts from adequate motives relative to his interest, and not on metaphysical speculations."

It was in America's interest no less than in Britain's not to hold to a rigid position. "All government, indeed every human benefit and enjoyment, every virtue and every prudent act, is founded on compromise and barter. We balance inconveniences; we give and take; we remit some rights, that we may enjoy others; and we choose rather to be happy citizens than subtle disputants. As we must give away some natural liberty to enjoy civil advantages, so we must sacrifice some civil liberties for the advantages to be derived from the communion and fellowship of a great empire." In the government of that empire, he declared, "magnanimity" was not seldom the "truest wisdom," for "a great empire and little minds go ill together." [43] Earlier he had said, "It is impossible to answer for bodies of men. But I am sure the natural effect of fidelity, clemency, kindness in governors is peace, good will, order, and esteem on the part of the governed." [44] Treated in this way, the colonies would continue to be held to England by "kindred blood," by the "close affection which grows from common names," by "similar privileges and equal protection." "Though light as air," these ties were, he said, "as strong as links of iron. Let the colonies always keep the idea of their civil rights associated with your government; they will cling and grapple to you, and no force under heaven will be of power to tear them from their allegiance." It is not "your letters of office, and your instructions and your suspending clauses," he told the House, "that hold together the great contexture of this mysterious whole. These things do not make your government. Dead instruments, passive tools as they are, it is the spirit of the English constitution that gives all their life and efficacy to them." His conclusion: "Let us get an American revenue as we have got an American empire. English privileges have made it all that it is; English privileges alone will make it all that it can be." [45]

Eight months later Burke made one last great effort to keep the "American empire" intact. The occasion was his second speech on conciliation delivered on November 16, 1775. It was a longer address than the first and, to judge by the increased support which it received, perhaps even more effective, although unfortunately it survives only in summary form. To conciliate the colonies, he was convinced that it was no longer enough merely to repeal the Acts of Parliament which they found offensive. If "more concession" was required, as he believed to be the case, it was because "injudicious coercion has made it necessary." For his part, Burke was willing to make two concessions which he had never entertained before, at least publicly. First, he proposed to "remove all doubt and uneasiness" in America on the subject of taxation. Taxation was the cause of the dispute; once that was removed as an issue, "the rest would not be difficult." From the start he had been willing to concede the right of colonial assemblies to tax themselves, reserving to Parliament only the right to tax imports and exports for purposes of regulating trade. Now, for the first time, he was even willing to give the colonies all revenue from regulatory duties to dispose of as they saw fit. His second concession was to recognize the Continental Congress as the *de facto* spokesman for the united colonies. The present ministry "could not succeed," he warned, if it tried to negotiate separately with the several colonies. He even proposed that Parliament give the Congress the constitutional standing which it lacked. In the future the colonies would be empowered, at the call of their governor, to send deputies to a "general meeting" with full power to bind "the whole body" to all acts approved by majority vote. On the general principle of parliamentary supremacy, however, he remained firm. He did not wish to see the Declaratory Act repealed for the reason, among others, that "the disgrace of an English Parliament could add nothing to the security of American liberty." Nor could he believe that "the desire for absolute independency was or could be general in the colonies." Independence was so contrary to their clearest interests, provided their liberties were preserved, that "he could scarcely credit them if they should assert it." [46]

But it was too late for such temperate counsel to prevail. America had already asserted its independence by its armed resistance to the Crown. An American Congress had met, a continental army had been raised, and a commander-in-chief placed in charge. British ships had been boarded, British forts taken and their arsenal seized, and British soldiers killed at Lexington, Concord, and Bunker Hill. Even as Burke spoke, an invading American army was preparing to occupy Montreal. Under the circumstances it is not remarkable that Burke's plan "for composing the present troubles" was defeated by a vote of only two-to-one; his earlier motions, advanced at a less critical time, had lost three-to-one. For a time he continued to hope that the Americans, then in what he called "the middle state of their affairs (much impaired but not perfectly ruined)," might be willing to accept peace on the generous terms which he had outlined in his November speech. During Parliament's Christmas recess in 1776, he discussed several plans with the Rockingham leaders. Benjamin Franklin, whom he knew and respected, was then in France, and for a time Burke considered "taking a turn to Paris" to sound him out on the possibility of a negotiated peace. When that scheme was opposed by some of his Lordship's friends, but not by Rockingham himself, Burke urged the party to carry out some other "settled plan of action or inaction." Two such plans were considered. Under both plans the Whig opposition would "secede" from Parliament when it reconvened in protest against the government's war policies. Under the second plan, however, one further step would be taken: the party leaders would appeal directly both to the King and to the rebels to accept the more conciliatory policies which Burke and his party had advanced. Before deciding how far to go, Burke advised Rockingham to consider carefully the risks involved. "We have the weight of king, lords, and commons in the other scale; we have against us, within a trifle, the whole body of the law; we oppose the more considerable part of the landed and mercantile interests; we contend, in a manner, against the whole church; we set our faces against great armies flushed with victory and navies who have tasted of civil spoil, and have a strong appetite for more; our strength, whatever it is, must depend for a good part of its effect upon events not very probable." [47]

Of the two plans, the second was the more drastic if only because of the hard-hitting language which Burke used in his draft of the two addresses. The address to the king was especially strong. Though it was to be sent in the name of several peers of the realm and several members of the House of Commons who professed only the highest respect and warmest affection toward His Majesty, they strongly condemned the ministers who ruled in his name. The disorders which prevailed in America, they declared, were the direct and inevitable result of the government's "misconduct," i.e., "to plans laid in error, pursued with obstinacy and conducted without wisdom." The recital of their specific wrongs was as damning an indictment in its way as the American Declaration of Independence. "The subversion of solemn, fundamental charters on a suggestion of abuse, without citation, evidence, or hearing; the total suspension of the commerce of a great maritime city, the capital of a great maritime province, during the pleasure of the Crown; the establishment of a military force not accountable to the ordinary tribunals of the country in which it was kept up . . . ;" the employment of foreign mercenary troops, "fierce and cruel" Indian tribes, and even African, slaves incited by Virginia's royal governor against the "brethren of our blood," [48] the "mode of proceeding by harsh laws and feeble armies" ("Force was sent out not sufficient to hold one town; laws were passed to inflame thirteen provinces"), and the "plunder" of the "whole trading property of America (even unoffending shipping in port)" by "sailors of your navy." Even if no previous cause of dissension had existed, these and other proceedings "were sufficient to produce great troubles; unjust at all times; they were then irrational." [49]

But the basic grievance from which all the others stemmed was the attempt made to tax the colonies without their consent. To this extent Americans were not free. This was not "merely the opinion of a very great number or even the majority, but the universal sense of the whole body of the people in those provinces." No matter how "false or disputable" it may appear to others, the sense of a whole people ought never be made to yield to the "abstract claims or even rights of *the supreme power*" or to the "theoretic reasonings of speculative men." The "only firm seat of all authority" lay "in the minds, affections, and interests of the people." It was neither just nor wise to defy sentiments which were so widely shared and so deeply felt. "Much power is tolerated and passes unquestioned where much is yielded to opinion. All is disputed where everything is enforced." The force of this argument was made stronger, not weaker, by the great distance which separated America from England. "Abuses of subordinate authority increase and all means of redress lessen as the distance of the subject removes him from the seat of the supreme power. What, in those circumstances, can save him from the last extremes of indignity and oppression, but something left in his own hands which may enable him to conciliate the favor and control the excesses of government?" It was no less important to Britain to leave the security of American prosperity largely in American hands. "To leave any real freedom to Parliament, freedom must be left to the colonies." The only substitute for civil liberty in America would be a military government which would become "an apt, powerful, and certain engine" for destroying freedom in England. "Great bodies of armed men," trained to despise popular assemblies in America, employed there to enforce taxes levied on an English people without their consent, and not answerable to their ordinary courts could hardly be expected to respect and protect those same institutions at home. "What, gracious sovereign, is the empire of America to us, or the empire of the world, if we lose our own liberties?" [50]

To that "gracious sovereign" the most galling part of the address may well have been its pointed reminder of his own limited authority. *Other* thrones may possibly have been founded "upon the principles of unconditional submission and passive obedience, on powers exercised without the concurrence of the people to be governed, on acts made in defiance of their prejudices and habits, on acquiescence procured by foreign mercenary troops and secured by standing armies." But *not*, the address insisted, the throne of England. It was not to "passive principles in our ancestors" from which George III derived his right to rule but from a revolution, the Glorious Revolution of 1688. "The people at that time re-entered into their original rights," because their freedom and safety, "the origin and cause of all laws," required it. No positive law then authorized the people to act as they did in deposing one monarch and installing another in his place, but none was needed. Their proceeding was "paramount and superior" to every such law because their freedom and security had been violated. "At that ever memorable and instructive period, the letter of the law was superseded in favor of the substance of liberty. To the free choice, therefore, of the people, without either king or Parliament, we owe that happy establishment out of which both king and Parliament were regenerated." The acts of Parliament confirming and ratifying that "happy settlement" originated in the "great principle of liberty." "Those statutes have not given us our liberties; our liberties have produced them." Every hour of his reign, the king was reminded, his title "stands upon the very same foundation on which it was at first laid, and we do not know a better on which it can possibly be placed." In every part of the empire, they boldly asserted, Englishmen enjoy "inherent rights which bind and regulate the Crown itself." [51]

Though "on the whole" Burke concurred heartily in the sentiments which he had expressed for his party, he anticipated that the
address would have "very important consequences." It was not at all
likely, he thought, that the court would "pass it over in silence, with
a real or affected contempt." If they did take notice, their "mildest
course" would be to use their parliamentary majority to censure the
Rockingham party and to stir their own constituencies to do likewise. Much more to be feared, he warned Rockingham, was "what a
Parliament omnipotent in power, influenced with party rage and
personal resentment, operating under the implicit military obedience of court discipline, is capable of." A prosecution for sedition
was not likely, he believed, because a jury could not be trusted to
convict, as fifteen years later during another revolution Tom Paine
would be convicted by an English jury. But neither impeachment
nor a bill of pains and penalties[52] presented any such problem for
the government; it would be able to select Rockingham and three
or four of his "most distinguished friends" and place them on trial
before Parliament itself. There, he thought, their conviction would
be assured. "The only question is whether the risk ought to be run
for the chance (and it is no more) of recalling the people of England
to their ancient principles, and to that personal interest which
formerly they took in all public affairs." If such a drastic step were
to be taken, he advised Rockingham, it should be done "with a full
view of the consequences and with minds and measures in a state of
preparation to meet them." [53]

It was not only the king who was to be addressed under the
second plan; so were the "British colonists in North America." The
risks involved, as Burke was aware, were at least as great, though of
a somewhat different kind. If to complain to the king about the
obstinate folly of his ministers could be considered seditious, to
give the Americans moral support in wartime would be deemed
worse. Yet this, in essence, is what the second address would have
done. The present war was not a rebellion but a "civil war" among
a "people of one origin and one character." "We do not call you
rebels and traitors. We do not call for the vengeance of the Crown
against you." On the contrary, the Americans were to be told, "we
highly revere the principles on which you act; though we lament
some of their effects. Armed as you are, we embrace you as our
friends and as our brethren by the best and dearest ties of relation."
As proof of that friendship, the addressers were able to cite their
"thorough detestation of the whole war," and especially the employment of foreign mercenaries and of "fierce tribes of savages and

cannibals . . . fleshing them in the slaughter of you," and the in-
citement of African slaves to "cut the throats of their masters." The
words, though Burke's own, might have come from Paine himself.
Even on the issues which led to the war, the addressers expressed
their sympathy for the American cause. They held to the same
standard of the "blessings of free government"; and they accepted
America's right to tax itself, even if it meant that England might be
cut off from all financial support, which, they hastened to add, they
were "far from supposing." The reason was this: "We know of no
road to your coffers but through your affections." Nor were these
warm sentiments confined to a small minority in England. Despite
the "corrupt influence treacherously employed" by "wicked men,"
a "large, and we trust the largest and soundest, part of this kingdom
perseveres in the most perfect unity of sentiments, principles, and
affections with you." [54]

But liberty was not their only concern, the addressers made
clear; union was no less so. It would be a "calamity" for America as
much as for England if they were to separate. The freedom which
Americans "so justly prize above all things" originated in England,
and only if it was "constantly fed from the original fountain" was it
likely to be preserved in "its native purity." Before embarking on
"untried forms of government" which appeal to "unstable minds"
for their novelty, America would do well to consider the advantages
of continued union with Britain. For several hundred years England
had been "great and happy" under its present limited monarchy, and
only under her continued rule could America expect to receive the
same blessings. "We apprehend you are not now, nor for ages, are
likely to be, capable of that form of constitution in an independent
state." Nor was it certain that the existing American union would
long endure in any condition without the authority and weight of
some "great and long respected body" to preserve a "just and fair
equality" among the former colonies. That "great and long respected
body," almost needless to say, was the British Parliament. Though it
may have fallen somewhat from its "independent spirit," Parliament
still retained its capacity for "renovating its principles and effecting
a self-reformation." In this way the "original scheme" of the constitution had often been corrected and its principles adapted to "suit
those changes which have successfully happened in the circumstances
of the nation or in the manners of the people." As a result, the constitution has admitted "innumerable improvements." One such improvement still needed was to give Americans a "solid security" for
their privileges and liberties against the abuse of power. Until that

time, the addressers were to say, "we do not advise you to an unconditional submission." Once given and ratified by Parliament, however, that pledge would lay the ground "for peace and forgiveness on our side and for a manly and liberal obedience on yours." In this "spirit of reconciliation" any remaining differences would be "easily and securely" adjusted. "Of this we give you our word, that . . . we at least, on these grounds, will never fail you." [55]

It is not at all likely that their American "brethren" would have heeded so general and so belated an appeal. In any event, neither this address nor the first was ever sent; the Rockingham party leaders, Burke among them, decided to confine any organized protest to a partial "secession" from Parliament. They were conspicuously absent when Parliament reconvened in January, 1777, and for the next few months they stayed away from any discussion of American affairs including the debate over the bill to deny Americans the ancient privilege of the writ of habeas corpus. Although they were free under the arrangement to attend the morning sessions to take part in discussions in which they had a personal interest, it was understood that they did so as private individuals, not as party members. Though with few exceptions most of the Opposition who considered themselves Rockingham Whigs adhered to the policy, many of their allies, including Charles James Fox and Lord Chatham, opposed the strategy and continued to oppose the Ministry from within Parliament. For this and no doubt other reasons, the secession proved ineffectual and was soon abandoned.[56] Worse yet, the withdrawal aroused even more popular resentment than Burke had anticipated, even in his own Bristol constituency. In some alarm Burke prepared a careful statement of his position on the American question which in part was a defense of his party's withdrawal from Parliament and also an attack on the punitive policies of the British government. He addressed it in the form of an open letter to the sheriffs of Bristol. For some time, he explained, he had been convinced that it was futile and frivolous to oppose any of the Ministry's measures dealing with America. "Everything proposed against America is supposed of course to be in favor of Great Britain." Even the failure of a policy was pressed as a reason for continuing it. Any suggestion to the contrary was considered "factious" by most within Parliament and by very many outside. Under these circumstances, he declared, "I cannot conscientiously support what is against my opinion nor prudently contend with what I know is irresistible." If he were absent from his seat only a single day, he trusted that his past conduct had proven that it was not owing to "indolence or love of dissipation." All that would be required to recall him to the duty which he had "quitted with regret" was the "slightest hope of doing good." [57]

Patiently and as eloquently as in his speeches on conciliation, Burke reviewed again his position on the American question. "Everything" that had been done in America, he said, had arisen from a "total misconception" of its people and their circumstances. "The whole of those maxims upon which we have made and continued this war must be abandoned." Only a "total renunciation" of the demand for "unconditional submission" would make it possible to reconcile, recover, and retain America, though nothing, he warned, could restore the two countries to their former situation. "That hope must be laid aside." He admitted that one of his first votes in Parliament had been to support the Declaratory Act which asserted Parliament's power to bind the American people "in all cases whatsoever." When challenged to explain why, after defending the act for more than a decade, he was now prepared to repeal it, he answered, "because a different state of things requires a different conduct." The concessions which America had been willing to accept at the start of the dispute would no longer suffice, because her "unsuspicious confidence" in Parliament had given way to "soreness, jealousy, and distrust." In proposing to repeal the Declaratory Act, Burke explained, "I parted with it as with a limb, but as a limb to save the body, and I would have parted with more, if more had been necessary—anything rather than a fruitless, hopeless, unnatural civil war." Even if this concession had led to permanent separation, he confessed that he would "prefer independency without war to independency with it." He had "so much trust in the inclinations and prejudices of mankind, and so little in anything else," that he would expect "ten times" more benefit to Britain from the "affection" of an independent America "than from her perfect submission to the Crown and Parliament, accompanied by her terror, disgust, and abhorrence. Bodies tied together by so unnatural a bond of union as mutual hatred are only connected to their ruin." [58]

And why was he so strongly opposed to the war with America? In every war, he explained, the "rules of moral obligation" are suspended, "and what is long suspended is in danger of being totally abrogated." The danger is especially great in civil wars, because they "vitiate" the politics of the people, "corrupt their morals," and "pervert even the natural taste and relish of equity and justice." A civil war also strikes "deepest of all into the manners of the people," which, while they remain intact, "correct the vices of law and soften

it at length to their own temper." This was precisely, he claimed,
what had already happened in the American war. "Every step we
have taken in this business has been made by trampling on some
maxim of justice or some capital principle of wise government." He
cited, as examples, acts of Parliament punishing American privateers
as pirates ("The general sense of mankind tells me that those offenses
which may possibly arise from mistaken virtue are not in the class
of infamous actions"), treating rebels as traitors and trying them in
England without resort to a common law jury ("[T]o try a man
under that act is, in effect, to condemn him unheard . . . ; such a
person may be executed according to form, but he can never be
tried according to justice") and denying Englishmen overseas recourse to writs of habeas corpus ("Liberty, if I understand it at all,
is a *general* principle, and the clear right of all the subjects within
the realm, or of none. Partial freedom seems to me a most invidious
mode of slavery"). All of these "ancient, honest juridicial principles
and institutions of England are so many clogs to check and retard
the headlong course of violence and oppression. They were invented
for this one good purpose, that what was not just should not be
convenient." In times of civil discord like the present, Burke pointed
out, people "are but too apt to forget their own future safety in
their desire of sacrificing their enemies" and to "admit the entrance
of that injustice of which they are not to be the immediate victims."
It is never the powerful who are in danger of irregular proceedings
but "the obnoxious and the suspected." No departure from justice
can be permitted on the "plea or pretense of *inconvenience or evil
example.*" The "true danger," he insisted, "is when liberty is nibbled
away for expedients and by parts." Indeed, he concluded, "nothing
is security to any individual but the common interest of all." [59]

In criticizing specific acts of Parliament, Burke made it clear
that he was not challenging its authority. From the start, he declared,
he had never the slightest doubt that Parliament possessed "unlimited legislative power" over the colonies. But he was also certain
that, where America was concerned, Parliament could not preserve
its power in any of its parts unless it was used with the "greatest
reserve," especially "in those delicate points in which the feelings of
mankind are the most irritable." [60] Though the "abstract idea of
that power" includes many things "which carry no absolute injustice
in themselves," it can no more be exercised when it runs "contrary
to the opinions and feelings of the people" than if Parliament in
that case had no power at all. If this was the case in England, where
Parliament's authority was accepted without question, it was no less

true in America where it was openly challenged. The "true end" of a legislature, he said, was "in effect, to follow, not to force the public inclination—to give a direction, a form, a technical dress, and a specific sanction to the general sense of the community." He was persuaded that "government was a practical thing, made for the happiness of mankind, and not . . . to gratify the schemes of visionary politicians." Yet there were people, he said, who have "split and anatomized the doctrine of free government, as if it were an abstract question concerning metaphysical liberty and necessity and not a matter of moral prudence and natural feeling." [61]

Civil freedom was not an "abstract speculation" hidden in the depth of "abstruse science" but a "blessing and a benefit" recognizable by men of "ordinary capacities." Unlike "those propositions in geometry and metaphysics which admit no medium, but must be true or false in all their latitude, social and civil freedom, like all other things in common life, are variously mixed and modified, enjoyed in very different degrees, and shaped into an infinite diversity of forms according to the temper and circumstances of every community." Liberty, pushed to the *extreme,* "which is its abstract perfection, but its real fault," is nowhere to be found, nor should it be, "because extremes, as we all know, in every point which relates either to our duties or satisfactions in life, are destructive both to virtue and enjoyment." [62] It was not possible in any case, he believed, to determine precisely the degree to which liberty must be restrained if it is to be enjoyed at all. "But it ought to be the constant aim of every wise public counsel to find out by cautious experiments, and rational, cool endeavors, with how little, not how much, of this restraint the community can subsist, for liberty is a good to be improved and not an evil to be lessened. It is not only a private blessing of the first order, but the vital spring and energy of the state itself, which has just so much life and vigor as there is liberty in it." [63]

Thus far, Burke had addressed himself to those, like the sheriffs of Bristol, who shared his views on American affairs. Next he turned to the Englishmen, of every description, who continued to support the war. To those who believed that the British cause was prospering in America, he had sober news. "Believe me, gentlemen, the way still before you is intricate, dark, and full of perplexed and treacherous mazes." As yet Britain and her "German allies of twenty hireling states" had contended only with the "unprepared strength" of its "own infant colonies." "But America is not yet subdued," he pointed out. Not a single village throughout the entire country had been won over except by force. "You have the ground you encamp

on, and you have no more. . . . You spread devastation, but you
do not enlarge the sphere of authority." In his judgment, Burke
said, this bad state of affairs would continue "as long as English
government is attempted to be supported over Englishmen by the
sword alone." Even if Britain should finally triumph, as he anticipated, the success of British arms would expose the failure of British
policy. "You will never see any revenue from America." For the
jingoes in his country who took a mindless, vicarious pride in every
success of British and Hessian arms, he had only scorn and contempt. He knew of nothing "more truly odious and disgusting than
an impotent, helpless creature, without civil wisdom or military skill,
without a consciousness of any other qualification for power but his
servility to it, bloated with pride and arrogance, calling for battles
which he is not to fight, contending for a violent dominion which
he can never exercise, and satisfied to be himself mean and miserable
in order to render others contemptible and wretched." [64] Tom
Paine, at his polemical best, could have put it no more pungently.

Much more formidable, as Burke was aware, were the critics who
complained that dissent of the kind he expressed had aided and
encouraged the rebellion. He, of course, flatly denied the charge.
"*General* rebellions and revolts of a whole people never were *encouraged*, now or at any time. They are always *provoked*." Even if
the charge were true, he rejected the inference to be drawn. "Does
anybody seriously maintain that, charged with my share of the
public councils, I am obliged not to resist projects which I think mischievous, lest men who suffer should be encouraged to resist? The
very tendency of such projects to produce rebellion is one of the
chief reasons against them. Shall that reason not be given?" Any
suggestion to the contrary, to his mind, was not true loyalty or
patriotism but servility. With those who expected all Englishmen,
whatever their sentiments might once have been, to close ranks
and support the government in time of war, Burke was equally
short. Before "unanimity can be [a] matter either of wish or congratulation," he said, "we ought to be pretty sure that we are engaged in a rational pursuit. Frenzy does not become a slighter dis-
temper on account of the number of those who may be infected with
it. Delusion and weakness produce not one mischief the less because
they are universal." It would have been happier for England, he
suggested, if dissent against the war had been more general and an
"American party" had been formed "to whom they could always
look for support." Only the most narrow partisan, he believed,
"would not wish that the Americans should from time to time carry

many points, and even some of them not quite reasonable, by the aid of any denomination of men here, rather than they should be driven to seek for protection against the fury of foreign mercenaries and the waste of savages in the arms of France." [65]

It is not surprising that Burke should be "charged," as he put it, "with being an American." He was even willing to plead guilty "if warm affection toward those over whom I claim any share of authority be a crime." [66] Later, even Paine, at the height of their quarrel, conceded that "with respect to America," Burke had been "very complimentary. He always contended, at least in my hearing, that the people of America are more enlightened than those of England, or of any other country in Europe." [67] Yet, as Burke also insisted with equal truth, no man was ever "more zealous" for the supremacy of Parliament and the prerogatives of the imperial Crown. Incompatible though these positions appeared, he was able to reconcile them in his enlightened conception of an empire bound together with the "cement of reciprocal esteem and regard." [68] Though the war dragged on for another five years, he continued to prove his attachment to both causes. He was one of the first in Parliament to urge publicly that Britain recognize American independence. Even before news of Burgoyne's surrender reached England, he told the House that whether members liked it or not, America was, in truth, already independent. Later, in February, 1778, he expressed his outrage again, in a three-hour speech, that Indians were still being used against Americans. Yet when peace finally came in 1782, he was sharply critical of some of the terms on which the war had been settled. He contended that too much territory had been conceded to the United States and too little concern shown for the plight of American Tories. In a direct test of his loyalties, those of the Empire prevailed.

PAINE AND FRANCE

Meanwhile, Tom Paine had developed an attachment for France which was to prove as decisive for his career as Burke's attachment to America had been for him. He had been secretary to Congress' Committee for Foreign Affairs during the time that an American commission was in France to enlist its political and logistical support of the Revolution. It was an important position, for which no exact counterpart exists today, since there was no chief executive to direct foreign policy. As Secretary for Foreign Affairs, as Paine liked to call himself, he was privy to most, if not all, political correspondence, even the most confidential. By his own account, "all the *political* letters from the American commissioners rested in my hands, and all that were officially written went from my office." [69] In any event, the French diplomatic and consular representatives saw in Paine a person of sufficient weight to be cultivated and, if possible, made useful. The French Minister Gérard, "offered Paine discreet financial inducements to write on the advantages for America in the alliance with France." [70] Paine did so, in his *Crisis VI* (October 20, 1778) in which he spoke of the alliance as "open, noble, and generous" and of France as "an affectionate friend and faithful ally." [71] If America alone could bring Britain to repeal the most obnoxious of her laws, as the North Ministry had offered to do in February, 1778, "united with France," she could force England to recognize her independence. Yet Paine needed no financial inducement to write favorably about France, nor did he accept any as long as he served Congress. "According to my opinion of things and principles," he later wrote, "a man needs no pecuniary inducement to do that to which the two-fold powers of duty and disposition naturally lead him on." [72] Indeed, he was soon to prove that he was as independent in his dealings with the French authorities as Burke had been with the New York Assembly.

The occasion was the famous Silas Deane affair, which has been called "the most notorious scandal of the American Revolution." [73] Deane, a Connecticut delegate to Congress, had been sent to France to obtain military supplies and, if possible, official recognition of American independence. The French government was not yet ready to risk war with Britain by supporting its rebellious colonies openly, but Louis XVI and his Bourbon uncle, Charles III of Spain, each secretly pledged a million livres for the purchase of arms and equipment, which Deane gratefully acknowledged for Congress. This much is known, but not whether the supplies were a gift or, in effect, a loan. The question has never been entirely resolved because of the secrecy in which the transaction was cloaked and the mixed motivation of those who took part in it. Some, though not all, of the circumstances came to light only after Benjamin Franklin and Arthur Lee had joined Deane in France as joint commissioners, but, understandably, the French government wished as little publicity as possible. In October, 1777, the French Foreign Minister, Count Vergennes, would only say that no payment would be expected for any of the aid provided thus far by the French government. But some of the supplies already provided had been financed by private interests headed by Caron de Beaumarchais, the French playwright. Since Beaumarchais and his associates had put up money of their own, Deane insisted that they were entitled to payment and, of course, a profit. This Arthur Lee denied after learning that Deane himself was also acting in the interests of American entrepreneurs, notably Robert Morris, the financier of the Revolution. His darkest suspicions now aroused, Lee openly charged Deane with fraud and even intimated that Franklin himself, that model of probity, might also be involved. When news of this wrangling reached Congress, Deane was recalled, ostensibly to report on European affairs generally, but in reality to give an account of his part in the transaction. On his return Deane requested an opportunity to present his case in person, but by that time Congress had been split into two hostile factions. When, as a result, Congress delayed giving him a hearing or even conducting an investigation, Deane took his case directly to the people through newspapers and handbills, denouncing his foes in Congress but offering no evidence that would clear his name.

It was inevitable, perhaps, that, given his combative disposition, Paine would be drawn into the controversy. Despite his friendship for Franklin, he sided entirely with Lee, partly in defense of his friends in Congress whom Deane had attacked and partly, no doubt, in the conviction that Deane was guilty of profiteering, if not indeed, fraud or worse. In any event, he took up his pen to attack not only Deane but Robert Morris and his associates. If he had stopped there, the whole controversy might have blown over without further damage to his own reputation or embarrassment to France. Instead, he stated categorically—and with seeming authority—that the French aid had been promised even before Deane had arrived in France in 1776. In doing so, he divulged the gist and at times, the precise language, of diplomatic correspondence he had sworn not to disclose.[74] Though Britain had known of the arrangement for more than a year, France was exposed to the other European powers as having supported rebellious colonies long before a formal alliance had made it legitimate. After trying unsuccessfully to get Paine to retract his statement, Minister Gérard protested to Congress against his "indiscreet" behavior and urged it to take appropriate action. Determined not to anger its ally, Congress called Paine before its bar, but he was allowed only to say whether he had in fact written the offensive article. Then after five days of debate, in which his friends did their best to defend him, Congress disavowed Paine and expressed its conviction that His Most Christian Majesty Louis XVI had *not* given America any supplies prior to the alliance. Paine resigned in protest on January 8, 1779, a victim of his own zeal and indiscretion, the touchiness of the French government, and the timidity of Congress.

Paine apparently held no grudge against Gérard for instigating the proceedings which cost him his position. Gérard, on his part, hastened to heal the breach lest Paine turn his formidable pen against France itself. Through an intermediary he offered to pay Paine the same salary he had received from the Congress if he would continue to write favorably about the alliance and to shun any political topics which, in Gérard's view, might be embarrassing to France. Though Paine regarded this a "very genteel and profitable offer," he declined it saying that "any service which I can render to either of the countries in alliance, or to both, I ever have done and shall readily do, and Mr. Gérard's *esteem* will be the only recompense I shall desire." In the next few days the offer was renewed several times "with considerable additions of advantage," but still Paine declined. Finally, at Gérard's invitation, the two men met on January 14, 1779. Though the subject of any financial remuneration was studiously avoided, or so Paine reported, Gérard professed "great respect" for Paine and said he would be glad for a chance to show "more solid marks" of his friendship.[75] Though Paine was careful not to give Gérard offense, he was determined not to be diverted from his campaign to discredit Deane and his associates in and out of the Congress. With even less restraint than before, he continued to attack Deane and to substantiate his charges by quoting from confidential documents formerly in his custody. Now it was Gérard's turn to feel aggrieved. Privately, he complained about Paine's "inconsistency and obstinance," and said that he had "defaulted in everything he promised." He was even less pleased by some of Paine's public remarks that summer. Gérard had intimated to Congress that it might be unwise to hold up peace until Britain was ready to recognize American fishing rights in the Newfoundland Banks. Paine cautioned Congress against treating Gérard "as if that gentleman was *our* Minister, instead of the Minister of His Most Christian Majesty," and complained that "*his* name" had been brought into a "variety of business" where it did not belong. "We seem in some instances to forget," he added, "that as France is the great ally of America, so America is the great ally of France."[76]

Eventually, Paine was able to resume his cordial relations with His Most Christian Majesty's representatives in America, but not until after two developments had taken place. The first was his three-month visit to France in the spring and summer of 1781. The Congress had decided to send Col. John Laurens there to obtain additional aid from the French court, and Laurens, son of a former president of the Congress and a close friend of Paine, asked the latter to go with him as his secretary. But Paine's foes in the Congress balked at giving him either rank or salary, so he had to make the trip unofficially at his own expense. From every standpoint the mission was successful. Though young and inexperienced in matters of diplomacy, Laurens handled himself well at the French court, and with Franklin's help he obtained much more aid than had been extended originally—six million livres as a gift and ten million more as a loan. For Paine the trip had rewards of another kind. He was able to renew his friendship with Franklin then under strain over the Deane affair, and he discovered, much to his satisfaction, that he was almost as well known in France as in America. When it came time to depart, Paine even considered staying on to work for the American cause in Europe, but in the end Laurens persuaded him to return. They arrived in Philadelphia in August with two and a half million livres in silver and two cargoes of supplies. Sixteen teams of oxen were required to transport the silver to the National Bank. Paine, on the other hand, reached home not only penniless but with his savings exhausted. At Bordentown he had to borrow a dollar to take the ferry across the Delaware.[77]

Even more gratifying than his acclaim in France was his vindication in the Deane affair. Deane had returned to Paris in July, 1780, exhausted after his long wrangle with the Congress and embittered over his failure to clear his name. Early the following summer he wrote eleven letters to friends in America, Robert Morris among them, denouncing the Revolution and, in effect, inviting them to do the same. Unfortunately for him, his letters were "intercepted," or so it seemed at the time, and published with the result that he was now discredited among his old associates. This gave Paine a chance to recall his prediction about Deane, that "As he rose like a rocket, he would fall like the stick," [78] a jibe which he liked so well that he applied it to Edmund Burke a decade later with much less justification. What neither Paine nor anyone else in America knew is that Deane, by that time, had become a paid British agent and had sent his letters to Lord North, the British prime minister, for his approval. What Deane himself did not realize apparently is that North arranged for the letters to be intercepted so that Deane's defection would have the greatest possible impact on American opinion. Financially, he was already ruined, but had his treason been known and not merely suspected by Paine and others, his disgrace would have been complete.[79]

Paine, meanwhile, had serious financial worries of his own. After losing his position with the Congress, he worked for nearly a year as a private clerk for a Philadelphia merchant and then served as clerk to the Pennsylvania legislative assembly until his trip to France. On his return, Paine let it be known that his pen was for hire in the right cause. He continued to publish his *Crisis* papers and newspaper articles, and from time to time he busied himself on a history of the revolution which he never completed, but none of these projects offered much prospect of a steady income. For a while this was provided under an agreement with Robert Morris, Robert Livingston, then Secretary for Foreign Affairs, and General Washington himself, under which Paine was to urge the state legislatures to support the war more vigorously. His salary, while it lasted, was $800 per year, paid quarterly. He also renewed his overtures to the new French Minister, the Chevalier de la Luzerne, who cautiously agreed to subsidize Paine if the latter would consult him prior to publication.[80] Paine's *Crisis* paper, XI, which he addressed mainly to the British Ministry in May, 1782, was entirely to Luzerne's liking. Britain had already tried to get France to break its alliance and now Paine feared that it was America's turn to be seduced from its fidelity to France. "Let the world and Britain know," he declared, "that we are neither to be bought nor sold." France had been more than "an open, noble, and manly" ally, he said; "she advocated the cause of America as if she had been America herself." The alliance was truly in America's interest to maintain, but it could also be defended on the higher ground of honor and principle. "Character is to us, in our present circumstances, of more importance than interest. We are a young nation, just stepping upon the stage of public life, and the eye of the world is upon us to see how we act." [81] Luzerne was also impressed by how favorably the pamphlet had been received. The reason, he thought, was that Paine had been content to "give form" to the "torrent of public opinion" and to give it a "firmer" foundation. It now seemed appropriate, he reported, to "nourish his patriotism" so that it could be made "more useful" from day to day.[82]

Before the war ended, Paine's patriotism was nourished on at least two other occasions. In August, 1782, he published a *Letter to the Abbé Raynal* on the affairs of North America. Raynal, one of the growing number of former French clerics to break with the old regime, had published a history of the American Revolution which had recently been translated into English. Paine found the work to be so riddled with errors that he wrote an extended critique to correct them. First, he denied Raynal's assertion that "the *whole* question" raised by the Revolution was "whether the mother country had, or had not, a right to lay, directly or indirectly, a *slight* tax upon the colonies." To the contrary, he insisted, it was not the tax as such, in any amount, against which America rebelled but the "principle" on which the right to tax had been grounded. The real question with America, he insisted, was whether she was to be bound *"in all cases whatsoever"* by the British Parliament as its Declaratory Act asserted. There was no despotism, he declared, to which this "iniquitous law" did not extend. "It stopped nowhere. It went to everything. It took in with it the whole life of a man, or, if I may so express it, an eternity of circumstances." Though those who executed the law, he conceded, might find it "convenient" to consult America's "manners and habits," which is precisely what Burke had been urging them to do, "the principle of the act made all tyranny legal." He also rejected Raynal's cynical suggestion that it was unnatural for a monarchy to ally itself with a republic which was fighting for its liberty or that a concern for the "happiness of mankind" had any part in its decision to do so. It was far sounder, Paine remarked, to examine the *consequences* of the alliance rather than the motives which produced it. Only a man who was "possessed of the mind of all the parties concerned" could possibly know their motivation. In any event, bad motives could never continue long to support a good cause. "Every object a man pursues is, for the time, a kind of mistress to his mind: if both are good or bad, the union is natural; but if they are in reverse, and neither can seduce nor yet reform the other, the opposition grows into dislike, and a separation follows." [83]

Nations are like individuals in a state of nature, Paine declared; "they are regulated by no fixed principle, governed by no compulsive law, and each does independently what it pleases or what it can." But nations have a greater capacity than "unconnected individuals" to behave in a civilized manner toward each other for the same reason that "it is somewhat easier to put together the materials of a machine after they are formed, than it was to form them from original matter." The progress of science, commerce, and letters had materially changed the condition of the world and "given a new cast to the mind of man, more than he appears to be sensible of." The boundaries of empires were "known and settled," and nations were no longer so likely to go to war for conquest or profit. Indeed, he declared, there was scarcely anything left for nations to quarrel about which did not arise from their prejudices; and even these, as the American Revolution and the French alliance had shown, were vulnerable to attack. Both events had already extended their influence from the New World to the Old. "Our style and manner of thinking have undergone a revolution more extraordinary than the political revolution of the country. We see with other eyes; we hear with other ears; and think with other thoughts, than those we formerly used. We can look back on our own prejudices as if they had been the prejudices of other people." [84]

For all of its wooliness, the *Letter* marked the first of several turning points in Paine's political thought. It was his first venture in what he called "metaphysical reasoning," and it was his first attempt to reach an international audience beyond the English-speaking world. [85] He had one hundred copies of the *Letter* sent to France where it appeared in four different translations. Although Paine had published the letter at his own expense, Luzerne paid him fifty guineas and "exhorted him to use his pen on objects of the same nature." More than a year later, after the war had ended, Paine received another "gratuity" for writing the last of his *Crisis* papers, the "Supernumerary Crisis" of December 9, 1783. [86] This time he answered a British pamphlet written by Lord Sheffield, a member of Parliament, who sought to persuade Americans to buy British goods and at the same time urged Parliament to forbid Americans to trade with the British West Indies. On the face of it, Paine observed, the appeal was an "absurdity" because "it offends, in the very act of endeavoring to ingratiate." This restriction on American trade was but a "gentle beginning of what America must expect, unless she guards her union with nicer care and stricter honor. United, she is formidable, and that with the least possible charge a nation can be so; separated, she is a medley of individual nothings, subject to the sport of foreign nations." [87]

With independence won, Paine's talents were no longer needed to bolster American morale and to preserve cordial relations with France, and he was obliged once more to find some regular means of support. In October, 1783, he addressed a memorial to Congress, which Washington himself endorsed, requesting that he be rewarded fairly for his services to the Revolution. Though his revolutionary tracts had been widely read, he claimed with some justice that he had not profited from their sale. Now that the war was over, he found his situation "singularly inconvenient," he said. "Trade I do not understand. Land I have none, or what is equal to none. I have exiled myself from one country without making a home of another; and I cannot help sometimes asking myself, what am I better off than a refugee, and that of the most extraordinary kind, a refugee from the country I have obliged and served, to that which can owe me no good will." [88] It was a moving appeal, but feeling over the Deane affair was still too strong in Congress for it to take action for another two years. Fortunately, two of the largest and wealthiest states came to his aid. In April, 1784, New York offered him his choice of two farms, and he chose a confiscated Tory estate near New Rochelle which he estimated to be worth at least one thousand guineas. In March, 1785, Pennsylvania awarded him 500 pounds as "temporary recompense" and promised to support any additional compensation which the Congress might see fit to make. When Congress finally acted, its response was as ungracious as it was belated. In October, 1785, it awarded Paine $3,000 as the "liberal gratification" to which it agreed he was entitled for his services. Actually, the sum represented only one-half of the amount he claimed to have spent out of his own pocket to serve Congress as secretary to its Committee for Foreign Affairs and as Col. Laurens' unofficial and unpaid companion and adviser. [89]

Though he continued to believe that he had been treated shabbily, Paine, nevertheless, was now in comfortable, if not well-to-do, circumstances. For the first time since he came to America he was able to lay aside his pen and pursue another lifelong interest. Even as a young man, he had been drawn to the study of science. Though his formal education was meager, he had a naturally inquisitive and inventive mind and a prodigious memory. At the age of twenty, while in London, he purchased a pair of globes out of his modest income and attended lectures on astronomy and natural philosophy. Later, by his own account, he made himself "master" not only of the globes but of the "orrery" which gave him a practical working knowledge of the universe. [90] In America his friendship with Benjamin Franklin and David Rittenhouse encouraged his natural bent for science, and he tried his hand at invention. As early as 1778 he began to think of ways to harness steam to propel vessels, and eight years later John Fitch thought enough of his abilities to offer him a partnership. [91] The first fruit of his newly acquired leisure was a smokeless candle designed to draw smoke out at the base. He and Franklin tested the candle to their satisfaction, but soon he became absorbed in a far more ambitious project—an iron bridge of a single arch. He was not the first to "invent" such a bridge, as his earlier biographers claimed, but at least the design was original. The arch combined a number of separate sections in much the same way that a spider's web is constructed, and in one model the arch had thirteen ribs to commemorate the thirteen original United States.[92]

Unable to get financial backing for his bridge in America, Paine decided to seek it in France. He left America in April, 1787, and it would be fifteen years before he returned. For a time he devoted his efforts almost entirely to promoting the bridge. At Franklin's suggestion he presented a model of the bridge to the Academy of Science in Paris, and it was favorably endorsed by the committee to which it was referred. But financing the bridge proved far more difficult. Since he had no personal contacts with the French court, he had to rely on his friends, especially Thomas Jefferson, then American Minister to France, and the Marquis de Lafayette, then a popular favorite for his dashing role in the American Revolution. For nearly a year they tried without success to interest the French government in building a bridge across the Seine based on Paine's model. Meanwhile, Paine had turned his thoughts to an engineering project of quite a different nature—building a "political bridge" between England and France. Certainly such a bridge was needed in 1787, for once again these traditional enemies were close to war, this time over Britain's support of the Dutch stadtholder and his Prussian allies against the Dutch "Patriot" party with which France was allied. Paine expressed his concern to the private secretary of the Cardinal de Brienne, then Finance Minister under Louis XVI, and offered his services to help bring about a "better understanding" between the two countries. Expecting soon to visit England, Paine asked specifically whether, if he should see any disposition there for friendlier relations with France, how far he might be authorized to say that the "same disposition" toward England prevailed in France. The secretary replied by letter in the "most unreserved manner," according to Paine, that he could say on Brienne's own authority that France had no wish to break with England if England offered no provocation.[93]

Before starting on his mission, Paine set down his views in writing. In a long letter to the Cardinal's secretary, he returned to the same theme he had developed in his *Letter to the Abbé Raynal.* It was in the interest of both France and England to gear their national economies to peace instead of war, as the ministries in both countries, he believed, fully understood. All that stood in the way of a "more friendly understanding" between the two countries were "the vulgar passions and prejudices of the commonality," meaning, of course, the common people. These prejudices were more deeply rooted in England than in France, he was convinced, because the affairs of France had never been fairly treated in the English newspapers and travel books. "Except Sterne," he declared, "there is scarcely a traveling English author, but who, on his return home, has [not] cherished and flattered those errors for the purpose of accommodating his work to the vulgar palates of his readers." It was understandable, therefore, why the English people were so easily incited to war against France. Nevertheless, he was encouraged by recent developments to believe that better relations were now possible between the two countries, and he pledged that he would do his best to promote them. He also promised that he would elaborate his views in a pamphlet intended to influence opinion in England.[94]

Paine kept his promise; indeed, the pamphlet was published so soon after his letter to Brienne's secretary as to warrant the conclusion that it was probably written beforehand. He called it *Prospects on the Rubicon* to express the hope that Britain, unlike Caesar, would stay on the "peaceable side" of that "figurative river." In doing so, he made the same appeal to enlightened self-interest which he had used so effectively in the *Crisis* papers. Quite apart from "all civil and moral considerations," a war between England and France could not possibly compensate either nation sufficiently, even if victorious, to recover its expenses. "War involves in its progress such a train of unforeseen and unsupposed circumstances, such a combination of foreign matters, that no human wisdom can calculate the end. It has but one thing certain, and that is increase of TAXES." Moreover, neither nation was in a condition to go to war, he maintained, and the Pitt ministry would make a grievous mistake if it assumed that France would be unable to defend itself because of the "confused" state of her "internal affairs" brought on by her financial and military support of the American Revolution. What neither Paine nor anyone else then realized was that the First and Second Estates—the nobles of the robe and sword—had already begun their resistance to any surrender of their ancient privileges which soon led to the first, aristocratic phase of the French Revolution. Far from being a source of weakness, he insisted, the "appearance of disorder in France is no more than one of the links in that great chain of circumstances by which nations acquire the summit of their greatness." Already, he declared, "a very extraordinary change" was taking place in the minds of the French people. If ever the "majesty of the nation" should be united with the "majesty of the sovereign" (for it was difficult, he explained, "to

express a new idea by old terms"), the power of the French government would be doubled; and its new "spirit" would make France
"exceedingly formidable." [95]

Actually, the idea which Paine advanced here was not new.
It was, in essence, the doctrine of the *bon roi* which the French
philosophes had propagated for years among the monarchs and
bourgeoisie of western Europe. It assumed that the best ordered
state was a union between an enlightened monarch and his people
in which the nobles were reduced to a subordinate role.[96] It was
not surprising that Voltaire and many of his fellow rationalists
should have placed their trust in such enlightened despots as Frederick the Great because they knew their own aristocracy too well
to expect reform from that quarter. For Paine to idealize monarchy,
however, was nothing short of astounding for he had repeatedly
expressed his contempt for hereditary government in any form:
"There is something exceedingly ridiculous in the composition of
monarchy," he had declared in *Common Sense;* "it first excludes a
man from the means of information, yet empowers him to act in
cases where the highest judgment is required. The state of a king
shuts him from the world; yet the business of a king requires him
to know it thoroughly." [97] Yet in the next few months he was not
only to repeat the doctrine but to apply it to Britain, despite his
verbal abuse of the "Royal Brute of Great Britain" during the
American Revolution. "The Regal Power is the Majesty of the
Nation collected to a center and residing in the Person exercising
the Regal Power," he wrote an English friend in February, 1782.
"The Right, therefore, of a Prince is a Right standing on the Right
of the whole Nation." The Power of the Crown, "standing on the
universal ground of the Nation," was necessary to mediate and to
balance the "distinct and opposite claims," one hereditary and the
other elective, of the "two orders of man—Peers and Commoners." [98]
A month previously, he told the same friend that the monarch,
though detached from and superior to all local interests and parties
in the nation, was "nearer related to the people than the Peers
are." [99]

BURKE AND PAINE

These were the political views which Paine brought to England
in the fall of 1787. It was his first visit to his native land in twelve
years, so he went directly to Thetford to see his aged parents, only
to learn that his father had recently died. Later he left a model of

his bridge with the Royal Society in London, as he had done with the Academy of Science in Paris. Only then, apparently, did he turn to his political mission. Late in September he wrote the Marquess of Lansdowne, who had been Prime Minister briefly after Rockingham's death in 1782. It was to Lansdowne, then the Earl of Shelburne, that Paine had addressed his *Crisis* XII. This time, of course, the message was quite different. He thanked Lansdowne for opposing England's war against America, and expressed the hope that "a few good men" on both sides would be able to still the clamor for war between England and France. Like other Englishmen, he had been brought up with "very wrong ideas" about France. "The people of that country," he was now convinced, "are a different kind of people to what they have been represented here." The "true interest" of both nations was to "agree and to trade instead of fight." He was not writing, he insisted, with any narrowly nationalistic bias. Though he expected to return to America, where his heart and what property he owned still lay, he was "a man who considers the world as his home, and the good of it in all places as his object." [100] It was a claim which he was soon to repeat. Later, though precisely when is not known, the two men met and exchanged views. Lansdowne was sufficiently pro-French to satisfy Paine apparently, but their relations soon cooled. In February, 1789, he was not as much in Lansdowne's "good graces" as he used to be, or so he reported to Jefferson. "He was always talking of a sort of reconnection of England and America, and my coldness and reserve on this subject checked communication." [101]

From the start, however, Paine appears to have rested most of his political hopes on another leader of the Parliamentary opposition—Edmund Burke himself. It was natural that he should do so. Burke was known throughout America as its greatest friend in Parliament, and perhaps in England as well. Paine himself had once quoted Burke in support of his view that the United States were "the greatest commonwealth on the face of the earth," [102] and he entertained no doubt, apparently, that his name was equally well known to Burke. In his *Letter to Bristol,* indeed, Burke had paid his wry respects to "the author of the celebrated pamphlet which prepared the minds of the people for independence." [103] When Paine presented himself to Burke some time during his first visit to England, he carried with him two letters which, in any event, would have assured him a warm welcome. The first was an introduction from Henry Laurens, whose son Paine had accompanied to Paris. Burke had befriended the elder Laurens after his capture and imprisonment in the Tower of London "on suspicion of high treason." Indeed, Burke had been largely responsible for his ultimate release.[104] The other was the letter from Cardinal de Brienne's private secretary authorizing Paine to say that France would reciprocate any disposition in England for better relations between the two countries. Nevertheless, it was naïve of Paine to have expected Burke to respond with any real enthusiasm to such an appeal. Staunch Whig that he was, Burke no doubt shared his party's traditional distrust of France, not so much for her commercial and colonial rivalry, as for repeated intrigues against the Hanoverian succession established by the Whig Revolution of 1688.[105] This prejudice against France, for it amounted to that, may actually have been reinforced, not dispelled, by his four brief visits to France over a lifetime. A devout Anglican, he had been alarmed in 1773 by the disrespect for religion which he heard openly expressed not only among the *philosophes* but in the leading salons in France. "The most horrible and cruel blow that can be offered to civil society," he warned Parliament on his return, "is through atheism. Do not promote diversity; when you have it, bear it; have as many sorts of religions as you find in your country; there is a reasonable worship in them all. The others, the infidels, are outlaws of the constitution, not of this country, but of the human race. They are never, never to be supported, never to be tolerated. Under the systematic attacks of these people, I see some of the props of good government already beginning to fail; I see propagated principles, which will not leave to religion even a toleration." [106]

Even on the subject of monarchy, if it ever arose, Burke would have found Paine's recent discovery of a "Regal Power standing on the Right of the whole Nation" entirely too royalist for his liking. The *bon roi* so much admired by the French *philosophes* was but a blood brother of the "Patriot King" so dear to English Tories which Burke had attacked early in his career.[107] To Burke the "majesty of the nation" was embodied not in the King alone but the King in Parliament, and of these Parliament was the senior partner. The plain fact is that though he venerated monarchy as an institution, Burke was not blind to the faults of individual monarchs, his own included. "Kings are naturally lovers of low company," he told the Commons in 1780. Indeed, many a Roman emperor had thrown himself into the hands of "an Italian eunuch, a mountebank, a fiddler, a player, or any regular practicioner of that tribe." Nor did Burke have any illusions about the nobility despite his long association with the most aristocratic of the Parliamentary connections.

"It must, indeed, be admitted that many of the nobility are as perfectly willing to act the part of flatterers, tale-bearers, parasites, pimps, and buffoons, as any of the lowest and vilest of mankind can possibly be." Nevertheless, he insisted, it was very important in every establishment to bring the prince into "daily and hourly" contact with "a great number of his first nobility," almost regardless of his own wishes.[108] Otherwise, Burke explained, the king in a pure monarchical government is prone to view his nobles with distrust and to shun them because only they are in a position to resist his will, whether for reasons of virtue, pride, or petulance. Once alienated from his nobles, a king has no other place to look for adulation but the common people. In doing so, however, he acts in ignorance of their faults, "which are as many as those of the great," Burke was convinced, "and much more decisive in their effects, when accompanied with power." Certainly, it was a mistake to assume that the people themselves would have no other ambition or interest than to support "the mild and parental authority by which they were invested, for the first time collectively, with real importance in the state, and protected in their peaceable and useful employments." It was precisely for this mistake, Burke was later to declare, that Louis XVI, "a perpetual example to all sovereigns," was ruined.[109]

It is not likely, of course, that either man expounded his political views fully at their first meeting, and for this reason, perhaps, it seems to have gone well.[110] On his return to England the following summer (1788) after seven months in France, Paine spent a week visiting Burke at his home in Beaconsfield. Though he would later deny it, Burke was much taken with Paine. While Paine was still a guest in his home, he told one friend with at least a slight touch of pride, "I am going to dine with the D[uke] of Portland in company with the great American Paine, whom I take with me," [111] and a few days later he wrote another friend that "the famous Mr. Paine, the author of Common Sense, the Crisis &c—and Secretary to the congress for foreign affairs" had been his guest for some time. "I was not sorry to see a man who was active in such an important scene." [112] Though Paine "was not without some attention to Politics," he was "much more deeply concerned" about his bridge— or so Burke believed. Paine had even more reason to be pleased by their new friendship. Not only had Burke extended his hospitality, he introduced Paine to some of his own inner circle of friends including Earl Fitzwilliam and the Duke of Portland who were not only very wealthy men but the principal leaders of the

Rockingham Whigs. For a time Paine may have been more impressed by their wealth than by their political eminence. It was now clear that the French government was in no position financially or even politically to build his bridge across the Seine. His last best hope now lay in England. Fortunately he was able to interest the Walker brothers, who operated one of the nation's leading iron works near Sheffield. While he was at their works that fall to examine the model under construction, Burke and his patron, Fitzwilliam, paid him a visit and he spent a few days at Fitzwilliam's country estate nearby. By January, 1789, he was able to report to Jefferson, then still in France as American Minister, that he was "in some intimacy with Mr. Burke" and the other leaders of the parliamentary opposition including Charles James Fox.[113] With this "line of acquaintance" and his first-hand knowledge of England, there was no need, he said, for the Congress to replace John Adams as minister to the English court. He was in a better position to act in that capacity, even unofficially, than "any other American," especially one far away. "If Congress should have any business to state to the government here, it can be easily done through their Minister at Paris"—meaning Jefferson himself; "but the seldomer the better." [114] Jefferson was agreeable to the proposal, but Washington, then President-elect, preferred to deal with the British ministry through Gouverneur Morris, one of Paine's bitter enemies.[115] Nevertheless Paine and Jefferson put their correspondence on a more formal basis and exchanged their assessment of the political situation in each country more fully and frequently than they had done before. This more or less tacit arrangement was to continue until Jefferson's recall later that same year.[116]

Burke and his friends had already found Paine a useful source of information. Though he had no official status Paine had let it be known that he had the ear not only of Jefferson but of Lafayette and other leading figures in France. Burke was not as well informed about France and its affairs as about America, Ireland, or even India, so he was all the more ready to rely on Paine's detailed and seemingly authoritative reports. For a time the news from France seems not to have given him much cause for alarm. The French Ministry, after failing in every other way to get the revenue which it needed so desperately, issued a call for the Estates General to convene in April, 1789, for the first time since 1614. This much, no doubt, Burke approved, though the Estates General bore little resemblance to the Parliament which he venerated. Not only were the clergy and nobility—the First and Second Estates—to meet separately, as they did not, of course, in the House of Lords, the Third Estate which represented the bourgeoisie, lacked the legal authority and proud tradition of the House of Commons. But what to Burke seemed merely an opportunity to bring France more nearly in line with the British constitution was to Paine an invitation to reform the whole society. He even dared hope that the French model of reform would be followed in England. During the regency crisis brought on by George III's temporary insanity in the winter of 1788–89, Paine "pressed" Burke to "propose a national convention, to be fairly elected, for the purpose of taking the state of the nation into consideration." [117] It is not known how Burke responded to the proposal, but he could not have taken it seriously. To Whigs of every persuasion, Parliament was, if not the nation itself, at least its embodiment and no other body was needed to take its interests into consideration.

Late in 1789 Paine returned to France to experience at first hand the excitement of the Revolution. To have "a share in two revolutions is living to some purpose," he had written Washington on the eve of his departure.[118] The second, bourgeois phase of the Revolution was still in full sway, and his friend Lafayette, though a noble, was one of its leading figures. In June the old Estates General had given way to a National Assembly in which the bourgeoisie were dominant. In July the Bastille had been captured, and the first threat of counterrevolution put down. In August the entire system of manorial rights and class privileges was swept away, and the Declaration of the Rights of Man and of the Citizen was proclaimed. By December the Gallican Church had been disestablished and its property taken over by the state. Officially, France was still a monarchy but it would remain so only as long as the intrigues of the royal family remained undiscovered. In this radically changed climate, Paine seems to have lost some of his zeal for the "Regal Power standing on the Right of the whole Nation," but he continued to speak favorably of Louis XVI and his Queen, Antoinette. On January 17, 1790, he wrote Burke from Paris that "the King has not felt himself so easy of late years as at present. His appearance shews it, the Queen's does not. Before he was accountable for every Extravagance of the Court, and chargeable with every misconduct. Now he knows what he is to do, and is on good terms with the Nation and the National Assembly." [119]

If Burke found this news reassuring, he was greatly alarmed by almost everything else which Paine reported during his second extended stay in France. Indeed, two of Paine's letters written early in 1790 may well explain why Burke decided to speak out against the Revolution as soon and as violently as he did. The first was the same letter in which Paine reported that Louis was "on good terms" with the nation. Much of what he wrote came as no surprise to Burke. The Revolution in France was "compleat," Paine believed, and the new constitution was "in a fair prospect" of becoming so. "The addresses and Congratulations which are every day arriving from all parts of France shew very effectively the attachment of the Nation to the National Assembly." Even the "exhausted Condition of the Treasury" was no cause for alarm, because it had been used to "force thereby a redress of Grievances." Thus, there was some "merit" in keeping the Treasury poor, as the "parliament of England ought to do in like Cases." Burke was cautioned not to rely on the English press for his information about French affairs. "Almost every thing related in the English papers as happening in Paris is either untrue or misrepresented." Certainly, they were wrong "to hold out the probability of a Counter-Revolution in France." No doubt, the "high Clergy and Pensioners" and many others of that stamp were discontented, but, he said, "their discontents amount to nothing." By the "destruction of the Feudal system," "pride" had been deprived of its power and "aristocracy of its authority, and it is as probable that those who pulled down the Bastille should build it up again and consent to be shut up in it, as that a Counter-Revolution should be worked.—The National Assembly has found out the Art of taking the public with them." [120]

What Burke did not realize, until he heard it from Paine, was that the seemingly moderate leaders of the Revolution would stop at nothing short of total reformation at home and abroad. In this judgment he may well have been influenced more by Jefferson's assessment of the situation the previous July which Paine had quoted than by Paine's own current evaluation. Jefferson had written Paine, three days before the Bastille fell, that the troops, supposedly loyal to the king, which had been sent to Paris to suppress the National Assembly, had instead shown "strong symptoms of being entirely with the people, so that nothing is apprehended from them." Through every stage of these transactions, he had reported, the National Assembly had shown "a coolness, wisdom, and resolution to set fire to the four Corners of the Kingdom and to perish with it themselves rather than to relinquish an iota from their plan of a total change of Government." As a consequence, Jefferson continued, they were "now in complete & undisputed possession of the sovereignty. The executive and the aristocracy are at their feet, the mass of the nation, the mass of the clergy, and the army are with them." All this, Paine reported almost verbatim to Burke.[121] His own contribution to Burke's alarm was to point out what the leaders of the Revolution were planning to do with their power. "The Assembly is now fixing the boundaries of the division of the Nation into 83 parts, Latitudinally and Longitudinally. It is intended by this arrangement to lose entirely the Name of Provinces and consequently of provincial distinction." Though "at present France appears to mind nothing but her own business," he added, "the Revolution in France is certainly a Fore-runner to other Revolutions in Europe.—Politically considered it is a new Mode of forming Alliances affirmatively with Countries and negatively with Courts." [122]

In retrospect, it now seems likely that Paine's letter of 17 February at least hastened Burke's decision to break with the Revolution. It is even more likely that a second letter sent soon afterward [123] caused him to break with Paine himself. Unfortunately, the letter has not survived, but its substance was reported in three presumably independent accounts. The first is a conversation with Burke on 21 May 1791 which Count Bentinck recorded in his journal. Burke is quoted as saying that "he had been in correspondence with Mr. Payne[124] who was then (in 1790) living at Paris, with the American Minister Jefferson, Fayette and the Jacobins, and that in one letter he stated how much good the propagation of the French opinions throughout Europe and England by ——— or Burke would advance the cause of Freedom." [125] The other two accounts came from Burke's earliest biographers. In Croly's summary of the letter, which he called—mistakenly, it would seem—one of Paine's "earliest missives" to Burke, Paine is said to have "eagerly urged [Burke] to introduce Revolution into England, by its established name of 'Reform!'" [126] In Bisset's still earlier account "Paine expressed his wishes that the British Opposition should coincide in the republican views, and *use parliamentary reform as the pretext.*" [127] All three accounts agree that Burke's response was emphatic, if not explosive. Bisset quotes Burke as replying, "Do you mean to propose that I, who have all my life fought for the constitution, should devote the wretched remains of my days to conspire its destruction? Do you not know that I have always opposed the things called reform; to be sure, because I did not think them reform?" [128] The reply which Croly attributed to Burke sounds much more like him, but, alas, the source is somewhat suspect: "Do you *really* imagine, Mr. Paine, that the constitution of this kingdom requires such innovations, or *could exist with them,* or that any *reflecting man would seriously engage in them?* You are aware that I have, all my life, opposed such schemes of reform, because I *know them not to be Reform."* [129] According to Bentinck, Burke was so offended at the "idea" that he "broke off all intercourse with Payne." [130]

Actually, Burke's break with Paine—and with the Revolution— was not so abrupt. By the winter of 1789–90 neither man should have had any illusions about the other where France was concerned. Certainly Paine had made no secret of his growing excitement over the prospect of another revolution. Burke, on his part, had made it clear that as an Englishman and a Whig, at that, he regarded France as a serious and formidable rival. This, no doubt, accounts for a remark which Paine made to Jefferson soon after his visit with Burke and the Duke of Portland in August, 1788: "I find the opposition as much warped in some respects as to Continental Politics as the Ministry." [131] Whether or not Burke was "warped" in his view of continental politics, he was at least slow to recognize the revolutionary spirit which was beginning to transform France. This we have on the authority of both men. "There was a time," Paine was soon to write, "when it was impossible to make Mr. Burke believe there would be any revolution in France. His opinion then was that the French had neither spirit to undertake it, nor fortitude to support. . . ." [132] Burke himself confessed his surprise at the revolutionary turn in French affairs. Indeed, his reaction to the storming of the Bastille was a mixture of astonishment and perplexity—"astonishment at a French struggle for Liberty" and perplexity in "not knowing whether to blame or applaud." Though he thought he saw "something like it in progress for several years," the whole affair was "one of the most curious matters of Speculation that ever was exhibited." The doubt in his mind was no longer whether the French had spirit but whether they would be able to restrain it. If the outbreak of "the old Parisian ferocity" was no more than a "sudden explosion," no inference, he thought, should be drawn from it. But if it stemmed from "character" rather than "accident," he declared, the French people were "not fit for Liberty" and needed "a Strong hand" to coerce them. "Men must have a certain fund of natural moderation to qualifye them for Freedom, else it become noxious to themselves and a perfect Nuisance to everybody else." It is not enough for a people to desire freedom to attain it, he insisted; wisdom is needed as well as spirit to form a "solid constitution." Whether the French had "wise heads" among them or whether those with such heads had "authority equal to their wisdom" was still to be seen.[133]

The question was still unresolved in Burke's mind at the end of the year, though his doubts had begun to harden. By November he was prepared to offer his first reasoned assessment of the events in France. The occasion was a letter from a young Frenchman, Charles-Jean-François Depont, who had once visited Burke and seems to have been a favorite of his. Depont had asked Burke for his opinion on French affairs, confident that the response would be favorable. Instead, Burke raised privately and tentatively most of the objections to the Revolution which soon he would proclaim publicly and unequivocally. Though he might have his prejudices about a nation's relative power, he would never envy its "internal freedom, security, and good order." The French people, like all others who desire liberty, deserved it, but the liberty to which they were entitled was not "solitary, unconnected, individual [or] selfish . . .[a]s if every Man was to regulate the whole of his Conduct by his own will." The liberty he meant was "*social* freedom," which indeed was "but another name for Justice, ascertained by wise Laws, and secured by well-constructed institutions." When, therefore, every citizen in France of any description was perfectly secure in his life, his property, and his person and free to express his sentiments "decently" on public affairs, Burke would be as "well pleased" as any one. And when the "great publick Assemblies" in France were "perfectly free themselves" from the "coercion of a Military Power of any description"; when they were not "driven to be the instruments of the Violence of others, from a sense of their own weakness"; when they were "not obliged to Resort to *confiscation* to supply the defects of *taxation*"; "when they look with horrour upon all Arbitrary decisions in their Legislative Capacity, striking at prescriptive Right [and] long undisturbed Possession"; when he saw France's sovereign legislative power acting "in this condition of deliberative freedom," he would gladly acknowledge it as "the collected Reason and Representative Majesty of the Commonwealth." Finally, when the Courts of Justice in France refrained from sitting in judgment "on the Lives, Liberties, Properties, or, estimation of their fellow Citizens" under conditions of "Suspense, fear and humiliation"; when they were not called upon to "put any Man to his trial upon undefined Crimes of State, not ascertain'd by any previous Rule, Statute or course of precedent"; when victims were not "snatched from the fury of the People, to be brought before a Tribunal itself subject to the effects of the same fury"; when he saw Tribunals made independent of "everything but Law, and with a clear Law for their direction," he would rejoice in seeing such a "happy order" established in France. But until the assemblies, judicatures, and municipalities of France acted or refrained from acting "in the particulars, upon the principles, and in the spirit" he had outlined, Depont was told, "I must delay my congratulations on your acquisition of Liberty. You had made a Revolution, but not a Reformation. You may have subverted Monarchy, but not recover'd freedom." [134]

Aware that his views were not at all what Depont had expected, Burke tried to soften their impact. It was only "natural," he declared, that the "astonishing scene" in France should have given rise in his mind "to many Reflexions and to some Emotions," but he was reluctant to express them with confidence and finality. His acquaintance with the "correct, political Map" of France was very imperfect, and in his "present want of knowledge," he could speak "only hypothetically." Besides, he had come to distrust his own judgment too much to press it on others unless they were aware of the "diffidence" with which it was offered. It was this same diffidence which allowed him to admit, without the slightest trace of self-pity, that his opinions carried "little weight" in his own country, even though he had "some share in a Publick Trust." This "self-distrust" he urged Depont to keep in mind as a "corrective" whenever Burke spoke with "more positiveness" than his "knowledge and situation" warranted. "If I should seem any where to express myself in the language of disapprobation," he begged his young friend, "be so good to consider it as no more than the expression of doubt." As a final assurance, he promised that he would not withhold a favorable judgment about the "new order" in France, merely because it was a "Democracy or rather a collection of Democracies" quite unlike the "qualified Monarchy" under which he had "long enjoyed a sober share of freedom." He was not so "narrow minded," he said, "as to be unable to conceive, that the same Object may be attain'd in many ways, and perhaps in ways very different from those which we have follow'd in this Country." England's "proud distinction, her Monopoly of fame" had been her "practical Constitution in which the grand secret had been found of reconciling a Government of real energy for all foreign and domestick Purposes, with the most perfect security to the liberty and safety of Individuals." But any government, whatever its name or form, which succeeded in uniting those advantages, deserved the applause of "all discerning Men." [135]

Yet within three months Burke's doubts had become certainties and his diffidence had given way to the most confident and sweeping of pronouncements about French affairs. Since no fresh acts of violence or pillage had occurred in the meantime, it seems likely that his now open hostility to the Revolution was brought about by his fear, which Paine's mid-winter letters from Paris had fed, that it was to be the "forerunner" of other revolutions in Europe, perhaps even in England. This fear, though no doubt exaggerated, was not entirely groundless. Dr. Richard Price, a Unitarian minister whom Burke was later to call a "political divine," had already preached his famous sermon to the Revolution Society in London congratulating France on the state of its affairs and expressing the hope that England would soon be moved by the same spirit of reform. Moved by Price's eloquence, the Society sent a congratulatory address of its own to the National Assembly, which then replied in kind. Both the sermon and the two addresses were published, and Burke read them about the same time he received Paine's letter of January 17. A few weeks later on February 9, he publicly denounced the Revolution. The occasion was the annual debate in the House of Commons on the Army Estimates. Fox and Sheridan, both of the Whig opposition, had openly praised the Revolution and the new democratic principles which it had instituted in the French army. Even Prime Minister Pitt declared that he looked forward to the day when a reconstructed France "would stand forward as one of the most brilliant powers in Europe." Burke disassociated himself completely from the sentiments which had been expressed. From the start, he declared, the leaders of the Third Estate had not been content to redress grievances and improve the fabric of their society. By insisting that all three orders be merged into a single National Assembly, they first rashly destroyed "all the balances and counterpoises which serve to fix the state and to give it a steady direction" and then "melted down the whole into one incongruous, ill-connected mass." This accomplished, they then "laid the axe to the root of all property, and consequently of all national prosperity, by the principles they established and the example they set, in confiscating all the possessions of the Church." In doing so, they had acted "with the most atrocious perfidy and breach of faith among all men." [136]

Not even the hallowed principles of the Revolution escaped his scorn. The Declaration of the Rights of Man and of the Citizen, so dear to Paine, Jefferson, and Lafayette, was so "pedantic" in its "abuse of elementary principles as would have disgraced boys at school." Worse yet, it was "a sort of *institute* and *digest* of anarchy" because in its name "every hold of authority by opinion, religious or civil," was being systematically destroyed. By "this mad declaration," the state had been subverted and the nation forced to suffer "calamities" which previously only countries long at war had ever been known to suffer "and which may in the end produce such a war, and perhaps many such." Only the direst necessity could ever justify such misconduct, and in France there was none. With the men who led the Revolution the choice had not been between "despotism and liberty"; the "peace and power" of France had not been sacrificed on the altar of freedom. "Freedom, and a better security for freedom than they have taken, they might have had without any sacrifice at all." They had not allowed the nation to suffer all these calamities in order to obtain a British constitution; rather "they plunged into those calamaties to prevent themselves from settling into that constitution, or into any thing resembling it." [137]

To Burke, obviously, much more was at stake than the outcome of a parliamentary debate. Ultimately, he was convinced, the same misfortunes which had already engulfed France would overtake England if sympathy for the Revolution continued to spread. Rather than see his country endangered, he warned prophetically that he would break with his closest friends and make common cause with his worst enemies. His speech in the House was but the start of a crusade to rouse his countrymen to their peril. He had the speech printed to reach a wider audience, and within a week he announced that he would deal with the Revolution more fully in a "public letter." When the letter was finally published later that year, it was entitled *Reflections on the Revolution in France and on the Proceedings in Certain Societies in London Relative to that Event In a Letter Intended to Have Been Sent to a Gentleman in Paris.* That "gentleman in Paris" was none other than his young friend, Depont, although for what Burke called "prudential considerations" he was not identified by name.[138]

Paine, then in Paris, seems to have been taken by surprise at the violence of Burke's speech in the House. On learning that Burke intended to write a more extended attack on the Revolution, he promised some of his friends in France that he would answer it. Not surprisingly, the promise was much more easily made than kept. He had already started to write a pamphlet of his own in defense of the Revolution which he intended to dedicate to George Washington.[139] But before it could be recast in suitable form, he had to wait eight months until Burke's own work was published. To Paine, it must have seemed a long and trying wait. For a time after his return to London in April, he was determined not to call on Burke "until his pamphlet comes out, or he gives it up." However, on at least one occasion he did, but with the understanding that no mention was to be made of French affairs.[140] Unwilling or unable to ask Burke himself, Paine had only secondhand reports about the progress of Burke's work. For a short time it seemed, as Paine confided to a friend, that after all his "vaporing," Burke would not publish his pamphlet. It was about this time that Paine said to one of Burke's friends, whom he met on the street, "I am exceedingly sorry to see a friend of ours so exceedingly wrong." To which the friend replied, "Time will show if he is." "He is already wrong," said Paine, "with respect to time past." [141] Finally, the suspense ended for Paine. On November 1, 1790, Burke's *Reflections* was published, and Paine hastened to reply. For the next few months he did little else. In March, 1791, his own reflections on the French Revolution and on "Mr. Burke" were published as Part I of *The Rights of Man*. It was followed nearly a year later by Part II which was inspired in part by Burke's contemptuous dismissal of his views in *An Appeal from the New to the Old Whigs* (1791). Thus began what has been called "perhaps the most crucial ideological debate ever carried on in English." [142] The Revolution which gave rise to that debate ended in disaster but its influence is still felt not only in France but throughout the world. Indeed, the issues which it raised are as timely today as when they were first debated by Burke and Paine. The debate was inconclusive in their day, and it continues to be inconclusive in ours. Nor is it likely that either side will ever completely and finally prevail. The conservative and liberal temperaments which Burke and Paine symbolize are equally authentic, hence equally valid expressions of man's political nature.[143]

PART I

THE CONSECRATED STATE OF EDMUND BURKE

Reflections on the Revolution in France,
abridged, arranged, and annotated
with excerpts added from Edmund Burke's
speeches and other writings.

Reflections on the Revolution in France

and on the *proceedings in certain
societies in London relative to
that event:* IN A LETTER *intended
to have been sent to a gentleman in Paris*

*It may not be unnecessary to inform the Reader, that the following
Reflections had their origin in a correspondence between the Author
and a very young gentleman at Paris, who did him the honor of
desiring his opinion upon the important transactions, which then,
and ever since, have so much occupied the attention of all men. An
answer was written some time in the month of October 1789; but
it was kept back upon prudential considerations. That letter is al-
luded to in the beginning of the following sheets. It has been since
forwarded to the person to whom it was addressed. The reasons for
the delay in sending it were assigned in a short letter to the same
gentleman. This produced on his part a new and pressing application for the Author's sentiments.*

*The Author began a second and more full discussion on the
subject. This he had some thoughts of publishing early in the last
spring; but the matter gaining upon him, he found that what he
had undertaken not only far exceeded the measure of a letter, but
that its importance required rather a more detailed consideration
than at that time he had any leisure to bestow upon it. However,
having thrown down his first thoughts in the form of a letter, and
indeed when he sat down to write, having intended it for a private*

71

letter, he found it difficult to change the form of address, when his sentiments had grown into a greater extent, and had received another direction. A different plan, he is sensible, might be more favorable to a commodious division and distribution of his matter.

Reflections
on the Revolution
in France

DEAR SIR,[1]

You are pleased to call again, and with some earnestness, for my thoughts on the late proceedings in France. I will not give you reason to imagine that I think my sentiments of such value as to wish myself to be solicited about them. They are of too little consequence to be very anxiously either communicated or withheld. It was from attention to you, and to you only, that I hesitated at the time, when you first desired to receive them. In the first letter I had the honor to write to you, and which at length I send, I wrote neither for nor from any description of men; nor shall I in this. My errors, if any, are my own. My reputation alone is to answer for them.

You see, Sir, by the long letter I have transmitted to you, that, though I do most heartily wish that France may be animated by a spirit of rational liberty, and that I think you bound, in all honest policy, to provide a permanent body, in which that spirit may reside, and an effectual organ, by which it may act, it is my misfortune to entertain great doubts concerning several material points in your late transactions.

You imagined, when you wrote last, that I might possibly be

reckoned among the approvers of certain proceedings in France, from the solemn public seal of sanction they have received from two clubs of gentlemen in London, called the Constitutional Society, and the Revolution Society.

I certainly have the honor to belong to more clubs than one in which the constitution of this kingdom and the principles of the Glorious Revolution are held in high reverence; and I reckon myself among the most forward in my zeal for maintaining that constitution and those principles in their utmost purity and vigor. It is because I do so, that I think it necessary for me that there should be no mistake. Those who cultivate the memory of our revolution,[2] and those who are attached to the constitution of this kingdom, will take good care how they are involved with persons who, under the pretext of zeal towards the Revolution and Constitution, too frequently wander from their true principles; and are ready on every occasion to depart from the firm but cautious and deliberate spirit which produced the one, and which presides in the other. Before I proceed to answer the more material particulars in your letter, I shall beg leave to give you such information as I have been able to obtain of the two clubs which have thought proper, as bodies, to interfere in the concerns of France; first assuring you, that I am not, and that I have never been, a member of either of those societies.

The first, calling itself the Constitutional Society, or Society for Constitutional Information,[3] or by some such title, is, I believe, of seven or eight years standing. The institution of this society appears to be of a charitable, and so far of a laudable, nature: it was intended for the circulation, at the expence of the members, of many books, which few others would be at the expense of buying; and which might lie on the hands of the booksellers, to the great loss of an useful body of men. Whether the books so charitably circulated, were ever as charitably read, is more than I know. Possibly several of them have been exported to France; and, like goods not in request here, may with you have found a market. I have heard much talk of the lights to be drawn from books that are sent from hence. What improvements they have had in their passage (as it is said some liquors are meliorated by crossing the sea) I cannot tell: But I never heard a man of common judgment, or the least degree of information, speak a word in praise of the greater part of the publications circulated by that society; nor have their proceedings been accounted, except by some of themselves, as of any serious consequence.

Your National Assembly seeems to entertain much the same opinion that I do of this poor charitable club. As a nation, you reserved the whole stock of your eloquent acknowledgments for the Revolution Society,[4] when their fellows in the Constitutional were, in equity, entitled to some share. Since you have selected the Revolution Society as the great object of your national thanks and praises, you will think me excusable in making its late conduct the subject of my observations. The National Assembly of France has given importance to these gentlemen by adopting them; and they return the favor, by acting as a committee in England for extending the principles of the National Assembly. Henceforward we must consider them as a kind of privileged persons, as no inconsiderable members in the diplomatic body. This is one among the revolutions which have given splendor to obscurity, and distinction to undiscerned merit. Until very lately I do not recollect to have heard of this club. I am quite sure that it never occupied a moment of my thoughts; nor, I believe, those of any person out of their own set. I find, upon enquiry, that on the anniversary of the Revolution in 1688, a club of dissenters,[5] but of what denomination I know not, have long had the custom of hearing a sermon in one of their churches; and that afterwards they spent the day cheerfully, as other clubs do, at the tavern. But I never heard that any public measure, or political system, much less that the merits of the constitution of any foreign nation, had been the subject of a formal proceeding at their festivals; until, to my inexpressible surprise, I found them in a sort of public capacity, by a congratulatory address, giving an authoritative sanction to the proceedings of the National Assembly in France. . . .

I flatter myself that I love a manly, moral, regulated liberty as well as any gentleman of that society, be he who he will; and perhaps I have given as good proofs of my attachment to that cause, in the whole course of my public conduct. I think I envy liberty as little as they do to any other nation.* But I cannot stand forward, and give

* [O]f all the loose terms in the world, liberty is the most indefinite. . . . It is not solitary, unconnected, individual, selfish liberty, as if every man was to regulate the whole of his conduct by his own will. The liberty I mean is *social* freedom. It is that state of things in which liberty is secured by the equality of restraint. A constitution of things in which the liberty of no man, and no body of men and no number of men, can find means to trespass on the liberty of any person, or any description of persons in the society. This kind of liberty is, indeed but another name for justice, ascertained by wise laws and secured by well-constructed institutions. *Letter to Charles-Jean François Dupont* (November 1789) in *The Correspondence of Edmund Burke*, ed. Thomas W. Copeland (Cambridge, Eng.: Cambridge University Press and Chicago: University of

praise or blame to any thing which relates to human actions, and human concerns, on a simple view of the object, as it stands stripped of every relation, in all the nakedness and solitude of metaphysical abstraction. Circumstances (which with some gentlemen pass for nothing) give in reality to every political principle its distinguishing color and discriminating effect. The circumstances are what render every civil and political scheme beneficial or noxious to mankind.* Abstractedly speaking, government, as well as liberty, is good; yet could I, in common sense, ten years ago, have felicitated France on enjoyment of a government (for she then had a government) without enquiry what the nature of that government was, or how it was administered? Can I now congratulate the same nation upon its freedom? Is it because liberty in the abstract may be classed amongst the blessings of mankind, that I am seriously to felicitate a madman, who has escaped from the protecting restraint and wholesome darkness of his cell, on his restoration to the enjoyment of light and liberty? Am I to congratulate a highwayman and murderer who has broke prison upon the recovery of his natural rights? This would be to act over again the scene of the criminals condemned to the galleys, and their heroic deliverer, the metaphysic Knight of the Sorrowful Countenance.[6]

When I see the spirit of liberty in action, I see a strong principle at work; and this, for a while, is all I can possibly know of it. The wild *gas,* the fixed air, is plainly broke loose: but we ought to suspend our judgment until the first effervescence is a little subsided, till the liquor is cleared, and until we see something deeper than the agitation of a troubled and frothy surface. I must be tolerably sure, before I venture publicly to congratulate men upon a blessing, that they have really received one. Flattery corrupts both the receiver and the giver; and adulation is not of more service to the people than to kings. I should therefore suspend my congratulations on the new liberty of France, until I was informed how it had been combined with government; with public force; with the discipline and obedi-

Chicago Press, 1958–1969), VI, 42; hereafter this work will be referred to as *Correspondence.* Spelling and punctuation modernized.

* I must see with mine own eyes, I must, in a manner, touch with my own hands, not only the fixed but the momentary circumstances, before I could venture to suggest any political project whatsoever. I must know the power and disposition to accept, to execute, to persevere. I must see all the aids, and all the obstacles. I must see the means of correcting the plan, where correctives would be wanted. I must see the things; I must see the men. *Letter To a Member of the National Assembly* (1791), II, 549.

ence of armies; with the collection of an effective and well-distributed revenue; with morality and religion; with the solidity of property; with peace and order; with civil and social manners. All these (in their way) are good things too; and, without them, liberty is not a benefit while it lasts, and is not likely to continue long. The effect of liberty to individuals is that they may do what they please: We ought to see what it will please them to do, before we risk congratulations, which may be soon turned into complaints. Prudence would dictate this in the case of separate insulated private men; but liberty, when men act in bodies, is *power*. Considerate people, before they declare themselves, will observe the use which is made of *power;* and particularly of so trying a thing as *new* power in *new* persons, of whose principles, tempers, and dispositions, they have little or no experience, and in situations where those who appear the most stirring in the scene may possibly not be the real movers. . . .

We are now in a condition to discern, with tolerable exactness, the true nature of the object held up to our imitation. If the prudence of reserve and decorum dictates silence in some circumstances, in others prudence of an higher order may justify us in speaking our thoughts. The beginnings of confusion with us in England are at present feeble enough; but with you, we have seen an infancy still more feeble, growing by moments into a strength to heap mountains upon mountains, and to wage war with Heaven itself. Whenever our neighbor's house is on fire, it cannot be amiss for the engines to play a little on our own. Better to be despised for too anxious apprehensions, than ruined by too confident a security.

Solicitous chiefly for the peace of my own country, but by no means unconcerned for yours I wish to communicate more largely, what was at first intended only for your private satisfaction. I shall still keep your affairs in my eye, and continue to address myself to you. Indulging myself in the freedom of epistolary intercourse, I beg leave to throw out my thoughts, and express my feelings, just as they arise in my mind, with very little attention to formal method. I set out with the proceedings of the Revolution Society; but I shall not confine myself to them. Is it possible I should? It looks to me as if I were in a great crisis, not of the affairs of France alone, but of all Europe, perhaps of more than Europe. All circumstances taken together, the French revolution is the most astonishing that has hitherto happened in the world. The most wonderful things are brought about in many instances by means the most absurd and ridiculous; in the most ridiculous modes; and apparently, by the most contemptible instruments. Every thing seems out of nature in this strange chaos of levity and ferocity, and of all sorts of crimes jumbled together with all sorts of follies. In viewing this monstrous tragi-comic scene, the most opposite passions necessarily succeed, and sometimes mix with each other in the mind; alternate contempt and indignation; alternate laughter and tears; alternate scorn and horror.

It cannot, however, be denied that to some this strange scene appeared in quite another point of view. Into them it inspired no other sentiments than those of exultation and rapture. They saw nothing in what has been done in France, but a firm and temperate exertion of freedom so consistent, on the whole, with morals and with piety, as to make it deserving not only of the secular applause of dashing Machiavelian politicians, but to render it a fit theme for all the devout effusions of sacred eloquence.

On the forenoon of the 4th of November last, Doctor Richard Price,[7] a non-conforming minister of eminence, preached at the dissenting meeting-house of the Old Jewry, to his club or society, a very extraordinary miscellaneous sermon, in which there are some good moral and religious sentiments, and not ill expressed, mixed up in a sort of porridge of various political opinions and reflections: but the revolution in France is the grand ingredient in the cauldron. . . . His doctrines affect our constitution in its vital parts. He tells the Revolution Society, in this political sermon, that his majesty "is almost the *only* lawful king in the world, because the *only* one who owes his crown to the *choice of his people*." . . .

Lest the foundation of the king's exclusive legal title should pass for a mere rant of adulatory freedom, the political Divine proceeds dogmatically to assert, that by the principles of the Revolution the people of England have acquired three fundamental rights, all which, with him, compose one system, and lie together in one short sentence; namely, that we have acquired a right

1. "To choose our own governors."
2. "To cashier them for misconduct."
3. "To frame a government for ourselves."

This doctrine, as applied to the prince now on the British throne, either is nonsense, and therefore neither true nor false, or it affirms a most unfounded, dangerous, illegal, and unconstitutional position. According to this spiritual doctor of politics, if His Majesty does not owe his crown to the choice of his people, he is no *lawful* king. Now nothing can be more untrue than that the crown of this kingdom is so held by His Majesty. . . . At sometime or other, to be sure, all the beginners of dynasties were chosen by those who called them to govern. There is ground enough for the opinion that all the kingdoms of Europe were, at a remote period, elective, with more or fewer limitations in the objects of choice; but whatever kings might have been here or elsewhere, a thousand years ago, or in whatever manner the ruling dynasties of England or France may have begun, the King of Great Britain is at this day king by a fixed rule of succession, according to the laws of his country; and while the legal conditions of the compact of sovereignty are performed by him (as they are performed) he holds his crown in contempt of the choice of the Revolution Society, who have not a single vote for a king amongst them, either individually or collectively; though I make no doubt they would soon erect themselves into an electoral college, if things were ripe to give effect to their claim. His Majesty's heirs and successors, each in his time and order, will come to the crown with the same contempt of their choice with which His Majesty has succeeded to that he wears. . . .

Unquestionably there was at the Revolution, in the person of King William, a small and a temporary deviation from the strict order of a regular hereditary succession; but it is against all genuine principles of jurisprudence to draw a principle from a law made in a special case, and regarding an individual person. *Privilegium non transit in exemplum.*[8] If ever there was a time favorable for establishing the principle, that a king of popular choice was the only legal king, without all doubt it was at the Revolution. Its not being done at that time is a proof that the nation was of opinion it ought not to be done at any time. There is no person so completely ignorant of our history as not to know that the majority in Parliament of both parties were so little disposed to any thing resembling that principle, that at first they were determined to place the vacant crown, not on the head of the Prince of Orange, but on that of his wife Mary, daughter of King James, the eldest born of the issue of that king, which they acknowledged as undoubtedly his. It would be to repeat a very trite story to recall to your memory all those circumstances which demonstrated that their accepting King William was not properly a *choice;* but, to all those who did not wish in effect to recall King James, or to deluge their country in blood, and again to bring their religion, laws, and liberties into the peril they had just escaped, it was an act of *necessity,* in the strictest moral sense in which necessity can be taken. . . .

The gentlemen of the Society of Revolutions see nothing in that of 1688 but the deviation from the constitution; and they take the deviation from the principle for the principle. They have little regard to the obvious consequences of their doctrine, though they must see, that it leaves positive authority in very few of the positive institutions of this country. When such an unwarrantable maxim is once established, that no throne is lawful but the elective, no one act of the princes who preceded their era of fictitious election can be valid. Do these theorists mean to imitate some of their predecessors, who dragged the bodies of our ancient sovereigns out of the quiet of their tombs? Do they mean to attaint and disable backwards all the kings that have reigned before the Revolution, and consequently to stain the throne of England with the blot of a continual usurpation? Do they mean to invalidate, annul, or to call into question, together with the titles of the whole line of our kings, that great body of our statute law which passed under those whom they treat as usurpers? to annul laws of inestimable value to our liberties —of as great value at least as any which have passed at or since the period of the Revolution? If kings, who did not owe their crown to the choice of their people, had no title to make laws, what will become of the Statute *de Tallagio Non Concedendo?*—of the *Petition of Right?*—of the Act of *Habeas Corpus?* [9] Do these new doctors of the rights of men presume to assert that King James the Second, who came to the crown as next of blood, according to the rules of a then unqualified succession, was not to all intents and purposes a lawful king of England, before he had done any of those acts which were justly construed into an abdication of his crown? If he was not, much trouble in Parliament might have been saved at the period these gentlemen commemorate. But King James was a bad king with a good title, and not an usurper. . . .

The second claim of the Revolution Society is "a right of cashiering their governors for *misconduct.*" Perhaps the apprehensions our ancestors entertained of forming such a precedent as that "of cashiering for misconduct," was the cause that the declaration of the act which implied the abdication of King James,[10] was, if it had any fault, rather too guarded, and too circumstantial. But all this guard, and all this accumulation of circumstances, serves to show the spirit of caution which predominated in the national councils, in a situation in which men irritated by oppression, and elevated by a triumph over it, are apt to abandon themselves to violent and extreme courses: it shows the anxiety of the great men who influenced the conduct of affairs at that great event, to make the Revolution a parent of settlement, and not a nursery of future revolutions.

No government could stand a moment, if it could be blown

down with any thing so loose and indefinite as an opinion of *"misconduct."* They who led at the Revolution grounded the virtual abdication of King James upon no such light and uncertain principle. They charged him with nothing less than a design, confirmed by a multitude of illegal overt acts, to *subvert the Protestant church and state,* and their *fundamental,* unquestionable laws and liberties: they charged him with having broken the *original contract* between king and people. This was more than *misconduct.* A grave and over-ruling necessity obliged them to take the step they took, and took with infinite reluctance, as under that most rigorous of all laws. Their trust for the future preservation of the constitution was not in future revolutions. The grand policy of all their regulations was to render it almost impracticable for any future sovereign to compel the states of the kingdom to have again recourse to those violent remedies. They left the crown what, in the eye and estimation of law, it had ever been, perfectly irresponsible. In order to lighten the crown still further, they aggravated responsibility on ministers of state. By the statute of the 1st of King William, sess. 2d, called *"the act for declaring the rights and liberties of the subject, and for settling the succession of the crown,"* [11] they enacted that the ministers should serve the crown on the terms of that declaration. They secured soon after the *frequent meetings of Parliament,* by which the whole government would be under the constant inspection and active control of the popular representative and of the magnates of the kingdom. In the next great constitutional act,[12] that of the 12th and 13th of King William, for the further limitation of the crown, and *better* securing the rights and liberties of the subject, they provided "that no pardon under the great seal of England should be pleadable to an impeachment by the commons in Parliament. The rule laid down for government in the Declaration of Right, the constant inspection of Parliament, the practical claim of impeachment, they thought infinitely a better security not only for their constitutional liberty, but against the vices of administration, than the reservation of a right so difficult in the practice, so uncertain in the issue, and often so mischievous in the consequences, as that of "cashiering their governors."

Dr. Price, in this sermon, condemns very properly the practice of gross, adulatory addresses to kings. Instead of this fulsome style, he proposes that His Majesty should be told, on occasions of congratulation, that "he is to consider himself as more properly the servant than the sovereign of his people." For a compliment, this new form of address does not seem to be very soothing. Those who are servants, in name, as well as in effect, do not like to be told of their situation, their duty, and their obligations. . . .

Kings, in one sense, are undoubtedly the servants of the people, because their power has no other rational end than that of the general advantage; but it is not true that they are, in the ordinary sense (by our constitution, at least) any thing like servants; the essence of whose situation is to obey the commands of some other, and to be removable at pleasure. But the king of Great Britain obeys no other person; all other persons are individually, and collectively too, under him, and owe to him a legal obedience. The law, which knows neither to flatter nor to insult, calls this high magistrate, not our servant, as this humble Divine calls him, but *"our sovereign Lord the King;"* and we, on our parts, have learned to speak only the primitive language of the law, and not the confused jargon of their Babylonian pulpits.

As he is not to obey us, but as we are to obey the law in him, our constitution has made no sort of provision towards rendering him, as a servant, in any degree responsible. Our constitution knows nothing of a magistrate like the *Justicia* of Aragon;[13] nor of any court legally appointed, nor of any process legally settled for submitting the king to the responsibility belonging to all servants. In this he is not distinguished from the commons and the lords, who, in their several public capacities, can never be called to an account for their conduct; although the Revolution Society chooses to assert, in direct opposition to one of the wisest and most beautiful parts of our constitution, that "a king is no more than the first servant of the public, created by it, *and responsible to it."* . . .

The third head of right, asserted by the pulpit of the Old Jewry, namely, the "right to form a government for ourselves," has, at least, as little countenance from any thing done at the Revolution, either in precedent or principle, as the two first of their claims. The Revolution was made to preserve our *ancient* indisputable laws and liberties, and that *ancient* constitution of government which is our only security for law and liberty. If you are desirous of knowing the spirit of our constitution, and the policy which predominated in that great period which has secured it to this hour, pray look for both in our histories, in our records, in our acts of Parliament, and journals of Parliament, and not in the sermons of the Old Jewry, and the after-dinner toasts of the Revolution Society. . . .

Our oldest reformation is that of Magna Carta [1215]. You will see that Sir Edward Coke,[14] that great oracle of our law, and indeed all the great men who follow him, to Blackstone,[15] are industrious to prove the pedigree of our liberties. They endeavor to prove that the ancient charter, the Magna Carta of King John, was connected with another positive charter from Henry I and that both the one and the other were nothing more than a re-affirmance of the still more ancient standing law of the kingdom. . . . In the famous law of the 3d of Charles I called the *Petition of Right* [1628] the Parliament says to the king, "Your subjects have *inherited* this freedom," claiming their franchises not on abstract principles "as the rights of men," but as the rights of Englishmen and as a patrimony derived from their forefathers. Selden,[16] and the other profoundly learned men, who drew this Petition of Right, were as well acquainted, at least, with all the general theories concerning the "rights of men," as any of the discoursers in our pulpits, or on your tribune; full as well as Dr. Price, or as the Abbé Sieyès.[17] But, for reasons worthy of that practical wisdom which superseded their theoretic science, they preferred this positive, recorded, *hereditary* title to all which can be dear to the man and the citizen, to that vague speculative right, which exposed their sure inheritance to be scrambled for and torn to pieces by every wild litigious spirit.

The same policy pervades all the laws which have since been made for the preservation of our liberties. In the 1st of William and Mary, in the famous statute called the Declaration of Right [1689], the two houses utter not a syllable of "a right to frame a government for themselves." You will see that their whole care was to secure the religion, laws, and liberties, that had been long possessed, and had been lately endangered. "Taking into their most serious consideration the *best* means for making such an establishment, that their religion, laws, and liberties, might not be in danger of being again subverted," they auspicate all their proceedings, by stating as some of those *best* means, "in the *first place*" to do "as their *ancestors in like cases have usually* done for vindicating their *ancient* rights and liberties, to *declare;*"—and then they pray the king and queen, "that it may be *declared* and enacted, that *all and singular* the rights and liberties *asserted and declared* are the true *ancient* and indubitable rights and liberties of the people of this kingdom."

You will observe, that from Magna Carta to the Declaration of Right, it has been the uniform policy of our constitution to claim and assert our liberties, as an *entailed inheritance* derived to us from our forefathers, and to be transmitted to our posterity as an estate specially belonging to the people of this kingdom without any reference whatever to any other more general or prior right. By this means our constitution preserves an unity in so great a diversity of its parts. We have an inheritable crown; an inheritable peerage; and an house of commons and a people inheriting privileges, franchises, and liberties, from a long line of ancestors. . . .

PREJUDICE AND REASON

Thanks to our sullen resistance to innovation, thanks to the cold sluggishness of our national character, we still bear the stamp of our forefathers. We have not (as I conceive) lost the generosity and dignity of thinking of the fourteenth century; nor as yet have we subtilized ourselves into savages. We are not the converts of Rousseau; we are not the disciples of Voltaire; Helvetius has made no progress amongst us.[18] Atheists are not our preachers; madmen are not our lawgivers. We know that *we* have made no discoveries; and we think that no discoveries are to be made in morality nor many in the great principles of government, nor in the ideas of liberty, which were understood long before we were born, altogether as well as they will be after the grave has heaped its mould upon our presumption, and the silent tomb shall have imposed its law on our pert loquacity. In England we have not yet been completely embowelled of our natural entrails; we still feel within us, and we cherish and cultivate, those inbred sentiments which are the faithful guardians, the active monitors of our duty, the true supporters of all liberal and manly morals. We have not been drawn and trussed, in order that we may be filled, like stuffed birds in a museum, with chaff and rags, and paltry, blurred shreds of paper about the rights of man.* We preserve the whole of our feelings still native and entire, unsophisticated by pedantry and infidelity. We have real hearts of flesh and blood beating in our bosoms. We fear God; we look up with awe to kings; with affection to parliaments; with duty to magistrates; with reverence to priests; and with respect to nobility. Why? Because when such ideas are brought before our minds, it is *natural* to be so affected; because all other feelings are false and spurious, and tend to corrupt our minds, to vitiate our primary morals, to render us unfit for rational liberty; and by teaching us a servile, licentious, and abandoned insolence, to be our low sport

---

* The pretended *rights of man*, which have made this havoc, cannot be the rights of the people. For to be a people, and to have these rights, are things incompatible. The one supposes the presence, the other the absence of a state of civil society. *An Appeal From the New to the Old Whigs* (1791), III, 95. [Burke's emphasis]

for a few holidays, to make us perfectly fit for, and justly deserving of slavery, through the whole course of our lives. You see, Sir, that in this enlightened age I am bold enough to confess, that we are generally men of untaught feelings; that instead of casting away all our old prejudices,[19] we cherish them to a very considerable degree, and, to take more shame to ourselves, we cherish them because they are prejudices; and the longer they have lasted, and the more generally they have prevailed, the more we cherish them. We are afraid to put men to live and trade each on his own private stock of reason; because we suspect that this stock in each man is small, and that the individuals would do better to avail themselves of the general bank and capital of nations, and of ages. Many of our men of speculation, instead of exploding general prejudices, employ their sagacity to discover the latent wisdom which prevails in them. If they find what they seek, and they seldom fail, they think it more wise to continue the prejudice, with the reason involved, than to cast away the coat of prejudice, and to leave nothing but the naked reason; because prejudice, with its reason, has a motive to give action to that reason, and an affection which will give it permanence. Prejudice is of ready application in the emergency; it previously engages the mind in a steady course of wisdom and virtue, and does not leave the man hesitating in the moment of decision, sceptical, puzzled, and unresolved. Prejudice renders a man's virtue his habit; and not a series of unconnected acts. Through just prejudice, his duty becomes a part of his nature. . . .

We know, and what is better we feel inwardly, that religion is the basis of civil society, and the source of all good and of all comfort. In England we are so convinced of this, that there is no rust of superstition, with which the accumulated absurdity of the human mind might have crusted it over in the course of ages, that ninety-nine in an hundred of the people of England would not prefer to impiety. We shall never be such fools as to call in an enemy to the substance of any system to remove its corruptions, to supply its defects, or to perfect its construction. If our religious tenets should ever want a further elucidation, we shall not call on atheism to explain them. We shall not light up our temple from that unhallowed fire. It will be illuminated with other lights. It will be perfumed with other incense than the infectious stuff which is imported by the smugglers of adulterated metaphysics. If our ecclesiastical establishment should want a revision, it is not avarice or rapacity, public or private, that we shall employ for the audit, or receipt, or application of its consecrated revenue.—Violently condemning neither the Greek nor the Armenian, nor, since heats are subsided, the Roman system of religion, we prefer the Protestant; not because we think it has less of the Christian religion in it, but because, in our judgment, it has more. We are protestants, not from indifference but from zeal.

We know, and it is our pride to know, that man is by his constitution a religious animal; that atheism is against, not only our reason but our instincts; and that it cannot prevail long. But if, in the moment of riot, and in a drunken delirium from the hot spirit drawn out of the alembic of hell, which in France is now so furiously boiling, we should uncover our nakedness by throwing off that Christian religion which has hitherto been our boast and comfort, and one great source of civilization amongst us, and among many other nations, we are apprehensive (being well aware that the mind will not endure a void) that some uncouth, pernicious, and degrading superstition, might take place of it.

For that reason, before we take from our establishment the natural human means of estimation, and give it up to contempt, as you have done, and in doing it have incurred the penalties you well deserve to suffer, we desire that some other may be presented to us in the place of it. We shall then form our judgment.

On these ideas, instead of quarrelling with establishments, as some do, who have made a philosophy and a religion of their hostility to such institutions, we cleave closely to them. We are resolved to keep an established church, an established monarchy, an established aristocracy, and an established democracy, each in the degree it exists, and in no greater. I shall show you presently how much of each of these we possess.

AN ESTABLISHED CHURCH

First, I beg leave to speak of our church establishment, which is the first of our prejudices, not a prejudice destitute of reason, but involving in it profound and extensive wisdom. I speak of it first. It is first, and last, and midst in our minds. For, taking ground on that religious system, of which we are now in possession, we continue to act on the early received, and uniformly continued sense of mankind. That sense not only, like a wise architect, has built up the august fabric of states, but like a provident proprietor, to preserve the structure from profanation and ruin, as a sacred temple, purged from all the impurities of fraud, and violence, and injustice, and tyranny, has solemnly and forever consecrated the commonwealth, and all that officiate in it. This consecration is made, that all who administer in the government of men, in which they stand in the person of God himself, should have high and worthy notions of their function and destination; that their hope should be full of immortality; that they should not look to the paltry pelf of the moment, nor to the temporary and transient praise of the vulgar, but to a solid, permanent existence, in the permanent part of their nature, and to a permanent fame and glory, in the example they leave as a rich inheritance to the world.

Such sublime principles ought to be infused into persons of exalted situations; and religious establishments provided, that may continually revive and enforce them. Every sort of moral, every sort of civil, every sort of politic institution, aiding the rational and natural ties that connect the human understanding and affections to the divine, are not more than necessary, in order to build up that wonderful structure, Man, whose prerogative it is, to be in a great degree a creature of his own making; and who when made as he ought to be made, is destined to hold no trivial place in the creation. But whenever man is put over men, as the better nature ought ever to preside, in that case more particularly, he should as nearly as possible be approximated to his perfection.

The consecration of the state, by a state religious establishment, is necessary also to operate with an wholesome awe upon free citizens; because, in order to secure their freedom, they must enjoy some determinate portion of power. To them therefore a religion connected with the state, and with their duty towards it, becomes even more necessary than in such societies, where the people by the terms of their subjection are confined to private sentiments, and the management of their own family concerns. All persons possessing any portion of power ought to be strongly and awfully impressed with an idea that they act in trust and that they are to account for their conduct in that trust to the one great master, author and founder of society.

This principle ought even to be more strongly impressed upon the minds of those who compose the collective sovereignty than upon those of single princes. Without instruments, these princes can do nothing. Whoever uses instruments, in finding helps, finds also impediments. Their power is therefore by no means complete, nor are they safe in extreme abuse. Such persons, however elevated by flattery, arrogance, and self-opinion, must be sensible that, whether covered or not by positive law, in some way or other they are accountable even here for the abuse of their trust. If they are not cut off by a rebellion of their people, they may be strangled by the very Janissaries[20] kept for their security against all other rebellion. Thus we have seen the king of France sold by his soldiers for an increase of pay. But where popular authority is absolute and unrestrained, the people have an infinitely greater, because a far better founded confidence in their own power. They are themselves, in a great measure, their own instruments. They are nearer to their objects. Besides, they are less under responsibility to one of the greatest controlling powers on earth, the sense of fame and estimation. The share of infamy that is likely to fall to the lot of each individual in public acts is small indeed; the operation of opinion being in the inverse ratio to the number of those who abuse power. Their own approbation of their own acts has to them the appearance of a public judgment in their favor. A perfect democracy is therefore the most shameless thing in the world. As it is the most shameless, it is also the most fearless. No man apprehends in his person he can be made subject to punishment. Certainly the people at large never ought: for as all punishments are for example towards the conservation of the people at large, the people at large can never become the subject of punishment by any human hand.* It is therefore of infinite importance that they should not be suffered to imagine that their will, any more than that of kings, is the standard of right and wrong. They ought to be persuaded that they are full as little entitled, and far less qualified, with safety to themselves, to use any arbitrary power whatsoever; that therefore they are not, under a false show of liberty but in truth to exercise an unnatural inverted domination, tyrannically to exact from those who officiate in the state, not an entire devotion to their interest, which is their right, but an abject submission to their occasional will, extinguishing thereby, in all those who serve them, all moral principle, all sense of dignity, all use of judgment, and all consistency of character, while by the very same process they give themselves up, a proper, a suitable, but a most contemptible prey, to the servile ambition of popular sycophants or courtly flatterers.

When the people have emptied themselves of all the lust of selfish will, which without religion it is utterly impossible they ever should, when they are conscious that they exercise, and exercise perhaps in an higher link of the order of delegation, the power, which

---

* I do not know the method of drawing up an indictment against an whole people. *Speech on Conciliation with America* (1775), p. 145.

to be legitimate must be according to that eternal immutable law, in which will and reason are the same, they will be more careful how they place power in base and incapable hands. In their nomination to office, they will not appoint to the exercise of authority, as to a pitiful job, but as to an holy function; not according to their sordid selfish interest, nor to their wanton caprice, nor to their arbitrary will; but they will confer that power (which any man may well tremble to give or to receive) on those only, in whom they may discern that predominant proportion of active virtue and wisdom, taken together and fitted to the charge, such, as in the great and inevitable mixed mass of human imperfections and infirmities, is to be found.

When they are habitually convinced that no evil can be acceptable, either in the act or the permission, to him whose essence is good, they will be better able to extirpate out of the minds of all magistrates, civil, ecclesiastical, or military, any thing that bears the least resemblance to a proud and lawless domination. . . .

These, my dear Sir, are, were, and I think long will be the sentiments of not the least learned and reflecting part of this kingdom. . . . They conceive that He who gave our nature to be perfected by our virtue, willed also the necessary means of its perfection—He willed therefore the state—He willed its connection with the source and original archetype of all perfection. They who are convinced of this His will, which is the law of laws and the sovereign of sovereigns, cannot think it reprehensible, that this our corporate fealty and homage, that this our recognition of a seigniory paramount, I had almost said this oblation of the state itself, as a worthy offering on the high altar of universal praise, should be performed as all public solemn acts are performed, in buildings, in music, in decoration, in speech, in the dignity of persons, according to the customs of mankind, taught by their nature; that is, with modest splendor, with unassuming state, with mild majesty and sober pomp. For those purposes they think some part of the wealth of the country is as usefully employed as it can be, in fomenting the luxury of individuals. It is the public ornament. It is the public consolation. It nourishes the public hope. The poorest man finds his own importance and dignity in it, while the wealth and pride of individuals at every moment makes the man of humble rank and fortune sensible of his inferiority, and degrades and vilifies his condition. It is for the man in humble life, and to raise his nature, and to put him in mind of a state in which the privileges of opulence will cease, when he will be equal by nature, and may be more than equal by virtue, that this portion of the general wealth of his country is employed and sanctified. . . .

It is on some such principles that the majority of the people of England, far from thinking a religious, national establishment unlawful, hardly think it lawful to be without one. . . . They do not consider their church establishment as convenient, but as essential to their state; not as a thing heterogeneous and separable; something added for accommodation; what they may either keep up or lay aside, according to their temporary ideas of convenience. They consider it as the foundation of their whole constitution, with which, and with every part of which, it holds an indissoluble union. Church and state are ideas inseparable in their minds, and scarcely is the one ever mentioned without mentioning the other.

It is from our attachment to a church establishment that the English nation did not think it wise to entrust that great fundamental interest of the whole to what they trust no part of their civil or military public service, that is to the unsteady and precarious contribution of individuals. They go further. They certainly never have suffered and never will suffer the fixed estate of the church to be converted into a pension, to depend on the treasury, and to be delayed, withheld, or perhaps to be extinguished by fiscal difficulties; which difficulties may sometimes be pretended for political purposes, and are in fact often brought on by the extravagance, negligence, and rapacity of politicians. The people of England think that they have constitutional motives, as well as religious, against any project of turning their independent clergy into ecclesiastical pensioners of state. They tremble for their liberty, from the influence of a clergy dependent on the crown; they tremble for the public tranquillity from the disorders of a factious clergy, if it were made to depend upon any other than the crown. They therefore made their church, like their king and their nobility, independent.

From the united considerations of religion and constitutional policy, from their opinion of a duty to make a sure provision for the consolation of the feeble and the instruction of the ignorant, they have incorporated and identified the estate of the church with the mass of *private property,* of which the state is not the proprietor, either for use or dominion, but the guardian only and the regulator. They have ordained that the provision of this establishment might be as stable as the earth on which it stands, and should not fluctuate with the Euripus[21] of funds and actions.

The men of England, the men, I mean, of light and leading in

England, whose wisdom (if they have any) is open and direct, would be ashamed, as of a silly deceitful trick, to profess any religion in name, which by their proceedings they appeared to contemn. If by their conduct (the only language that rarely lies) they seemed to regard the great ruling principle of the moral and the natural world, as a mere invention to keep the vulgar in obedience, they apprehend that by such a conduct they would defeat the politic purpose they have in view. They would find it difficult to make others to believe in a system to which they manifestly gave no credit themselves. The Christian statesmen of this land would indeed first provide for the *multitude;* because it is the *multitude;* and is therefore, as such, the first object in the ecclesiastical institution, and in all institutions. They have been taught that the circumstance of the gospel's being preached to the poor was one of the great tests of its true mission. They think, therefore, that those do not believe it, who do not take care it should be preached to the poor. But as they know that charity is not confined to any one description, but ought to apply itself to all men who have wants, they are not deprived of a due and anxious sensation of pity to the distresses of the miserable great. They are not repelled through a fastidious delicacy, at the stench of their arrogance and presumption, from a medicinal attention to their mental blotches and running sores. They are sensible that religious instruction is of more consequence to them than to any others; from the greatness of the temptation to which they are exposed; from the important consequences that attend their faults; from the contagion of their ill example; from the necessity of bowing down the stubborn neck of their pride and ambition to the yoke of moderation and virtue; from a consideration of the fat stupidity and gross ignorance concerning what imports men most to know, which prevails at courts, and at the head of armies, and in senates, as much as at the loom and in the field.

The English people are satisfied that to the great the consolations of religion are as necessary as its instructions. They too are among the unhappy. They feel personal pain and domestic sorrow. In these they have no privilege, but are subject to pay their full contingent to the contributions levied on mortality. They want this sovereign balm under their gnawing cares and anxieties, which being less conversant about the limited wants of animal life, range without limit, and are diversified by infinite combinations in the wild and unbounded regions of imagination. Some charitable dole is wanting to these, our often very unhappy brethren, to fill the gloomy void that reigns in minds which have nothing on earth to hope or fear; something to relieve in the killing languor and over-labored lassitude of those who have nothing to do; something to excite an appetite to existence in the palled satiety which attends on all pleasures which may be bought, where nature is not left to her own process, where even desire is anticipated, and therefore fruition defeated by meditated schemes and contrivances of delight; and no interval, no obstacle, is interposed between the wish and the accomplishment.

The people of England know how little influence the teachers of religion are likely to have with the wealthy and powerful of long standing, and how much less with the newly fortunate, if they appear in a manner no way assorted to those with whom they must associate, and over whom they must even exercise, in some cases, something like an authority. What must they think of that body of teachers, if they see it in no part above the establishment of their domestic servants? If the poverty were voluntary, there might be some difference. Strong instances of self-denial operate powerfully on our minds; and a man who has no wants has obtained great freedom and firmness, and even dignity. But as the mass of any description of men are but men, and their poverty cannot be voluntary,* that disrespect which attends upon all Lay poverty, will not depart from the Ecclesiastical. Our provident constitution has therefore taken care that those who are to instruct presumptuous ignorance, those who are to be censors over insolent vice, should neither incur their contempt, nor live upon their alms; nor will it tempt the rich to a neglect of the true medicine of their minds. For these reasons, while we provide first for the poor, and with a parental solicitude, we have not relegated religion (like something we were ashamed to show) to obscure municipalities or rustic villages. No! We will have her to exalt her mitred front in courts and parliaments. We will have her mixed throughout the whole mass of life, and blended with all the classes of society. The people of England will show to the haughty potentates of the world, and to their talking sophisters,[22] that a free, a generous, an informed nation, honors the high magistrates of its church; that it will not suffer the insolence of wealth and titles, or any other species of proud pretension, to look down with scorn upon what they look up to with reverence; nor presume to trample on that acquired personal nobility, which they intend always to be, and which often is the fruit, not the reward, (for what

---

* The laboring people are poor only because they are numerous. Numbers in their nature imply poverty. *Thoughts on Scarcity* (1795), V, 84.

can be the reward?) of learning, piety, and virtue. They can see, without pain or grudging, an archbishop precede a duke. They can see a Bishop of Durham, or a Bishop of Winchester, in possession of ten thousand pounds a year; and cannot conceive why it is in worse hands than estates to the like amount in the hands of this Earl, or that Squire; although it may be true, that so many dogs and horses are not kept by the former, and fed with the victuals which ought to nourish the children of the people. It is true the whole church revenue is not always employed, and to every shilling, in charity, nor perhaps ought it; but something is generally so employed. It is better to cherish virtue and humanity, by leaving much to free will, even with some loss to the object, than to attempt to make men mere machines and instruments of a political benevolence.* The world on the whole will gain by a liberty, without which virtue cannot exist.

When once the commonwealth has established the estates of the church as property, it can, consistently, hear nothing of the more or the less. Too much and too little are treason against property. What evil can arise from the quantity in any hand, while the supreme authority has the full, sovereign superintendence over this, as over all property, to prevent every species of abuse; and, whenever it notably deviates, to give to it a direction agreeable to the purposes of its institution? . . .

With these ideas rooted in their minds, the commons of Great Britain, in the national emergencies, will never seek their resource from the confiscation of the estates of the church and poor. Sacrilege and proscription are not among the ways and means in our committee of supply. The Jews in Change Alley have not yet dared to hint their hopes of a mortgage on the revenues belonging to the see of Canterbury. I am not afraid that I shall be disavowed, when I assure you that there is not *one* public man in this kingdom, whom you would wish to quote; no not one of any party or description, who does not reprobate the dishonest, perfidious, and cruel confiscation[23] which the National Assembly has been compelled to make of that property which it was their first duty to protect. . . .

The confiscators truly have made some allowance to their victims from the scraps and fragments of their own tables from which

* To provide for us in our necessities is not in the power of government. It would be a vain presumption in statesmen to think they can do it. The people maintain them, and not they the people. It is in the power of government to prevent much evil; it can do very little positive good in this, or perhaps in anything else. *Thoughts on Scarcity* (1795), V, 83.

they have been so harshly driven, and which have been so bountifully spread for a feast to the harpies of usury. But to drive men from independence to live on alms is itself great cruelty. That which might be a tolerable condition to men in one state of life, and not habituated to other things, may, when all these circumstances are altered, be a dreadful revolution; and one to which a virtuous mind would feel pain in condemning any guilt except that which would demand the life of the offender. But to many minds this punishment of *degradation* and *infamy* is worse than death. Undoubtedly it is an infinite aggravation of this cruel suffering, that the persons who were taught a double prejudice in favor of religion by education and by the place they held in the administration of its functions, are to receive the remnants of their property as alms from the profane and impious hands of those who had plundered them of all the rest; to receive (if they are at all to receive) not from the charitable contributions of the faithful, but from the insolent tenderness of known and avowed Atheism, the maintenance of religion, measured out to them on the standard of the contempt in which it is held; and for the purpose of rendering those who receive the allowance vile and of no estimation in the eyes of mankind.

But this act of seizure of property, it seems, is a judgment in law, and not a confiscation. They have, it seems, found out in the academies of the *Palais Royale*[24] and the *Jacobins*[25] that certain men had no right to the possessions which they held under law, usage, the decisions of courts, and the accumulated prescription of a thousand years. They say that ecclesiastics are fictitious persons, creatures of the state, whom at pleasure they may destroy, and of course limit and modify in every particular; that the goods they possess are not properly theirs, but belong to the state which created the fiction; and we are therefore not to trouble ourselves with what they may suffer in their natural feelings and natural persons, on account of what is done towards them in this their constructive character. Of what import is it, under what names you injure men, and deprive them of the just emoluments of a profession, in which they were not only permitted but encouraged by the state to engage; and upon the supposed certainty of which emoluments they had formed the plan of their lives, contracted debts, and led multitudes to an entire dependence upon them? . . .

It is not with much credulity I listen to any, when they speak evil of those whom they are going to plunder. I rather suspect that vices are feigned or exaggerated, when profit is looked for in their punishment. An enemy is a bad witness; a robber is a worse. Vices and abuses there were undoubtedly in that order, and must be. It was an old establishment, and not frequently revised. But I saw no crimes in the individuals that merited confiscation of their substance, nor those cruel insults and degradations, and that unnatural persecution which have been substituted in the place of meliorating regulation.

If there had been any just cause for this new religious persecution, the atheistic libellers, who act as trumpeters to animate the populace to plunder, do not love any body so much as not to dwell with complacence on the vices of the existing clergy. This they have not done. They find themselves obliged to rake into the histories of former ages (which they have ransacked with a malignant and profligate industry) for every instance of oppression and persecution which has been made by that body or in its favor, in order to justify, upon very iniquitous, because very illogical principles of retaliation, their own persecutions, and their own cruelties. After destroying all other genealogies and family distinctions, they invent a sort of pedigree of crimes. It is not very just to chastise men for the offenses of their natural ancestors; but to take the fiction of ancestry in a corporate succession, as a ground for punishing men who have no relation to guilty acts, except in names and general descriptions, is a sort of refinement in injustice belonging to the philosophy of this enlightened age. The Assembly punishes men, many, if not most, of whom abhor the violent conduct of ecclesiastics in former times as much as their present persecutors can do, and who would be as loud and as strong in the expression of that sense, if they were not well aware of the purposes for which all this declamation is employed.

Corporate bodies are immortal for the good of the members, but not for their punishment. Nations themselves are such corporations. As well might we in England think of waging inexpiable war upon all Frenchmen for the evils which they have brought upon us in the several periods of our mutual hostilities. You might, on your part, think yourselves justified in falling upon all Englishmen on account of the unparalleled calamities brought upon the people of France by the unjust invasions of our Henries and our Edwards. Indeed we should be mutually justified in this exterminatory war upon each other, full as much as you are in the unprovoked persecution of your present countrymen, on account of the conduct of men of the same name in other times.

We do not draw the moral lessons we might from history. On the contrary, without care it may be used to vitiate our minds and to destroy our happiness. In history a great volume is unrolled for our instruction, drawing the materials of future wisdom from the past errors and infirmities of mankind. It may, in the perversion, serve for a magazine, furnishing offensive and defensive weapons for parties in church and state, and supplying the means of keeping alive, or reviving dissensions and animosities, and adding fuel to civil fury. History consists, for the greater part, of the miseries brought upon the world by pride, ambition, avarice, revenge, lust, sedition, hypocrisy, ungoverned zeal, and all the train of disorderly appetites, which shake the public with the same

——— troublous storms that toss
The private state, and render life unsweet.[25a]

These vices are the *causes* of those storms. Religion, morals, laws, prerogatives, privileges, liberties, rights of men, are the *pretexts*. The pretexts are always found in some specious appearance of a real good. You would not secure men from tyranny and sedition, by rooting out of the mind the principles to which these fraudulent pretexts apply? If you did, you would root out every thing that is valuable in the human breast. As these are the pretexts, so the ordinary actors and instruments in great public evils are kings, priests, magistrates, senates, parliaments, national assemblies, judges, and captains. You would not cure the evil by resolving that there should be no more monarchs, nor ministers of state, nor of the gospel; no interpreters of law; no general officers; no public councils. You might change the names. The things in some shape must remain. A certain *quantum* of power must always exist in the community, in some hands, and under some appellation. Wise men will apply their remedies to vices, not to names; to the causes of evil which are permanent, not to the occasional organs by which they act, and the transitory modes in which they appear. Otherwise you will be wise historically, a fool in practice. Seldom have two ages the same fashion in their pretexts and the same modes of mischief. Wickedness is a little more inventive. While you are discussing fashion, the fashion is gone by. The very same vice assumes a new body. The spirit transmigrates; and, far from losing its principle of life by the change of its appearance, it is renovated in its new organs with the fresh vigor of a juvenile activity. It walks abroad; it continues its ravages; while you are gibbeting the carcass, or demolishing the tomb. You are terrifying yourself with ghosts and apparitions, while your house is the haunt of robbers. It is thus with all those, who, attending only to the shell and husk of history, think they are waging war with intolerance, pride, and cruelty, while, under color of abhorring the ill principles of antiquated parties, they are authorizing and feeding the same odious vices in different factions, and perhaps in worse. . . .

Such is the effect of the perversion of history, by those, who, for the same nefarious purposes, have perverted every other part of learning. But those who will stand upon that elevation of reason, which places centuries under our eye, and brings things to the true point of comparison, which obscures little names, and effaces the colors of little parties, and to which nothing can ascend but the spirit and moral quality of human actions, will say to the teachers of the Palais Royale: the Cardinal of Lorraine[26] was the murderer of the sixteenth century; you have the glory of being the murderers in the eighteenth; and this is the only difference between you. But history, in the nineteenth century, better understood, and better employed, will, I trust, teach a civilized posterity to abhor the misdeeds of both these barbarous ages. It will teach future priests and magistrates not to retaliate upon the speculative and inactive atheists of future times, the enormities committed by the present practical zealots and furious fanatics of that wretched error, which, in its quiescent state, is more than punished, whenever it is embraced. It will teach posterity not to make war upon either religion or philosophy, for the abuse which the hypocrites of both have made of the two most valuable blessings conferred upon us by the bounty of the universal Patron, who in all things eminently favors and protects the race of man.

If your clergy, or any clergy, should show themselves vicious beyond the fair bounds allowed to human infirmity, and to those professional faults which can hardly be separated from professional virtues, though their vices never can countenance the exercise of oppression, I do admit that they would naturally have the effect of abating very much of our indignation against the tyrants who exceed measure and justice in their punishment. I can allow in clergymen, through all their divisions, some tenaciousness of their own opinion; some overflowings of zeal for its propagation; some predilection to their own state and office; some attachment to the interest of their own corps; some preference to those who listen with docility to their doctrines, beyond those who scorn and deride them. I allow all this, because I am a man who have to deal with men, and who would not, through a violence of toleration, run into the greatest of all intolerance. I must bear with infirmities until they fester into crimes.

Undoubtedly, the natural progress of the passions, from frailty to vice, ought to be prevented by a watchful eye and a firm hand. But is it true that the body of your clergy had past those limits of a just allowance? From the general style of your late publications of all sorts, one would be led to believe that your clergy in France were a sort of monsters; an horrible composition of superstition, ignorance, sloth, fraud, avarice, and tyranny. But is this true? Is it true that the lapse of time, the cessation of conflicting interests, the woeful experience of the evils resulting from party rage, have had no sort of influence gradually to meliorate their minds? Is it true that they were daily renewing invasions on the civil power, troubling the domestic quiet of their country, and rendering the operations of its government feeble and precarious? Is it true that the clergy of our times have pressed down the laity with an iron hand, and were, in all places, lighting up the fires of a savage persecution? Did they by every fraud endeavor to increase their estates? Did they use to exceed the due demands on estates that were their own? Or, rigidly screwing up right into wrong, did they convert a legal claim into a vexatious extortion? When not possessed of power, were they filled with the vices of those who envy it? Were they inflamed with a violent litigious spirit of controversy? Goaded on with the ambition of intellectual sovereignty, were they ready to fly in the face of all magistracy, to fire churches, to massacre the priests of other descriptions, to pull down altars, and to make their way over the ruins of subverted governments to an empire of doctrine, sometimes flattering, sometimes forcing the consciences of men from the jurisdiction of public institutions into a submission to their personal authority, beginning with a claim of liberty and ending with an abuse of power?

These, or some of these, were the vices objected, and not wholly without foundation, to several of the churchmen of former times, who belonged to the two great parties [Catholics and Protestants] which then divided and distracted Europe.

If there was in France, as in other countries there visibly is, a great abatement, rather than any increase of these vices, instead of loading the present clergy with the crimes of other men, and the odious character of other times, in common equity they ought to be praised, encouraged, and supported, in their departure from a spirit which disgraced their predecessors, and for having assumed a temper of mind and manners more suitable to their sacred function. . . .

But the present ruling power has shown a disposition only to plunder the church. It has punished *all* prelates, which is to favor the vicious, at least in point of reputation. It has made a degrading pensionary establishment, to which no man of liberal ideas or liberal condition will destine his children. It must settle into the lowest classes of the people. As with you the inferior clergy are not numerous enough for their duties; as these duties are, beyond measure, minute and toilsome; as you have left no middle classes of clergy at their ease, in future nothing of science or erudition can exist in the Gallican [French Catholic] church. To complete the project, without the least attention to the rights of patrons, the Assembly has provided in future an elective clergy; an arrangement which will drive out of the clerical profession all men of sobriety; all who can pretend to independence in their function or their conduct; and which will throw the whole direction of the public mind into the hands of a set of licentious, bold, crafty, factious, flattering wretches, of such condition and such habits of life as will make their contemptible pensions (in comparison of which the stipend of an exciseman[27] lucrative and honorable) an object of low and illiberal intrigue. Those officers, whom they still call bishops, are to be elected to a provision comparatively mean, through the same arts, (that is, electioneering arts) by men of all religious tenets that are known or can be invented. The new lawgivers have not ascertained anything whatsover concerning their qualifications, relative either to doctrine or to morals; no more than they have done with regard to the subordinate clergy; nor does it appear but that both the higher and the lower may, at their discretion, practise or preach any mode of religion or irreligion that they please. I do not yet see what the jurisdiction of bishops over their subordinates is to be; or whether they are to have any jurisdiction at all.

In short, Sir, it seems to me that this new ecclesiastical establishment is intended only to be temporary, and preparatory to the utter abolition, under any of its forms, of the Christian religion, whenever the minds of men are prepared for this last stroke against it, by the accomplishment of the plan for bringing its ministers into universal contempt. They who will not believe that the philosophical fanatics who guide in these matters have long entertained such a design are utterly ignorant of their character and proceedings. These enthusiasts do not scruple to avow their opinion that a state can subsist without any religion better than with one; and that they are able to supply the place of any good which may be in it, by a project of their own—namely, by a sort of education they have imagined, founded in a knowledge of the physical wants of men, progressively carried to an enlightened self-interest, which, when well understood, they tell us will identify with an interest more enlarged and public.[28]

The scheme of this education has been long known. Of late they distinguish it (as they have got an entire new nomenclature of technical terms) by the name of a *Civic Education*. . . .

Those of you who have robbed the clergy think that they shall easily reconcile their conduct to all Protestant nations; because the clergy, whom they have thus plundered, degraded, and given over to mockery and scorn, are of the Roman Catholic, that is, of *their own* pretended persuasion. I have no doubt that some miserable bigots will be found here as well as elsewhere, who hate sects and parties different from their own, more than they love the substance of religion; and who are more angry with those who differ from them in their particular plans and systems, than displeased with those who attack the foundation of our common hope. . . .

We hear these new teachers continually boasting of their spirit of toleration. That those persons should tolerate all opinions, who think none to be of estimation, is a matter of small merit. Equal neglect is not impartial kindness. The species of benevolence, which arises from contempt, is no true charity. There are in England abundance of men who tolerate in the true spirit of toleration. They think the dogmas of religion, though in different degrees, are all of moment; and that amongst them there is, as amongst all things of value, a just ground of preference. They favor, therefore, and they tolerate. They tolerate, not because they despise opinions, but because they respect justice. They would reverently and affectionately protect all religions, because they love and venerate the great principle upon which they all agree, and the great object to which they are all directed. They begin more and more plainly to discern that we have all a common cause, as against a common enemy. They will not be so misled by the spirit of faction, as not to distinguish what is done in favor of their subdivision, from those acts of hostility, which, through some particular description, are aimed at the whole corps, in which they themselves, under another denomination, are included. It is impossible for me to say what may be the character of every description of men amongst us. But I speak for the greater part; and for them, I must tell you, that sacrilege is no part of their doctrine of good works; that, so far from calling you into their fellowship on such title, if your professors are admitted to their communion, they must carefully conceal their doctrine of the lawfulness of the proscription of innocent men; and that they must make restitution of all stolen goods whatsoever. Till then they are none of ours. . . .

PROPERTY AND PRESCRIPTION

It is true that this particular part of your general confiscation does not affect England as a precedent in point, but the reason applies; and it goes a great way. The Long Parliament[29] confiscated the lands of deans and chapters in England on the same ideas upon which your Assembly set to sale the lands of the monastic orders. But it is in the principle of injustice that the danger lies, and not in the description of persons on whom it is first exercised. I see, in a country very near us, a course of policy pursued, which sets justice, the common concern of mankind, at defiance. With the National Assembly of France, possession is nothing; law and usage are nothing. I see the National Assembly openly reprobate the doctrine of prescription, which one of the greatest of their own lawyers[30] tells us, with great truth, is a part of the law of nature. He tells us that the positive ascertainment of its limits, and its security from invasion, were among the causes for which civil society itself has been instituted. If prescription be once shaken, no species of property is secure, when it once becomes an object large enough to tempt the cupidity of indigent power. I see a practice perfectly correspondent to their contempt of this great fundamental part of natural law. I see the confiscators begin with bishops, and chapters, and monasteries; but I do not see them end there. I see the princes of the blood, who, by the oldest usages of that kingdom, held large landed estates, (hardly with the compliment of a debate) deprived of their possessions, and in lieu of their stable independent property, reduced to the hope of some precarious, charitable pension, at the pleasure of an assembly, which of course will pay little regard to the rights of pensioners at pleasure, when it despises those of legal proprietors. Flushed from the insolence of their first inglorious victories, and pressed by the distresses caused by their lust of unhallowed lucre, disappointed but not discouraged, they have at length ventured completely to subvert all property of all descriptions throughout the extent of a great kingdom. They have compelled all men, in all transactions of commerce, in the disposal of lands, in civil dealing, and through the whole communion of life, to accept as perfect payment and good and lawful tender, the symbols of their speculations on a projected sale of their plunder. What vestiges of liberty or property have they left? The tenant-right of a cabbage-garden, a year's interest in a hovel, the good-will of an alehouse, or a baker's shop, the very shadow of a constructive property, are more ceremoniously treated in our Parliament than with you the oldest and most valuable landed possessions, in the hands of the most respectable personages, or than the whole body of the monied and commercial interest of your country. We entertain an high opinion of the legislative authority; but we have never dreamt that parliaments had any right whatever to violate property, to overrule prescription, or to force a currency of their own fiction in the place of that which is real, and recognized by the law of nations. But you, who began with refusing to submit to the most moderate restraints, have ended by establishing an unheard of despotism. I find the ground upon which your confiscators go is this: that indeed their proceedings could not be supported in a court of justice; but that the rules of prescription cannot bind a legislative assembly. So that this legislative assembly of a free nation sits, not for the security, but for the destruction of property, and not of property only, but of every rule and maxim which can give it stability, and of those instruments which can alone give it circulation. . . .

It is not the confiscation of our church property from this example in France that I dread, though I think this would be no trifling evil. The great source of my solicitude is, lest it should ever be considered in England as the policy of a state, to seek a resource in confiscations of any kind; or that any one description of citizens should be brought to regard any of the others, as their proper prey. Nations are wading deeper and deeper into an ocean of boundless debt. Public debts, which at first were a security to governments, by interesting many in the public tranquillity, are likely in their excess to become the means of their subversion. If governments provide for these debts by heavy impositions, they perish by becoming odious to the people. If they do not provide for them, they will be undone by the efforts of the most dangerous of all parties; I mean an extensive discontented monied interest, injured and not destroyed. The men who compose this interest look for their security, in the first instance, to the fidelity of government; in the second, to its power. If they find the old governments effete, worn out, and with their springs relaxed, so as not to be of sufficient vigor for their purposes, they may seek new ones that shall be possessed of more energy; and this energy will be derived, not from an acquisition of resources, but from a contempt of justice. Revolutions are favorable to confiscation; and it is impossible to know under what obnoxious names the next confiscations will be authorized. I am sure that the principles predominant in France extend to very many persons and descriptions of persons in all countries who think their innoxious indolence their security. This kind of innocence in proprietors may be argued into inutility; and inutility into an unfitness for their estates. Many parts of Europe are in open disorder. In many others there is a hollow murmuring under ground; a confused movement is felt that threatens a general earthquake in the political world. Already confederacies and correspondences of the most extraordinary nature are forming in several countries. In such a state of things we ought to hold ourselves upon our guard.* In all mutations (if mutations must be) the circumstance which will serve most to blunt the edge of their mischief, and to promote what good may be in them, is, that they should find us with our minds tenacious of justice, and tender of property.

But it will be argued that this confiscation in France ought not to alarm other nations. They say it is not made from wanton rapacity; that it is a great measure of national policy, adopted to remove an extensive, inveterate, superstitious mischief. It is with the greatest difficulty that I am able to separate policy from justice. Justice is itself the great standing policy of civil society; and any eminent departure from it, under any circumstances, lies under the suspicion of being no policy at all.

When men are encouraged to go into a certain mode of life by the existing laws, and protected in that mode as in a lawful occupation—when they have accommodated all their ideas, and all their habits to it—when the law had long made their adherence to its rules a ground of reputation, and their departure from them a ground of disgrace and even of penalty—I am sure it is unjust in legislature, by an arbitrary act, to offer a sudden violence to their minds and their feelings; forcibly to degrade them from their state and condition, and to stigmatize with shame and infamy that character and those customs which before had been made the measure of their happiness and honor. If to this be added an expulsion from their habitations, and a confiscation of all their goods, I am not sagacious enough to discover how this despotic sport, made of the feelings, consciences, prejudices, and properties of men, can be discriminated from the rankest tyranny. . . .

There are moments in the fortune of states when particular

* We are at war with a system, which, by its essence, is inimical to all other governments, and which makes peace or war, as peace or war may best contribute to their subversion. It is with an *armed doctrine* that we are at war. It has, by its essence, a faction of opinion, and of interest, and of enthusiasm, in every country. *First Letter on a Regicide Peace* (1796), V, 164–65.

men are called to make improvements by great mental exertion. In those moments, even when they seem to enjoy the confidence of their prince and country, and to be invested with full authority, they have not always apt instruments. A politician, to do great things looks for a *power,* what our workmen call a *purchase;* and if he finds that power, in politics as in mechanics he cannot be at a loss to apply it. In the monastic institutions, in my opinion, was found a great *power* for the mechanism of politic benevolence. There were revenues with a public direction; there were men wholly set apart and dedicated to public purposes, without any other than public ties and public principles; men without the possibility of converting the estate of the community into a private fortune; men denied to self-interests, whose avarice is for some community; men to whom personal poverty is honor, and implicit obedience stands in the place of freedom. In vain shall a man look to the possibility of making such things when he wants them. The winds blow as they list. These institutions are the products of enthusiasm; they are the instruments of wisdom. Wisdom cannot create materials; they are the gifts of nature or of chance; her pride is in the use. The perennial existence of bodies corporate and their fortunes are things particularly suited to a man who has long views; who meditates designs that require time in fashioning; and which propose duration when they are accomplished. He is not deserving to rank high, or even to be mentioned in the order of great statesmen, who, having obtained the command and direction of such a power as existed in the wealth, the discipline, and the habits of such corporations, as those which you have rashly destroyed, cannot find any way of converting it to the great and lasting benefit of his country. . . .

But the institutions savor of superstition in their very principle; and they nourish it by a permanent and standing influence. This I do not mean to dispute; but this ought not to hinder you from deriving from superstition itself any resources which may thence be furnished for the public advantage. You derive benefits from many dispositions and many passions of the human mind, which are of as doubtful a color in the moral eye as superstition itself. It was your business to correct and mitigate every thing which was noxious in this passion, as in all the passions. But is superstition the greatest of all possible vices? In its possible excess I think it becomes a very great evil. It is, however, a moral subject; and of course admits of all degrees and all modifications. Superstition is the religion of feeble minds; and they must be tolerated in an intermixture of it, in some trifling or some enthusiastic shape or other, else you will deprive weak minds of a resource found necessary to the strongest. The body of all true religion consists, to be sure, in obedience to the will of the Sovereign of the world; in a confidence in his declarations; and an imitation of his perfections. The rest is our own. It may be prejudicial to the great end; it may be auxiliary. Wise men, who as such, are not *admirers* (not admirers at least of the *Munera Terræ*)[31] are not violently attached to these things, nor do they violently hate them. Wisdom is not the most severe corrector of folly. They are the rival follies, which mutually wage so unrelenting a war; and which make so cruel a use of their advantages, as they can happen to engage the immoderate vulgar on the one side or the other in their quarrels. Prudence would be neuter; but if, in the contention between fond attachment and fierce antipathy concerning things in their nature not made to produce such heats, a prudent man were obliged to make a choice of what errors and excesses of enthusiasm he would condemn or bear, perhaps he would think the superstition which builds, to be more tolerable than that which demolishes—that which adorns a country, than that which deforms it—that which endows, than that which plunders—that which disposes to mistaken beneficence, than that which stimulates to real injustice—that which leads a man to refuse to himself lawful pleasures, than that which snatches from others the scanty subsistence of their self-denial. Such, I think, is very nearly the state of the question between the ancient founders of monkish superstition, and the superstition of the pretended philosophers of the hour.

AN HEREDITARY CROWN

The people of England will not ape the fashions they have never tried; nor go back to those which they have found mischievous on trial. They look upon the legal hereditary succession of their crown as among their rights, not as among their wrongs; as a benefit, not as a grievance; as a security for their liberty, not as a badge of servitude. They look on the frame of their commonwealth, *such as it stands,* to be of inestimable value; and they conceive the undisturbed succession of the crown to be a pledge of the stability and perpetuity of all the other members of our constitution.

I shall beg leave, before I go any further, to take notice of some paltry artifices, which the abettors of election as the only lawful title to the crown, are ready to employ, in order to render the support of the just principles of our constitution a task somewhat invidious. These sophisters substitute a fictitious cause, and feigned personages, in whose favor they suppose you engaged, whenever you defend the inheritable nature of the crown. It is common with them to dispute as if they were in a conflict with some of those exploded fanatics of slavery, who formerly maintained, what I believe no creature now maintains, "that the crown is held by divine, hereditary, and indefeasible right."—These old fanatics of single arbitrary power[32] dogmatized as if hereditary royalty was the only lawful government in the world, just as our new fanatics* of popular arbitrary power, maintain that a popular election is the sole lawful source of authority. The old prerogative enthusiasts, it is true, did speculate foolishly, and perhaps impiously too, as if monarchy had more of a divine sanction than any other mode of government; and as if a right to govern by inheritance were in strictness *indefeasible* in every person, who should be found in the succession to a throne, and under every circumstance, which no civil or political right can be. But an absurd opinion concerning the king's hereditary right to the crown does not prejudice one that is rational, and bottomed upon solid principles of law and policy. . . .

Nothing can reconcile men to their proceedings and projects but the supposition that there is no third option between them; and some tyranny as odious as can be furnished by the records of history, or by the invention of poets. This prattling of theirs hardly deserves the name of sophistry. It is nothing but plain impudence. Have these gentlemen never heard, in the whole circle of the worlds of theory and practice, of any thing between the despotism of the monarch and the despotism of the multitude? Have they never heard of a monarchy directed by laws, controlled and balanced by the great hereditary wealth and hereditary dignity of a nation; and both again controlled by a judicious check from the reason and feeling of the people at large acting by a suitable and permanent organ? Is it then impossible that a man may be found who, without criminal ill intention, or pitiable absurdity, shall prefer such a mixed and tempered government to either of the extremes; and who may repute that nation to be destitute of all wisdom and of all virtue, which, having in its choice to obtain such a government with ease,

---

* It must always have been discoverable by persons of reflection, but it is now obvious to the world, that a theory concerning government may become as much a cause of fanaticism as a *dogma* in religion. There is a boundary to men's passions when they act from feeling; none whatever when they are under the influence of imagination. *An Appeal from the New to the Old Whigs* (1791), III, 98–99.

or rather to confirm it when actually possessed, thought proper to commit a thousand crimes, and to subject their country to a thousand evils, in order to avoid it? Is it then a truth so universally acknowledged, that a pure democracy is the only tolerable form into which human society can be thrown, that a man is not permitted to hesitate about its merits, without the suspicion of being a friend to tyranny, that is, of being a foe to mankind?

I do not know under what description to class the present ruling authority in France. It affects to be a pure democracy, though I think it in a direct train of becoming shortly a mischievous and ignoble oligarchy. But for the present I admit it to be a contrivance of the nature and effect of what it pretends to. I reprobate no form of government merely upon abstract principles.* There may be situations in which the purely democratic form will become necessary. There may be some (very few, and very particularly circumstanced) where it would be clearly desirable. This I do not take to be the case of France, or of any other great country. Until now, we have seen no examples of considerable democracies. The ancients were better acquainted with them. Not being wholly unread in the authors, who had seen the most of those constitutions, and who best understood them, I cannot help concurring with their opinion that an absolute democracy, no more than absolute monarchy, is to be reckoned among the legitimate forms of government. They think it rather the corruption and degeneracy, than the sound constitution of a republic. If I recollect rightly, Aristotle observes that a democracy has many striking points of resemblance with a tyranny.[33] Of this I am certain, that in a democracy, the majority of the citizens is capable of exercising the most cruel oppressions upon the minority, whenever strong divisions prevail in that kind of polity, as they often must; and that oppression of the minority will extend to far greater numbers, and will be carried on with much greater fury, than can almost ever be apprehended from the dominion of a single sceptre. In such a popular persecution, individual sufferers

* I never govern myself, no rational man ever did govern himself, by abstractions and universals. . . . A statesman differs from a professor in an university; the latter has only the general view of society; the former, the statesman, has a number of circumstances to combine with those general ideas and to take into his consideration. Circumstances are infinite, are infinitely combined, are variable and transient: he who does not take them into consideration is not erroneous, but stark mad; . . . he is metaphysically mad. *Speech on the Petition of the Unitarians* (1792), VI, 113–14.

are in a much more deplorable condition than in any other. Under a cruel prince they have the balmy compassion of mankind to assuage the smart of their wounds; they have the plaudits of the people to animate their generous constancy under their sufferings: but those who are subjected to wrong under multitudes are deprived of all external consolation. They seem deserted by mankind; overpowered by a conspiracy of their whole species.

But admitting democracy not to have that inevitable tendency to party tyranny, which I suppose it to have, and admitting it to possess as much good in it when unmixed, as I am sure it possesses when compounded with other forms; does monarchy, on its part, contain nothing at all to recommend it? I do not often quote Bolingbroke,[34] nor have his works in general left any permanent impression on my mind. He is a presumptuous and a superficial writer. But he has one observation, which, in my opinion, is not without depth and solidity. He says that he prefers a monarchy to other governments; because you can better ingraft any description of republic on a monarchy than any thing of monarchy upon the republican forms. I think him perfectly in the right. The fact is so historically; and it agrees well with the speculation.

I know how easy a topic it is to dwell on the faults of departed greatness. By a revolution in the state, the fawning sycophant of yesterday is converted into the austere critic of the present hour. But steady independent minds, when they have an object of so serious a concern to mankind as government under their contemplation, will disdain to assume the part of satirists and declaimers. They will judge of human institutions as they do of human characters. They will sort out the good from the evil, which is mixed in mortal institutions as it is in mortal men.

Your government in France, though usually, and I think justly, reputed the best of the unqualified or ill-qualified monarchies, was still full of abuses. These abuses accumulated in a length of time, as they must accumulate in every monarchy not under the constant inspection of a popular representative. I am no stranger to the faults and defects of the subverted government of France; and I think I am not inclined by nature or policy to make a panegyric upon any thing which is a just and natural object of censure. But the question is not now of the vices of that monarchy, but of its existence. Is it then true that the French government was such as to be incapable or undeserving of reform; so that it was of absolute necessity the whole fabric should be at once pulled down, and the area cleared for the erection of a theoretic experimental edifice in its place? All

France was of a different opinion in the beginning of the year 1789. The instructions to the representatives to the States-General,[35] from every district in that kingdom, were filled with projects for the reformation of that government, without the remotest suggestion of a design to destroy it. Had such a design been then even insinuated, I believe there would have been but one voice, and that voice for rejecting it with scorn and horror. Men have been sometimes led by degrees, sometimes hurried into things, of which, if they could have seen the whole together, they never would have permitted the most remote approach. When those instructions were given, there was no question but that abuses existed, and that they demanded a reform; nor is there now. In the interval between the instructions and the revolution, things changed their shape; and in consequence of that change, the true question at present is whether those who would have reformed, or those who have destroyed, are in the right?

To hear some men speak of the late monarchy of France, you would imagine that they were talking of Persia bleeding under the ferocious sword of Tahmas Kouli Khân;[36] or at least describing the barbarous anarchic despotism of Turkey, where the finest countries in the most genial climates in the world are wasted by peace more than any countries have been worried by war; where arts are unknown, where manufactures languish, where science is extinguished, where agriculture decays, where the human race itself melts away and perishes under the eye of the observer. Was this the case of France? I have no way of determining the question but by a reference to facts. Facts do not support this resemblance. Along with much evil, there is some good in monarchy itself; and some corrective to its evil, from religion, from laws, from manners, from opinions, the French monarchy must have received, which rendered it (though by no means a free, and therefore by no means a good constitution) a despotism rather in appearance than in reality. . . .

Indeed, when I consider the face of the kingdom of France, the multitude and opulence of her cities, the useful magnificence of her spacious high roads and bridges, the opportunity of her artificial canals and navigations opening the conveniences of maritime communication through a solid continent of so immense an extent; when I turn my eyes to the stupendous works of her ports and harbors, and to her whole naval apparatus, whether for war or trade; when I bring before my view the number of her fortifications, constructed with so bold and masterly a skill, and made and maintained at so prodigious a charge, presenting an armed front and impenetrable barrier to her enemies upon every side; when I recollect how very small a part of that extensive region is without cultivation, and to what complete perfection the culture of many of the best productions of the earth have been brought in France; when I reflect on the excellence of her manufactures and fabrics, second to none but ours, and in some particulars not second; when I contemplate the grand foundations of charity, public and private; when I survey the state of all the arts that beautify and polish life; when I reckon the men she has bred for extending her fame in war, her able statesmen, the multitude of her profound lawyers and theologians, her philosophers, her critics, her historians and antiquaries, her poets, and her orators sacred and profane, I behold in all this something which awes and commands the imagination, which checks the mind on the brink of precipitate and indiscriminate censure, and which demands, that we should very seriously examine what and how great are the latent vices that could authorise us at once to level so spacious a fabric with the ground. I do not recognize, in this view of things, the despotism of Turkey. Nor do I discern the character of a government that has been, on the whole, so oppressive, or so corrupt, or so negligent, as to be utterly unfit *for all reformation.* I must think such a government well deserved to have its excellencies heightened; its faults corrected; and its capacities improved into a British constitution. . . .

That a man should rejoice and triumph in the destruction of an absolute monarchy,—that in such an event he should overlook the captivity, disgrace, and degradation of an unfortunate prince, and the continual danger to a life which exists only to be endangered,—that he should overlook the utter ruin of whole orders and classes of men, extending itself directly, or in its nearest consequences, to at least a million of our kind, and to at least the temporary wretchedness of a whole community,—I do not deny to be in some sort natural; because, when people see a political object which they ardently desire but in one point of view, they are apt extremely to palliate or underrate the evils which may arise in obtaining it. This is no reflection on the humanity of those persons. Their good nature[37] I am the last man in the world to dispute. It only shows that they are not sufficiently informed or sufficiently considerate. When they come to reflect seriously on the transaction, they will think themselves bound to examine what the object is that has been acquired by all this havoc. They will hardly assert that the destruction of an absolute monarchy is a thing good in itself, without any sort of reference to the antecedent state of things, or to consequences which result from the change,—without any consideration whether under its ancient rule a country was to a considerable degree flourishing and populous, highly cultivated and highly commercial, and whether, under that domination, though personal liberty had been precarious and insecure, property at least was never violated. They cannot take the moral sympathies of the human mind along with them, in abstractions separated from the good or evil condition of the state, from the quality of actions, and the character of the actors. None of us love absolute and uncontrolled monarchy; but we could not rejoice at the sufferings of a Marcus Aurelius or a Trajan, who were absolute monarchs, as we do when Nero is condemned by the Senate to be punished . . . nor, when that monster was obliged to fly with his wife Sporus, and to drink puddle, were men affected in the same manner as when the venerable Galba, with all his faults and errors, was murdered by a revolted mercenary soldiery. With such things before our eyes, our feelings contradict our theories; and when this is the case, the feelings are true, and the theory is false.* . . .

[*An Appeal from the New to the Old Whigs* (1791), III, 14–15.]

It is now sixteen or seventeen years since I saw the Queen of France,[38] then the dauphiness, at Versailles; and surely never lighted on this orb, which she hardly seemed to touch, a more delightful vision. I saw her just above the horizon, decorating and cheering the elevated sphere she just began to move in,—glittering like the morning-star, full of life, and splendor, and joy. Oh! what a revolution! and what a heart must I have, to contemplate without emotion that elevation and that fall! Little did I dream when she added titles of veneration to those of enthusiastic, distant, respectful love, that she should ever be obliged to carry the sharp antidote against disgrace concealed in that bosom; little did I dream that I should live to see such disasters fallen upon her in a nation of gallant men, in a nation of men of honor and of cavaliers. I thought ten thousand swords must have leaped from their scabbards to avenge even a look that threatened her with insult.— But the age of chivalry is gone.— That of sophisters, economists, and calculators, has succeeded; and the glory of Europe is extinguished for ever. Never, never more, shall we behold that generous loyalty to rank and sex, that proud submission, that dignified obedience, that subordination of the heart, which kept alive, even in servitude itself, the spirit of an

---

* Never was there a jar or discord between genuine sentiment and sound policy. Never, no, never did Nature say one thing and Wisdom say another. Nor are sentiments of elevation in themselves turgid and unnatural. Nature is never more truly herself than in her grandest forms. *Third Letter on a Regicide Peace* (1796–97), V, 278.

exalted freedom. The unbought grace of life, the cheap defense of nations, the nurse of manly sentiment and heroic enterprise is gone! It is gone, that sensibility of principle, that chastity of honor, which felt a stain like a wound, which inspired courage while it mitigated ferocity, which ennobled whatever it touched, and under which vice itself lost half its evil, by losing all its grossness.

This mixed system of opinion and sentiment had its origin in the ancient chivalry; and the principle, though varied in its appearance by the varying state of human affairs, subsisted and influenced through a long succession of generations, even to the time we live in. If it should ever be totally extinguished, the loss I fear will be great. It is this which has given its character to modern Europe. It is this which has distinguished it under all its forms of government, and distinguished it to its advantage, from the states of Asia, and possibly from those states which flourished in the most brilliant periods of the antique world. It was this, which, without confounding ranks, had produced a noble equality, and handed it down through all the gradations of social life. It was this opinion which mitigated kings into companions, and raised private men to be fellows with kings. Without force or opposition, it subdued the fierceness of pride and power; it obliged sovereigns to submit to the soft collar of social esteem, compelled stern authority to submit to elegance, and gave a dominating vanquisher of laws, to be subdued by manners.

But now all is to be changed. All the pleasing illusions, which made power gentle and obedience liberal, which harmonized the different shades of life, and which, by a bland assimilation, incorporated into politics the sentiments which beautify and soften private society, are to be dissolved by this new conquering empire of light and reason. All the decent drapery of life is to be rudely torn off. All the super-added ideas, furnished from the wardrobe of a moral imagination, which the heart owns and the understanding ratifies as necessary to cover the defects of our naked shivering nature, and to raise it to dignity in our own estimation, are to be exploded as a ridiculous, absurd, and antiquated fashion.

On this scheme of things, a king is but a man; a queen is but a woman; a woman is but an animal; and an animal not of the highest order. All homage paid to the sex in general as such, and without distinct views, is to be regarded as romance and folly. Regicide, and parricide, and sacrilege, are but fictions of superstition, corrupting jurisprudence by destroying its simplicity. The murder of a king,* or a queen, or a bishop, or a father, are only common homicide; and if the people are by any chance, or in any way gainers by it, a sort of homicide much the most pardonable, and into which we ought not to make too severe a scrutiny.

On the scheme of this barbarous philosophy, which is the offspring of cold hearts and muddy understandings† and which is as void of solid wisdom, as it is destitute of all taste and elegance, laws are to be supported only by their own terrors, and by the concern, which each individual may find in them from his own private speculations, or can spare to them from his own private interests. In the groves of *their* academy,[39] at the end of every vista you see nothing but the gallows. Nothing is left which engages the affections on the part of the commonwealth. On the principles of this mechanic philosophy, our institutions can never be embodied, if I may use the expression, in persons; so as to create in us love, veneration, admiration, or attachment. But that sort of reason which banishes the affections is incapable of filling their place. These public affections, combined with manners, are required sometimes as supplements, sometimes as correctives, always as aids to law. The precept given by a wise man, as well as a great critic, for the construction of poems, is equally true as to states. *Non satis est pulchra esse poemata, dulcia sunto.*[39a] There ought to be a system of manners in every nation which a well-formed mind would be disposed to relish. To make us love our country, our country ought to be lovely.

But power of some kind or other will survive the shock in which manners and opinions perish; and it will find other and worse means for its support. The usurpation which, in order to subvert ancient institutions, has destroyed ancient principles, will hold power by arts similar to those by which it has acquired it. When the old feudal and chivalrous spirit of *Fealty,* which, by

* In spite of their solemn declarations, their soothing addresses, and the multiplied oaths which they have taken and forced others to take, they will assassinate the king when his name no longer be necessary to their designs; but not a moment sooner. *Letter to a Member of the National Assembly* (1791), II, 533. [That moment came two years later when Louis XVI was guillotined after he was tried for treason and found guilty.]

† This sort of people are so taken up with their theories about the rights of man, that they have totally forgot his nature. . . . Their liberty is not liberal. Their science is presumptuous ignorance. Their humanity is savage and brutal. . . . By hating vices too much, they come to love men too little. *Reflections on the Revolution in France,* (1790), pp. 74, 90, 199.

freeing kings from fear, freed both kings and subjects from the precautions of tyranny, shall be extinct in the minds of men, plots and assassinations will be anticipated by preventive murder and preventive confiscation, and that long roll of grim and bloody maxims, which form the political code of all power, not standing on its own honor, and the honor of those who are to obey it. Kings will be tyrants from policy when subjects are rebels from principle. . . .

AN ARISTOCRACY OF
WEALTH AND TALENT

The advocates for this revolution, not satisfied with exaggerating the vices of their ancient government, strike at the fame of their country itself, by painting almost all that could have attracted the attention of strangers, I mean their nobility and their clergy, as objects of horror. If this were only a libel, there had not been much in it. But it has practical consequences. . . . Nothing is more certain than that our manners, our civilization, and all the good things which are connected with manners, and with civilization, have, in this European world of ours, depended for ages upon two principles and were indeed the result of both combined; I mean the spirit of a gentleman, and the spirit of religion.* The nobility and the clergy, the one by profession, the other by patronage, kept learning in existence, even in the midst of arms and confusions, and while governments were rather in their causes than formed. Learning paid back what it received to nobility and to priesthood, and paid it with usury, by enlarging their ideas and by furnishing their minds. Happy if they had all continued to know their indissoluble union and their proper place! Happy if learning, not debauched by ambition, had been satisfied to continue the instructor, and not aspired to be the master! Along with its natural protectors and guardians, learning will be cast into the mire, and trodden down under the hoofs of a swinish multitude[40]. . . .

I do not pretend to know France as correctly as some others;

---

* Manners are of more importance than laws. Upon them, in a great measure, the laws depend. The law touches us but here and there, and now and then. Manners are what vex or soothe, corrupt or purify, exalt or debase, barbarize or refine us, by a constant, steady, uniform, insensible operation, like that of the air we breathe in. They give their whole form and color to our lives. *First Letter on a Regicide Peace* (1796), V. 208.

but I have endeavored through my whole life to make myself acquainted with human nature; otherwise I should be unfit to take even my humble part in the service of mankind. In that study I could not pass by a vast portion of our nature, as it appeared modified in a country but twenty-four miles from the shore of this island. On my best observation, compared with my best enquiries, I found your nobility for the greater part composed of men of a high spirit and of a delicate sense of honor, both with regard to themselves individually, and with regard to their whole corps, over whom they kept, beyond what is common in other countries, a censorial eye. They were tolerably well-bred; very officious,[41] humane, and hospitable; in their conversation frank and open; with a good military tone; and reasonably tinctured with literature, particularly of the authors in their own language. Many had pretensions far above this description. I speak of those who were generally met with.

As to their behavior to the inferior classes, they appeared to me to comport themselves towards them with good-nature, and with something more nearly approaching to familiarity, than is generally practised with us in the intercourse between the higher and lower ranks of life. To strike any person, even in the most abject condition, was a thing in a manner unknown, and would be highly disgraceful. Instances of other ill-treatment of the humble part of the community were rare; and as to attacks made upon the property or the personal liberty of the commons, I never heard of any whatsoever from *them;* nor, while the laws were in vigor under the ancient government, would such tyranny in subjects have been permitted.

Denying, as I am well warranted to do, that the nobility had any considerable share in the oppression of the people, in cases in which real oppression existed, I am ready to admit that they were not without considerable faults and errors. A foolish imitation of the worst part of the manners of England, which impaired their natural character without substituting in its place what perhaps they meant to copy, has certainly rendered them worse than formerly they were. Habitual dissoluteness of manners continued beyond the pardonable period of life was more common amongst them than it is with us; and it reigned with the less hope of remedy, though possibly with something of less mischief, by being covered with more exterior decorum. They countenanced too much that licentious philosophy which has helped to bring on their ruin. There was another error amongst them more fatal. Those of the commons, who approached to or exceeded many of the nobility in point of wealth, were not fully admitted to the rank and estimation which wealth, in reason and good policy, ought to bestow in every country; though I think not equally with that of other nobility. The two kinds of aristocracy were too punctiliously kept asunder; less so, however, than in Germany and some other nations.

This separation, as I have already taken the liberty of suggesting to you, I conceive to be one principal cause of the destruction of the old nobility. The military, particularly, was too exclusively reserved for men of family. But after all, this was an error of opinion, which a conflicting opinion would have rectified. A permanent assembly, in which the commons had their share of power, would soon abolish whatever was too invidious and insulting in these distinctions; and even the faults in the morals of the nobility would have been probably corrected by the greater varieties of occupation and pursuit to which a constitution by orders would have given rise. . . .

All this violent cry against the nobility I take to be a mere work of art. To be honored and even privileged by the laws, opinions, and inveterate usages of our country, growing out of the prejudice of ages, has nothing to provoke horror and indignation in any man. Even to be too tenacious of those privileges is not absolutely a crime. The strong struggle in every individual to preserve possession of what he has found to belong to him and to distinguish him, is one of the securities against injustice and despotism implanted in our nature. It operates as an instinct to secure property, and to preserve communities in a settled state. What is there to shock in this? Nobility is a graceful ornament to the civil order. It is the Corinthian capital of polished society. *Omnes boni nobilitati semper favemus*,[41a] was the saying of a wise and good man. It is indeed one sign of a liberal and benevolent mind to incline to it with some sort of partial propensity. He feels no ennobling principle in his own heart who wishes to level all the artificial institutions which have been adopted for giving a body to opinion and permanence to fugitive esteem. It is a sour, malignant, envious disposition, without taste for the reality, or for any image or representation of virtue, that sees with joy the unmerited fall of what had long flourished in splendor and in honor. . . . Believe me, Sir, those who attempt to level, never equalize.* In all societies, consisting of various descriptions of citizens, some description must be uppermost. The levellers there-

---

* Such is the event of all compulsory equalizations. They pull down what is above. They never raise what is below; and they depress high and low together beneath the level of what was originally the lowest. *Thoughts on Scarcity* (1795), V, 90.

fore only change and pervert the natural order of things; they load the edifice of society, by setting up in the air what the solidity of the structure requires to be on the ground. The associations of tailors and carpenters, of which the republic (of Paris, for instance) is composed, cannot be equal to the situation into which, by the worst of usurpations, an usurpation on the prerogatives of nature, you attempt to force them.

The Chancellor of France at the opening of the States said, in a tone of oratorical flourish, that all occupations were honorable. If he meant only that no honest employment was disgraceful, he would not have gone beyond the truth. But in asserting that any thing is honorable, we imply some distinction in its favor. The occupation of an hair-dresser, or of a working tallow-chandler, cannot be a matter of honor to any person—to say nothing of a number of other more servile employments. Such descriptions of men ought not to suffer oppression from the state; but the state suffers oppression, if such as they, either individually or collectively, are permitted to rule. In this you think you are combating prejudice, but you are at war with nature.*

I do not, my dear Sir, conceive you to be of that sophistical captious spirit, or of that uncandid dullness, as to require, for every general observation or sentiment, an explicit detail of the correctives and exceptions, which reason will presume to be included in all the general propositions which come from reasonable men. You do not imagine that I wish to confine power, authority, and distinction to blood, and names, and titles. No, Sir. There is no qualification for government but virtue and wisdom, actual or presumptive. Wherever they are actually found, they have, in whatever state, condition, profession or trade, the passport of Heaven to human place and hon-

---

* *Ecclesiasticus,* Chap. xxxviii, verses 24, 25. "The wisdom of a learned man cometh by opportunity of leisure: and he that hath little business shall become wise."—"How can he get wisdom that holdeth the plough, and that glorieth in the goad; that driveth oxen; and is occupied in their labors; and whose talk is of bullocks?" Ver. 27. "So every carpenter and work-master that laboreth night and day," etc. Ver. 33. "They shall not be sought for public counsel nor sit high in the congregation: they shall not sit on the judge's seat, nor understand the sentence of judgement; they cannot declare justice and judgement, and they shall not be found where parables are spoken." Ver. 34. "But they will maintain the state of the world."

I do not determine whether this book be canonical, as the Gallican church (till lately) has considered it, or apocryphal, as here it is taken. I am sure it contains a great deal of sense and truth. Burke, *Reflections,* p. 56.

or. Woe to the country which would madly and impiously reject
the service of the talents and virtues, civil, military, or religious, that
are given to grace and to serve it; and would condemn to obscurity
every thing formed to diffuse lustre and glory around a state. Woe
to that country, too, that passing into the opposite extreme, considers
a low education, a mean contracted view of things, a sordid mercenary occupation, as a preferable title to command. Every thing
ought to be open; but not indifferently to every man. No rotation;
no appointment by lot; no mode of election operating in the spirit
of sortition or rotation[42] can be generally good in a government
conversant in extensive objects. Because they have no tendency,
direct or indirect, to select the man with a view to the duty, or to
accommodate the one to the other, I do not hesitate to say that the
road to eminence and power, from obscure condition, ought not to
be made too easy, nor a thing too much of course. If rare merit be
the rarest of all rare things, it ought to pass through some sort of
probation. The temple of honor ought to be seated on an eminence. If it be open through virtue, let it be remembered too, that
virtue is never tried but by some difficulty, and some struggle. . . .
    Nothing is a due and adequate representation of a state that
does not represent its ability as well as its property. But as ability
is a vigorous and active principle, and as property is sluggish, inert,
and timid, it never can be safe from the invasions of ability, unless
it be, out of all proportion, predominant in the representation.*
It must be represented too in great masses of accumulation, or it is
not rightly protected. The characteristic essence of property, formed
out of the combined principles of its acquisition and conservation,
is to be *unequal*. The great masses therefore which excite envy, and
tempt rapacity, must be put out of the possibility of danger. Then
they form a natural rampart about the lesser properties in all their
gradations. The same quantity of property, which is by the natural
course of things divided among many, has not the same operation.
Its defensive power is weakened as it is diffused. In this diffusion
each man's portion is less than what, in the eagerness of his desires,
he may flatter himself to obtain by dissipating the accumulations
of others. The plunder of the few would indeed give but a share

---

* I readily admit (indeed I should lay it down as a fundamental principle)
that in a republican government, which has a democratic basis, the rich do
require an additional security above what is necessary to them in monarchies.
They are subject to envy, and through envy to oppression. Burke, *Reflections*,
p. 207.

inconceivably small in the distribution to the many. But the many are not capable of making this calculation; and those who lead them to rapine never intend this distribution.

The power of perpetuating our property in our families is one of the most valuable and interesting circumstances belonging to it, and that which tends the most to the perpetuation of society itself. It makes our weakness subservient to our virtue; it grafts benevolence even upon avarice. The possessors of family wealth, and of the distinction which attends hereditary possession (as most concerned in it) are the natural securities for this transmission. With us, the House of Peers is formed upon this principle. It is wholly composed of hereditary property and hereditary distinction; and made therefore the third of the legislature;[43] and in the last event, the sole judge of all property in all its subdivisions. The House of Commons too, though not necessarily, yet in fact, is always so composed in the far greater part. Let those large proprietors be what they will, and they have their chance of being amongst the best, they are at the very worst, the ballast in the vessel of the commonwealth. For though hereditary wealth, and the rank which goes with it, are too much idolized by creeping sycophants, and the blind abject admirers of power, they are too rashly slighted in shallow speculations of the petulant, assuming, short-sighted coxcombs of philosophy. Some decent regulated preeminence, some preference (not exclusive appropriation) given to birth, is neither unnatural nor unjust nor impolitic. . . .

A true natural aristocracy is not a separate interest in the state, or separable from it. It is an essential integrant part of any large body rightly constituted. It is formed out of a class of legitimate presumptions, which, taken as generalities, must be admitted for actual truths. To be bred in a place of estimation; to see nothing low and sordid from one's infancy; to be taught to respect one's self; to be habituated to the censorial inspection of the public eye; to look early to public opinion; to stand upon such elevated ground as to be enabled to take a large view of the wide-spread and infinitely diversified combinations of men and affairs in a large society; to have leisure to read, to reflect, to converse; to be enabled to draw the court and attention of the wise and learned, wherever they are to be found; to be habituated in armies to command and to obey; to be taught to despise danger in the pursuit of honor and duty; to be formed to the greatest degree of vigilance, foresight, and circumspection, in a state of things in which no fault is committed with impunity and the slightest mistakes draw on the most ruinous consequences; to be led to a guarded and regulated conduct, from a sense that you are considered as an instructor of your fellow-

citizens in their highest concerns, and that you act as a reconciler between God and man; to be employed as an administrator of law and
justice, and to be thereby among the first benefactors to mankind; to
be a professor of high science, or of liberal and ingenuous art; to be
among rich traders, who from their success are presumed to have
sharp and vigorous understandings, and to possess the virtues of dili-
gence, order, constancy, and regularity, and to have cultivated an
habitual regard to commutative justice: these are the circumstances of
men that form what I should call a *natural* aristocracy, without which
there is no nation.

The state of civil society which necessarily generates this aristocracy is a state of Nature,—and much more truly so than a savage and
incoherent mode of life. For man is by nature reasonable; and he is
never perfectly in his natural state, but when he is placed where reason
may be best cultivated and most predominates. Art is man's nature.
We are as much, at least, in a state of Nature in formed manhood as
in immature and helpless infancy. Men, qualified in the manner I
have just described, form in Nature, as she operates in the common
modification of society, the leading, guiding, and governing part. It
is the soul to the body, without which the man does not exist. To
give, therefore, no more importance, in the social order, to such descriptions of men than that of so many units is a horrible usurpation. . . .

[*An Appeal from the New to the Old Whigs* (1791), III, 85–87.]

To keep a balance between the power of acquisition on the part
of the subject, and the demands he is to answer on the part of the
state, is a fundamental part of the skill of a true politician. The
means of acquisition are prior in time and in arrangement. Good
order is the foundation of all good things. To be enabled to acquire,
the people, without being servile, must be tractable and obedient.
The magistrate must have his reverence, the laws their authority.
The body of the people must not find the principles of natural
subordination by art rooted out of their minds. They must respect
that property of which they cannot partake. They must labor to
obtain what by labor can be obtained; and when they find, as they
commonly do, the success disproportioned to the endeavor, they
must be taught their consolation in the final proportions of eternal
justice. Of this consolation, whoever deprives them, deadens their
industry, and strikes at the root of all acquisition as of all conservation. He that does this is the cruel oppressor, the merciless enemy of
the poor and wretched; at the same time that by his wicked speculations he exposes the fruits of successful industry, and the accumula-

tions of fortune, to the plunder of the negligent, the disappointed, and the unprosperous. . . .

RIGHTS AND DUTIES

The factions now so busy among us, in order to divest men of all love for their country, and to remove from their minds all duty with regard to the state, endeavor to propagate an opinion, that the *people,* in forming their commonwealth, have by no means parted with their power over it. This is an impregnable citadel, to which these gentlemen retreat, whenever they are pushed by the battery of laws and usages and positive conventions. Indeed, it is such, and of so great force, that all they have done in defending their outworks is so much time and labor thrown away. Discuss any of their schemes, their answer is: It is the act of the *people,* and that is sufficient. Are we to deny to a *majority* of the people the right of altering even the whole frame of their society, if such should be their pleasure? They may change it, say they, from a monarchy to a republic to-day, and to-morrow back again from a republic to a monarchy; and so backward and forward as often as they like. They are masters of the commonwealth, because in substance they are themselves the commonwealth. The French Revolution, say they, was the act of the majority of the people; and if the majority of any other people, the people of England, for instance, wish to make the same change, they have the same right.

Just the same, undoubtedly. That is, none at all. Neither the few nor the many have a right to act merely by their will, in any matter connected with duty, trust, engagement, or obligation. The Constitution of a country being once settled upon some compact, tacit or expressed, there is no power existing of force to alter it, without the breach of the covenant, or the consent of all the parties. Such is the nature of a contract. And the votes of a majority of the people, whatever their infamous flatterers may teach in order to corrupt their minds, cannot alter the moral any more than they can alter the physical essence of things. The people are not to be taught to think lightly of their engagements to their governors; else they teach governors to think lightly of their engagements towards them. In that kind of game, in the end, the people are sure to be losers. To flatter them into a contempt of faith, truth, and justice is to ruin them; for in these virtues consists their whole safety. To flatter any man, or any part of mankind, in any description, by asserting that in engagements he or they are free, while any other human creature is bound, is ultimately to vest the rule of morality in the pleasure of those who ought to be rigidly submitted to it,—to subject the sovereign reason of the world to the caprices of weak and giddy men.

But, as no one of us men can dispense with public or private faith, or with any other tie of moral obligation, so neither can any number of us. The number engaged in crimes, instead of turning them into laudable acts, only augments the quantity and intensity of the guilt. I am well aware that men love to hear of their power, but have an extreme disrelish to be told of their duty. This is of course; because every duty is a limitation of some power. Indeed, arbitrary power is so much to the depraved taste of the vulgar, of the vulgar of every description, that almost all the dissensions which lacerate the commonwealth are not concerning the manner in which it is to be exercised, but concerning the hands in which it is to be placed. Somewhere they are resolved to have it. Whether they desire it to be vested in the many or the few depends with most men upon the chance which they imagine they themselves may have of partaking in the exercise of that arbitrary sway, in the one mode or in the other.

It is not necessary to teach men to thirst after power. But it is very expedient that by moral instruction they should be taught, and by their civil constitutions they should be compelled, to put many restrictions upon the immoderate exercise of it, and the inordinate desire. The best method of obtaining these two great points forms the important, but at the same time the difficult problem to the true statesman. He thinks of the place in which political power is to be lodged with no other attention than as it may render the more or the less practicable its salutary restraint and its prudent direction. For this reason, no legislator, at any period of the world, has willingly placed the seat of active power in the hands of the multitude; because there it admits of no control, no regulation, no steady direction whatsoever. The people are the natural control on authority; but to exercise and to control together is contradictory and impossible.

As the exorbitant exercise of power cannot, under popular sway, be effectually restrained, the other great object of political arrangement, the means of abating an excessive desire of it, is in such a state still worse provided for. The democratic commonwealth is the foodful nurse of ambition. Under the other forms it meets with many restraints. Whenever, in states which have had a democratic basis, the legislators have endeavored to put restraints upon ambition, their methods were as violent as in the end they were ineffectual,—as violent, indeed, as any of the most jealous despotism could invent. The ostracism[44] could not very long save itself, and much less the state which it was meant to guard, from the attempts of ambition,—one of the natural, inbred, incurable distempers of a powerful democracy.

But to return from this short digression,—which, however, is not wholly foreign to the question of the effect of the will of the majority upon the form or the existence of their society. I cannot too often recommend it to the serious consideration of all men who think civil society to be within the province of moral jurisdiction, that, if we

owe to it any duty, it is not subject to our will. Duties are not voluntary. Duty and will are even contradictory terms. Now, though civil
society might be at first a voluntary act, (which in many cases it undoubtedly was,) its continuance is under a permanent standing covenant, coexisting with the society; and it attaches upon every individual
of that society, without any formal act of his own. This is warranted
by the general practice, arising out of the general sense of mankind.
Men without their choice derive benefits from that association; without their choice they are subjected to duties in consequence of these
benefits; and without their choice they enter into a virtual obligation
as binding as any that is actual. Look through the whole of life and
the whole system of duties. Much the strongest moral obligations are
such as were never the results of our option. . . . When we marry,
the choice is voluntary, but the duties are not matter of choice: they
are dictated by the nature of the situation. Dark and inscrutable are
the ways by which we come into the world. The instincts which give
rise to this mysterious process of Nature are not of our making. But
out of physical causes, unknown to us, perhaps unknowable, arise
moral duties, which, as we are able perfectly to comprehend, we are
bound indispensably to perform. Parents may not be consenting to
their moral relation; but, consenting or not, they are bound to a long
train of burdensome duties towards those with whom they have never
made a convention of any sort. Children are not consenting to their
relation; but their relation, without their actual consent, binds them
to its duties,—or rather it implies their consent, because the presumed
consent of every rational creature is in unison with the predisposed
order of things. Men come in that manner into a community with the
social state of their parents, endowed with all the benefits, loaded
with all the duties of their situation. If the social ties and ligaments,
spun out of those physical relations which are the elements of the
commonwealth, in most cases begin, and always continue, independently of our will, so, without any stipulation on our own part, are we
bound by that relation called our country, which comprehends (as it
has been well said) "all the charities of all." * 45 Nor are we left without powerful instincts to make this duty as dear and grateful to us as it
is awful and coercive. Our country is not a thing of mere physical
locality. It consists, in a great measure, in the ancient order into
which we are born. We may have the same geographical situation, but
another country; as we may have the same country in another soil.

* Men are not tied to one another by papers and seals. They are led to
associate by resemblances, by conformities, by sympathies. It is with nations as
with individuals. Nothing is so strong a tie of amity between nation and nation
as correspondence in laws, customs, manners and habits of life. They have more
than the force of treaties in themselves. They are obligations written in the heart.
First Letter on a Regicide Peace (1796), V, 213–14.

The place that determines our duty to our country is a social, civil relation. . . .

I admit, indeed, that in morals, as in all things else, difficulties will sometimes occur. Duties will sometimes cross one another. Then questions will arise, which of them is to be placed in subordination? which of them may be entirely superseded? These doubts give rise to that part of moral science called *casuistry,* which . . . requires a very solid and discriminating judgment, great modesty and caution, and much sobriety of mind in the handling; else there is a danger that it may totally subvert those offices which it is its object only to methodize and reconcile. Duties, at their extreme bounds, are drawn very fine, so as to become almost evanescent. In that state some shade of doubt will always rest on these questions, when they are pursued with great subtilty. But the very habit of stating these extreme cases is not very laudable or safe; because, in general, it is not right to turn our duties into doubts. They are imposed to govern our conduct, not to exercise our ingenuity; and therefore our opinions about them ought not to be in a state of fluctuation, but steady, sure, and resolved. . . .

MAJORITIES AND MINORITIES

We hear much, from men who have not acquired their hardiness of assertion from the profundity of their thinking, about the omnipotence of a *majority,* in such a dissolution of an ancient society as has taken place in France. But among men so disbanded there can be no such thing as majority or minority, or power in any one person to bind another. The power of acting by a majority, which the gentlemen theorists seem to assume so readily, after they have violated the contract out of which it has arisen, (if at all it existed,) must be grounded on two assumptions: first, that of an incorporation produced by unanimity; and secondly, a unanimous agreement that the act of a mere majority (say of one) shall pass with them and with others as the act of the whole.

We are so little affected by things which are habitual, that we consider this idea of the decision of a *majority* as if it were a law of our original nature. But such constructive whole, residing in a part only, is one of the most violent fictions of positive law that ever has been or can be made on the principles of artificial incorporation. Out of civil society Nature knows nothing of it; nor are men, even when arranged according to civil order, otherwise than by very long training, brought at all to submit to it. The mind is brought far more easily to acquiesce in the proceedings of one man, or a few, who act under a general procuration for the state, than in the vote of a victorious majority in councils in which every man has his share in the deliberation. For there the beaten party are exasperated and soured by the previous contention, and mortified by the conclusive defeat. This mode of decision, where wills may be so nearly equal, according to circumstances, the smaller number may be the stronger force, and where apparent reason may be all upon one side, and on the other little else than impetuous appetite,—all this must be the result of a very particular and special convention, confirmed afterwards by long habits of obedience, by a sort of discipline in society, and by a strong hand, vested with stationary, permanent power to enforce this sort of constructive general will. What organ it is that shall declare the corporate mind is so much a matter of positive arrangement, that several states, for the validity of several of their acts, have required a proportion of voices much greater than that of a mere majority. These proportions are so entirely governed by convention that in some cases the minority decides. The laws in many countries to *condemn* require more than a mere majority; less than an equal number to *acquit*. In our judicial trials we require unanimity either to condemn or to absolve. In some incorporations one man speaks for the whole; in others, a few. . . .

Among these nice, and therefore dangerous points of casuistry, may be reckoned the question so much agitated in the present hour: Whether, after the people have discharged themselves of their original power by a habitual delegation, no occasion can possibly occur which may justify the resumption of it? This question, in this latitude, is very hard to affirm or deny; but I am satisfied that no occasion can justify such a resumption, which would not equally authorize a dispensation with any other moral duty, perhaps with all of them together. However, if in general it be not easy to determine concerning the lawfulness of such devious proceedings, which must be ever on the edge of crimes, it is far from difficult to foresee the perilous consequences of the resuscitation of such a power in the people. The practical consequences of any political tenet go a great way in deciding upon its value. Political problems do not primarily concern truth or falsehood. They relate to good or evil. What in the result is likely to produce evil is politically false; that which is productive of good, politically true.

Believing it, therefore, a question at least arduous in the theory, and in the practice very critical, it would become us to ascertain as well as we can what form it is that our incantations are about to call up from darkness and the sleep of ages. When the supreme authority of the people is in question, before we attempt to extend or to confine it, we ought to fix in our minds, with some degree of distinctness, an idea of what it is we mean, when we say, the PEOPLE.

In a state of *rude* Nature there is no such thing as a people. A number of men in themselves have no collective capacity. The idea of a people is the idea of a corporation. It is wholly artificial, and made, like all other legal fictions, by common agreement. What the particular nature of that agreement was is collected from the form into which the particular society has been cast. Any other is not *their* covenant.

When men, therefore, break up the original compact or agreement which gives its corporate form and capacity to a state, they are no longer a people,—they have no longer a corporate existence,—they have no longer a legal coactive force to bind within, nor a claim to be recognized abroad. They are a number of vague, loose individuals, and nothing more. With them all is to begin again. Alas! they little know how many a weary step is to be taken before they can form themselves into a mass which has a true politic personality.

As in the abstract it is perfectly clear, that, out of a state of civil society, majority and minority are relations which can have no existence, and that, in civil society, its own specific conventions in each corporation determine what it is that constitutes the people, so as to make their act the signification of the general will,—to come to particulars, it is equally clear that neither in France nor in England has the original or any subsequent compact of the state, expressed or implied, constituted *a majority of men, told by the head,*[46] to be the acting people of their several communities. And I see as little of policy or utility as there is of right, in laying down a principle that a majority of men told by the head are to be considered as the people, and that as such their will is to be law. What policy can there be found in arrangements made in defiance of every political principle? To enable men to act with the weight and character of a people, and to answer the ends for which they are incorporated into that capacity, we must suppose them (by means immediate or consequential) to be in that state of habitual social discipline in which the wiser, the more expert, and the more opulent conduct, and by conducting enlighten and protect, the weaker, the less knowing, and the less provided with the goods of fortune. . . . When great multitudes act together, under that discipline of Nature, I recognize the PEOPLE. I acknowledge something that perhaps equals, and ought always to guide, the sovereignty of convention. In all things the voice of this grand chorus of national harmony ought to have a mighty and decisive influence. . . .

When the multitude are not under this discipline, they can scarcely be said to be in civil society.* Give once a certain constitution of things which produces a variety of conditions and circumstances in a state, and there is in Nature and reason a principle which, for

---

* But when you disturb this harmony—when you break up this beautiful order, this array of truth and Nature, as well as of habit and prejudice—when you separate the common sort of men from their proper chieftains, so as to form them into an adverse army, I no longer know that venerable object called the people in such a disbanded race of deserters and vagabonds. For a while they may be terrible, indeed, but in such a manner as wild beasts are terrible. The mind owes to them no sort of submission. *An Appeal from the New to the Old Whigs* (1791), III, 87.

their own benefit, postpones, not the interest, but the judgment, of those who are *numero plures*, to those who are *virtute et honore majores*.^{46a} Numbers in a state (supposing, which is not the case in France, that a state does exist) are always of consideration,—but they are not the whole consideration. . . .

[*An Appeal from the New to the Old Whigs* (1791), III, 76–87 *passim*.]

It is said that twenty-four millions ought to prevail over two hundred thousand. True; if the constitution of a kingdom be a problem of arithmetic. This sort of discourse does well enough with the lamp-post for its second: to men who *may* reason calmly, it is ridiculous. . . .⁴⁷ The legislators who framed the ancient republics knew that their business was too arduous to be accomplished with no better apparatus than the metaphysics of an undergraduate and the mathematics and arithmetic of an exciseman.* They had to do with men, and they were obliged to study human nature. They had to do with citizens, and they were obliged to study the effects of those habits which are communicated by the circumstances of civil life. They were sensible that the operation of this second nature on the first produced a new combination; and thence arose many diversities among men, according to their birth, their education, their professions, the periods of their lives, their residence in towns or in the country, their several ways of acquiring and of fixing property, and according to the quality of the property itself, all which rendered them as it were so many different species of animals. From hence they thought themselves obliged to dispose their citizens into such classes, and to place them in such situations in the state as their peculiar habits might qualify them to fill, and to allot to them such appropriated privileges as might secure to them what their specific occasions required, and which might furnish to each description such force as might protect it in the conflict caused by the diversity of interests that must exist and must contend in all complex society. . . .

It is here that your modern legislators have gone deep into the negative series, and sunk even below their own nothing. As the first sort of legislators attended to the different kinds of citizens, and combined them into one commonwealth, the others, the metaphysical

---

* They have much, but bad, metaphysics; much, but bad, geometry; much, but false, proportionate arithmetic; but if it were all as exact as metaphysics, geometry, and arithmetic ought to be, and if their schemes were perfectly consistent in all their parts, it would make only a more fair and sightly vision. *Reflections*, p. 212.

and alchemistical legislators, have taken the direct contrary course. They have attempted to confound all sorts of citizens, as well as they could, into one homogeneous mass; and then they divided this their amalgam into a number of incoherent republics.[48] They reduce men to loose counters merely for the sake of simple telling, and not to figures whose power is to arise from their place in the table. The elements of their own metaphysics might have taught them better lessons. The troll of their categorical table might have informed them that there was something else in the intellectual world besides *substance* and *quantity*. They might learn from the catechism of metaphysics that there were eight heads more,[49] in every complex deliberation, which they have never thought of, though these, of all the ten, are the subject on which the skill of man can operate any thing at all. . . .

THE COMMONS AND
THEIR REPRESENTATION

I see that your example is held out to shame us. I know that we are supposed a dull sluggish race, rendered passive by finding our situation tolerable; and prevented by a mediocrity of freedom[50] from ever attaining to its full perfection. Your leaders in France began by affecting to admire, almost to adore, the British constitution; but as they advanced they came to look upon it with a sovereign contempt. The friends of your National Assembly among us have full as mean an opinion of what was formerly thought the glory of their country. The Revolution Society has discovered that the English nation is not free. They are convinced that the inequality in our representation is a "defect in our constitution so *gross and palpable,* as to make it excellent chiefly in *form* and *theory.*" That a representation in the legislature of a kingdom is not only the basis of all constitutional liberty in it, but of *"all legitimate government;* that without it a *government* is nothing but an *usurpation;"*—that "when the representation is *partial,* the kingdom possesses liberty only *partially;* and if extremely partial it gives only a *semblance;* and if not only extremely partial, but corruptly chosen, it becomes a *nuisance.*" Dr. Price considers this inadequacy of representation as our *fundamental grievance;* and though, as to the corruption of this semblance of representation, he hopes it is not yet arrived to its full perfection of depravity, he fears that "nothing will be done towards gaining for us this *essential blessing,* until some *great abuse of power* again provokes our resentment, or some *great calamity* again alarms our fears, or perhaps till the acquisition of a *pure and equal representation by other countries,* while we are *mocked* with the *shadow,* kindles our shame." To this he subjoins a note in these words: "A representation, chosen chiefly by the Treasury, and a *few* thousands of the *dregs* of the people, who are generally paid for their votes."

You will smile here at the consistency of those democratists, who, when they are not on their guard, treat the humbler part of the community with the greatest contempt, while, at the same time, they pretend to make them the depositories of all power. It would require a long discourse to point out to you the many fallacies that lurk in the generality and equivocal nature of the terms "inadequate representation." I shall only say here, in justice to that old-fashioned constitution, under which we have long prospered, that our representation has been found perfectly adequate to all the purposes for which a representation of the people can be desired or devised.* I defy the enemies of our constitution to show the contrary. To detail the particulars in which it is found so well to promote its ends, would demand a treatise on our practical constitution. I state here the doctrine of the Revolutionists, only that you and others may see, what an opinion these gentlemen entertain of the constitution of their country, and why they seem to think that some great abuse of power, or some great calamity, as giving a chance for the blessing of a constitution according to their ideas, would be much palliated to their feelings; you see *why they* are so much enamored of your fair and equal representation, which being once obtained, the same effects might follow. You see they consider our House of Commons as only "a semblance," "a form," "a theory," "a shadow," "a mockery," perhaps "a nuisance."

These gentlemen value themselves on being systematic and not without reason. They must therefore look on this gross and palpable defect of representation, this fundamental grievance (so they call it) as a thing not only vicious in itself, but as rendering our whole government absolutely *illegitimate,* and not at all better than a downright *usurpation.* Another revolution, to get rid of this illegitimate and usurped government, would of course be perfectly justifiable,

---

* If there is a doubt whether the House of Commons represents perfectly the whole commons of Great Britain (I think there is none), there can be no question but that the Lords and Commons together represent the sense of the whole people to the Crown and to the world. *Third Letter on a Regicide Peace* (1796–97), V, 295.

if not absolutely necessary. Indeed their principle, if you observe it with any attention, goes much further than to an alteration in the election of the House of Commons; for, if popular representation, or choice, is necessary to the *legitimacy* of all government, the House of Lords is, at one stroke, bastardized and corrupted in blood. That house is no representative of the people at all, even in "semblance or in form." The case of the Crown is altogether as bad. In vain the Crown may endeavor to screen itself against these gentlemen by the authority of the establishment made on the Revolution. The Revolution which is resorted to for a title, on their system, wants a title itself. The Revolution is built, according to their theory, upon a basis not more solid than our present formalities, as it was made by a House of Lords not representing any one but themselves; and by a House of Commons exactly such as the present, that is, as they term it, by a mere "shadow and mockery" of representation. . . .

> The House of Commons, in that light, undoubtedly, is no representative of the people, as a collection of individuals. Nobody pretends it, nobody can justify such an assertion. When you come to examine into this claim of right, founded on the right of self-government in each individual, you find the thing demanded infinitely short of the principle of the demand. What! *one third* only of the legislature, and of the government no share at all? What sort of treaty of partition is this for those who have an inherent right to the whole? Give them all they ask, and your grant is still a cheat: for how comes only a third to be their younger-children's fortune in this settlement? How came they neither to have the choice of kings or lords, or judges, or generals, or admirals, or bishops, or priests, or ministers, or justices of peace? Why, what have you to answer in favor of the prior rights of the crown and peerage but this: Our Constitution is a prescriptive constitution; it is a constitution whose sole authority is, that it has existed time out of mind? . . . Prescription is the most solid of all titles, not only to property, but which is to secure that property, to government. They harmonize with each other, and give mutual aid to one another. It is accompanied with another ground of authority in the constitution of the human mind, presumption. It is a presumption in favor of any settled scheme of government against any untried project, that a nation has long existed and flourished under it. It is a better presumption even of the *choice* of a nation,—far better than any sudden and temporary arrangement by actual election. Because a nation is not an idea only of local extent and individual momentary aggregation, but it is an idea of continuity which extends in time as well as in numbers and in space. And this is a choice not of one day or one set of people, not a tumultuary and giddy choice; it is a deliberate election of ages and of generations; it is a constitution

made by what is ten thousand times better than choice; it is made by
the peculiar circumstances, occasions, tempers, dispositions, and moral,
civil, and social habitudes of the people, which disclose themselves
only in a long space of time. It is a vestment which accommodates
itself to the body. Nor is prescription of government formed upon
blind, unmeaning prejudices. For man is a most unwise and a most
wise being. The individual is foolish; the multitude, for the moment,
is foolish, when they act without deliberation; but the species is wise,
and, when time is given to it, as a species, it almost always acts right.

The reason for the Crown as it is, for the lords as they are, is
my reason for the commons as they are, the electors as they are. Now
if the Crown, and the lords, and the judicatures are all prescriptive,
so is the House of Commons of the very same origin, and of no other.
We and our electors have their powers and privileges both made and
circumscribed by prescription, as much to the full as the other parts;
and as such we have always claimed them, and on no other title. The
House of Commons is a legislative body corporate by prescription, not
made upon any given theory, but existing prescriptively, just like the
rest. This prescription has made it essentially what it is, an aggregate
collection of three parts, knights, citizens, burgesses. . . .

The more frequently this affair is discussed, the stronger the
case appears to the sense and the feelings of mankind. I have no more
doubt than I entertain of my existence, that this very thing, which is
stated as an horrible thing, is the means of the preservation of our
Constitution while it lasts,—of curing it of many of the disorders
which, attending every species of institution, would attend the principle of an exact local representation, or a representation on the
principle of numbers. If you reject personal representation, you are
pushed upon expedience; and then what they wish us to do is, to
prefer their speculations on that subject to the happy experience of
this country, of a growing liberty and a growing prosperity for five
hundred years.

[*Speech on Reform of Representation of the Commons in Parliament*
(1782), VI, 146–47, 148–49.]

With us, when we elect popular representatives, we send them
to a council, in which each man individually is a subject, and submitted to a government complete in all its ordinary functions. With
you the elective assembly is the sovereign, and the sole sovereign:
all the members are therefore integral parts of this sole sovereignty.
But with us it is totally different. With us the representative,
separated from the other parts, can have no action and no existence.
The government is the point of reference of the several members and
districts of our representation. This is the center of our unity. This
government of reference is a trustee for the *whole,* and not for the

parts. So is the other branch of our public council, I mean the House of Lords. With us the king and the lords are several and joint securities for the equality of each district, each province, each city. When did you hear in Great Britain of any province suffering from the inequality of its representation; what district from having no representation at all?

> . . . [C]an you fairly and distinctly point out what one evil or grievance has happened which you can refer to the representative not following the opinion of his constituents? What one symptom do we find of this inequality? But it is not an arithmetical inequality with which we ought to trouble ourselves. If there be a moral, a political equality, this is the *desideratum* in our Constitution, and in every constitution in the world. Moral inequality is as between places and between classes. Now, I ask, what advantage do you find that the places which abound in representation possess over others in which it is more scanty, in security for freedom, in security for justice, or in any one of those means of procuring temporal prosperity and eternal happiness, the ends for which society was formed? Are the local interests of Cornwall and Wiltshire, for instance, their roads, canals, their prisons, their police, better than Yorkshire, Warwickshire, or Staffordshire? Warwick has members: is Warwick or Stafford more opulent, happy, or free than Newcastle, or than Birmingham? Is Wiltshire the pampered favorite, while Yorkshire, like the child of the bondwoman, is turned out to the desert? . . . Is a committee of Cornwall, &c., thronged, and the others deserted? No. You have an equal representation, because you have men equally interested in the prosperity of the whole, who are involved in the general interest and the general sympathy; and, perhaps, these places furnishing a superfluity of public agents and administrators, (whether in strictness they are representatives or not I do not mean to inquire, but they are agents and administrators,) they will stand clearer of local interests, passions, prejudices, and cabals than the others, and therefore preserve the balance of the parts, and with a more general view and a more steady hand than the rest. . . .
>
> [*Speech on Reform of Representation of the Commons in Parliament* (1782), VI, 149–50.]

Certainly, Gentlemen, it ought to be the happiness and glory of a representative to live in the strictest union, the closest correspondence, and the most unreserved communication with his constituents. Their wishes ought to have great weight with him; their opinions high respect; their business unremitted attention. It is his duty to sacrifice his repose, his pleasure, his satisfactions, to theirs—and above all, ever, and in all cases, to prefer their interest to his own.

But his unbiased opinion, his mature judgment, his enlightened conscience, he ought not to sacrifice to you, to any man, or to any set of men living. These he does not derive from your pleasure—no, nor from the law and the constitution. They are a trust from Providence, for the abuse of which he is deeply answerable. Your representative owes you, not his industry only, but his judgment; and he betrays, instead of serving you, if he sacrifices it to your opinion.* . . .

To deliver an opinion is the right of all men; that of constituents is a weighty and respectable opinion, which a representative ought always to rejoice to hear, and which he ought always most seriously to consider. But *authoritative* instructions, *mandates* issued, which a member is bound blindly and implicitly to obey, to vote, and to argue for, though contrary to the clearest conviction of his judgment and conscience; these are things utterly unknown to the laws of this land, and which arise from a fundamental mistake of the whole order and tenor of our constitution.†

Parliament is not a *congress* of ambassadors from different and hostile interests, which interests each must maintain, as an agent and advocate, against other agents and advocates; but Parliament is a *deliberative* assembly of *one* nation, with *one* interest, that of the whole—where not local purposes, not local prejudices, ought to guide but the general good, resulting from the general reason of the whole. You choose a member, indeed; but when you have chosen him he is not a member of Bristol,[51] but he is a member of *Parliament*. If the local constituent should have an interest or should form a hasty opinion evidently opposite to the real good of the rest of the community, the member for that place ought to be as far as any other from any endeavor to give it effect. . . .

[*An Address to the Electors of Bristol* (1774), I, 446–48.]

* Faithful watchmen we ought to be over the rights and privileges of the people. But our duty, if we are qualified for it as we ought, is to give them information, and not to receive it from them: we are not to go to school to them, to learn the principles of law and government. . . . I reverentially look up to the opinion of the people, and with an awe that is almost superstitious. I should be ashamed to show my face before them, if I changed my ground as they cried up or cried down men or things or opinions—if I wavered and shifted about with every change, and joined in it or opposed as best answered any low interest or passion—if I held them up hopes which I knew I never intended, or promised what I well knew I could not perform. *Speech on the Duration of Parliaments* (1780), VI, 134–35.

† For my own part, in which I have meditated upon that subject, I cannot, indeed, take upon me to say I have the honor *to follow* the sense of the people. The truth is *I met it on the way,* while I was pursuing their interest according to my own ideas. I am happy beyond expression to find that my intentions have so far coincided with theirs. . . . *Speech on the Plan for Economical Reform* (1780), II, 66. [Burke's emphasis]

To govern according to the sense and agreeably to the interests of the people is a great and glorious object of government. This object cannot be obtained but through the medium of popular election; and popular election is a mighty evil. It is such and so great an evil, that, though there are few nations whose monarchs were not originally elective, very few are now elected. They are the distempers of elections that have destroyed all free states. To cure these distempers is difficult, if not impossible; the only thing, therefore, left to save the commonwealth is to prevent their return too frequently. The objects in view are to have Parliaments as frequent as they can be without distracting them in the prosecution of public business: on one hand, to secure their dependence upon the people; on the other, to give them that quiet in their minds and that ease in their fortunes as to enable them to perform the most arduous and most painful duty in the world with spirit, with efficiency, with independency, and with experience, as real public counsellors, not as the canvassers at a perpetual election. . . .

Theory, I know, would suppose that every general election is to the representative a day of judgment, in which he appears before his constituents to account for the use of the talent with which they intrusted him, and for the improvement he has made of it for the public advantage. It would be so, if every corruptible representative were to find an enlightened and incorruptible constituent. But the practice and knowledge of the world will not suffer us to be ignorant that the Constitution on paper is one thing, and in fact and experience is another. We must know that the candidate, instead of trusting at his election to the testimony of his behavior in Parliament, must bring the testimony of a large sum of money, the capacity of liberal expense in entertainments, the power of serving and obliging the rulers of corporations, of winning over the popular leaders of political clubs, associations, and neighborhoods. It is ten thousand times more necessary to show himself a man of power than a man of integrity, in almost all the elections with which I have been acquainted. Elections, therefore, become a matter of heavy expense; and if contests are frequent, to many they will become a matter of an expense totally ruinous, which no fortunes can bear, but least of all the landed fortunes, incumbered as they often, indeed as they mostly are, with debts, with portions, with jointures,[52] and tied up in the hands of the possessor by the limitations of settlement. It is a material, it is in my opinion a lasting consideration, in all the questions concerning election. Let no one think the charges of elections a trivial matter.[53]

The charge, therefore, of elections ought never to be lost sight of in a question concerning their frequency; because the grand object you seek is independence. Independence of mind will ever be more or less influenced by independence of fortune; and if every three years the exhausting sluices of entertainments, drinkings, open houses, to say nothing of bribery, are to be periodically drawn up and renewed,—if government favors, for which now, in some shape or other, the whole race of men are candidates, are to be called for upon every occasion, I see that private fortunes will be washed away, and every, even to the least, trace of independence borne down by the torrent. . . .

Gentlemen, I know, feel the weight of this argument; they agree that this would be the consequence of more frequent elections, if things were to continue as they are. But they think the greatness and frequency of the evil would itself be a remedy for it,—that, sitting but for a short time, the member would not find it worth while to make such vast expenses, while the fear of their constituents will hold them the more effectually to their duty.

To this I answer that experience is full against them. . . . A seat in this House, for good purposes, for bad purposes, for no purposes at all, (except the mere consideration derived from being concerned in the public counsels,) will ever be a first-rate object of ambition in England. Ambition is no exact calculator. Avarice itself does not calculate strictly, when it games. One thing is certain: that in this political game the great lottery of power is that into which men will purchase with millions of chances against them. In Turkey, where the place, where the fortune, where the head itself are so insecure that scarcely any have died in their beds for ages, so that the bowstring is the natural death of bashaws, yet in no country is power and distinction (precarious enough, God knows, in all) sought for with such boundless avidity,—as if the value of place was enhanced by the danger and insecurity of its tenure. Nothing will ever make a seat in this House not an object of desire to numbers by any means or at any charge, but the depriving it of all power and all dignity. This would do it. This is the true and only nostrum for that purpose. But a House of Commons without power and without dignity, either in itself or in its members, is no House of Commons for the purposes of this Constitution.

[*Speech on the Duration of Parliaments* (1780), VI, 132–33, 136–37, 139, 140–41.]

THE REAL RIGHTS OF MAN

The effects of the incapacity shown by the popular leaders in all the great members of the commonwealth are to be covered with the "all-atoning name" of liberty. In some people I see great liberty indeed; in many, if not in the most, an oppressive degrading servitude. But what is liberty without wisdom, and without virtue? It is the greatest of all possible evils; for it is folly, vice, and madness, without tuition or restraint. Those who know what virtuous liberty is cannot bear to see it disgraced by incapable heads, on account of their having high-sounding words in their mouths. Grand, swelling sentiments of liberty, I am sure I do not despise. They warm the heart; they enlarge and liberalize our minds; they animate our courage in a time of conflict. Old as I am, I read the fine raptures of Lucan and Corneille[54] with pleasure. Neither do I wholly condemn the little arts and devices of popularity.* They facilitate the carrying of many points of moment; they keep the people together; they refresh the mind in its exertions; and they diffuse occasional gaiety over the severe brow of moral freedom. Every politician ought to sacrifice to the graces; and to join compliance with reason. But in such an undertaking as that in France, all these subsidiary sentiments and artifices are of little avail.

The pretended rights of these theorists are all extremes; and in proportion as they are metaphysically true, they are morally and politically false. The rights of men are in a sort of *middle,* incapable of definition, but not impossible to be discerned. The rights of men in governments are their advantages; and these are often in balances between differences of good; in compromises sometimes between good and evil, and sometimes, between evil and evil.† Political reason is a computing principle; adding, substracting, multiplying, and dividing, morally and not metaphysically or mathematically, true moral denominations.

By these theorists the right of the people is almost always sophistically confounded with their power. The body of the community, whenever it can come to act, can meet with no effectual resistance; but till power and right are the same, the whole body of them has

---

* No man carries further than I do the policy of making government pleasing to the people. But the widest range of this politic complaisance is confined within the limits of justice. I would not only consult the interest of the people, but I would cheerfully gratify their humors. We are all a sort of children that must be soothed and managed. I think I am not austere or formal in my nature. I would bear, I would even myself play my part in, any innocent buffooneries, to divert them. But I will never act the tyrant for their amusement. If they will mix malice in their sports, I shall never consent to throw them any living, sentient creature whatsoever, no, not so much as a kitling, to torment. *Speech at Britol Previous to the Election* (1780), II, 167.

† All government, indeed every human benefit and enjoyment, every virtue and every prudent act, is founded on compromise and barter. We balance inconveniences; we give and take; we remit some rights, that we may enjoy others; and we choose rather to be happy citizens than subtle disputants. *Speech on Conciliation with America* (1775), II, 173.

no right inconsistent with virtue, and the first of all virtues, prudence. Men have no right to what is not reasonable, and to what is not for their benefit. . . .

Far am I from denying in theory; full as far is my heart from withholding in practice (if I were of power to give or to withhold) the *real* rights of men. In denying their false claims of right, I do not mean to injure those which are real, and are such as their pretended rights would totally destroy. If civil society be made for the advantage of man, all the advantages for which it is made become his right. It is an institution of beneficence; and law itself is only beneficence acting by a rule. Men have a right to live by that rule; they have a right to justice as between their fellows, whether their fellows are in politic function or in ordinary occupation. They have a right to the fruits of their industry; and to the means of making their industry fruitful. They have a right to the acquisitions of their parents; to the nourishment and improvement of their offspring; to instruction in life, and to consolation in death. Whatever each man can separately do, without trespassing upon others, he has a right to do for himself; and he has a right to a fair portion of all which society, with all its combinations of skill and force, can do in his favor. In this partnership all men have equal rights; but not to equal things. He that has but five shillings in the partnership has as good a right to it, as he that has five hundred pounds has to his larger proportion. But he has not a right to an equal dividend in the product of the joint stock; and as to the share of power, authority, and direction which each individual ought to have in the management of the state, that I must deny to be amongst the direct original rights of man in civil society; for I have in my contemplation the civil social man, and no other. It is a thing to be settled by convention.

If civil society be the offspring of convention, that convention must be its law. That convention must limit and modify all the descriptions of constitution which are formed under it. Every sort of legislative, judicial, or executory power are its creatures. They can have no being in any other state of things; and how can any man claim, under the conventions of civil society, rights which do not so much as suppose its existence? Rights which are absolutely repugnant to it? One of the first motives to civil society, and which becomes one of its fundamental rules, is *that no man should be judge in his own cause.* By this each person has at once divested himself of the first fundamental right of uncovenanted man, that is, to judge for himself, and to assert his own cause. He abdicates all right to be his own governor. He inclusively, in a great measure, abandons the right of self-defence, the first law of nature. Men cannot enjoy the rights of an uncivil and of a civil state together. That he may obtain justice he gives up his right of determining what it is in points the most essential to him. That he may secure some liberty, he makes a surrender in trust of the whole of it.

Government is not made in virtue of natural rights, which may and do exist in total independence of it, and exist in much greater clearness, and in a much greater degree of abstract perfection: but their abstract perfection is their practical defect. By having a right to every thing they want every thing. Government is a contrivance of human wisdom to provide for human *wants*. Men have a right that these wants should be provided for by this wisdom. Among these wants is to be reckoned the want, out of civil society, of a sufficient restraint upon their passions. Society requires not only that the passions of individuals should be subjected, but that even in the mass and body as well as in the individuals, the inclinations of men should frequently be thwarted, their will controlled, and their passions brought into subjection.* This can only be done *by a power out of themselves;* and not, in the exercise of its function, subject to that will and to those passions which it is its office to bridle and subdue. In this sense the restraints on men, as well as their liberties, are to be reckoned among their rights. But as the liberties and the restrictions vary with times and circumstances, and admit of infinite modifications, they cannot be settled upon any abstract rule; and nothing is so foolish as to discuss them upon that principle.†

The moment you abate any thing from the full rights of men, each to govern himself, and suffer any artificial positive limitation upon those rights, from that moment the whole organization of government becomes a consideration of convenience. This it is which makes the constitution of a state, and the due distribution of its powers, a matter of the most delicate and complicated skill. It

* Men are qualified for civil liberty in exact proportion to their disposition to put moral chains upon their own appetites. . . . Society cannot exist unless a controlling power upon will and appetite be placed somewhere, and the less of it there is within, the more there must be without. It is ordained in the eternal constitution of things, that men of intemperate minds cannot be free. Their passions forge their fetters. *Letter to a Member of the National Assembly* (1791), II, 555.

† I am not here going into the distinctions of rights, nor attempting to mark their boundaries. I do not enter into these metaphysical distinctions: I hate the very sound of them. *Speech on American Taxation* (1774), II, 110.

requires a deep knowledge of human nature and human necessities, and of the things which facilitate or obstruct the various ends which are to be pursued by the mechanism of civil institutions. The state is to have recruits to its strength, and remedies to its distempers. What is the use of discussing a man's abstract right to food or to medicine? The question is upon the method of procuring and administering them. In that deliberation I shall always advise to call in the aid of the farmer and the physician, rather than the professor of metaphysics. . . .

These metaphysic rights entering into common life, like rays of light which pierce into a dense medium, are, by the laws of nature, refracted from their straight line. Indeed in the gross and complicated mass of human passions and concerns, the primitive rights of men undergo such a variety of refractions and reflections, that it becomes absurd to talk of them as if they continued in the simplicity of their original direction. The nature of man is intricate; the objects of society are of the greatest possible complexity; and therefore no simple disposition or direction of power can be suitable either to man's nature, or to the quality of his affairs.* When I hear the simplicity of contrivance aimed at and boasted of in any new political constitutions, I am at no loss to decide that the artificers are grossly ignorant of their trade, or totally negligent of their duty. The simple governments are fundamentally defective, to say no worse of them. If you were to contemplate society in but one point of view, all these simple modes of polity are infinitely captivating. In effect each would answer its single end much more perfectly than the more complex is able to attain all its complex purposes. But it is better that the whole should be imperfectly and anomalously answered than that, while some parts are provided for with great exactness, others might be totally neglected, or perhaps materially injured, by the over-care of a favorite member. . . .

THE CONSECRATED STATE

To make a government requires no great prudence. Settle the seat of power; teach obedience: and the work is done. To give freedom is still more easy. It is not necessary to guide; it only requires to let go the rein. But to form a *free government;* that is, to temper

---

* [P]olitics ought to be adjusted, not to human reasonings, but to human nature of which the reason is but a part, and by no means the greatest part. *Observations on the Present State of the Nation* (1769), 49.

together these opposite elements of liberty and restraint in one consistent work, requires much thought, deep reflection, a sagacious,
powerful, and combining mind. . . .

The science of constructing a commonwealth, or renovating it,
or reforming it, is, like every other experimental science, not to be
taught *a priori*.* Nor is it a short experience that can instruct us in
that practical science; because the real effects of moral causes are not
always immediate; but that which in the first instance is prejudicial
may be excellent in its remoter operation; and its excellence may
arise even from the ill effects it produces in the beginning. The
reverse also happens; and very plausible schemes, with very pleasing
commencements, have often shameful and lamentable conclusions.
In states there are often some obscure and almost latent causes,
things which appear at first view of little moment, on which a very
great part of its prosperity or adversity may most essentially depend.
The science of government being therefore so practical in itself, and
intended for such practical purposes, a matter which requires experience, and even more experience than any person can gain in his
whole life, however sagacious and observing he may be, it is with
infinite caution that any man ought to venture upon pulling down
an edifice which has answered in any tolerable degree for ages the
common purposes of society, or on building it up again, without
having models and patterns of approved utility before his eyes. . . .

[O]ne of the first and most leading principles on which the commonwealth and the laws are consecrated is lest the temporary possessors and life-renters in it, unmindful of what they have received
from their ancestors, or of what is due to their posterity, should act
as if they were the entire masters; that they should not think it
amongst their rights to cut off the entail, or commit waste on the
inheritance, by destroying at their pleasure the whole original fabric
of their society; hazarding to leave to those who come after them,
a ruin instead of an habitation—and teaching these successors as
little to respect their contrivances, as they had themselves respected
the institutions of their forefathers. By this unprincipled facility of
changing the state as often, and as much, and in as many ways as

---

* I do not put abstract ideas wholly out of any question; because I well
know that under that name I should dismiss principles, and that without the guide
and light of sound, well-understood principles, all reasonings in politics, as in
everything else, would be only a confused jumble of particular facts and details,
without the means of drawing out any sort of theoretical or practical conclusion.
Speech on the Petition of the Unitarians (1792), VI, 113–14.

there are floating fancies or fashions, the whole chain and continuity of the commonwealth would be broken. No one generation could link with the other. Men would become little better than the flies of a summer.*

And first of all the science of jurisprudence, the pride of the human intellect, which, with all its defects, redundancies, and errors, is the collected reason of ages, combining the principles of original justice with the infinite variety of human concerns, as a heap of old exploded errors, would be no longer studied. Personal self-sufficiency and arrogance (the certain attendants upon all those who have never experienced a wisdom greater than their own) would usurp the tribunal. Of course, no certain laws, establishing invariable grounds of hope and fear, would keep the actions of men in a certain course, or direct them to a certain end. Nothing stable in the modes of holding property, or exercising function, could form a solid ground on which any parent could speculate in the education of his offspring, or in a choice for their future establishment in the world. No principles would be early worked into the habits. As soon as the most able instructor had completed his laborious course of institution, instead of sending forth his pupil, accomplished in a virtuous discipline, fitted to procure him attention and respect in his place in society, he would find every thing altered; and that he had turned out a poor creature to the contempt and derision of the world, ignorant of the true grounds of estimation. Who would insure a tender and delicate sense of honor to beat almost with the first pulses of the heart, when no man could know what would be the test of honor in a nation, continually varying the standard of its coin? No part of life would retain its acquisitions. Barbarism with regard to science and literature, unskilfulness with regard to arts and manufactures, would infallibly succeed to the want of a steady education and settled principle; and thus the commonwealth itself would, in a few generations, crumble away, be disconnected into the dust and powder of individuality, and at length dispersed to all the winds of heaven.

To avoid therefore the evils of inconstancy and versatility, ten thousand times worse than those of obstinacy and the blindest prejudice, we have consecrated the state, that no man should approach

---

* Individuals pass like shadows; but the commonwealth is fixed and stable. The difference, therefore, of today and tomorrow, which to private people is immense, to the state is nothing. *Speech on the Plan for Economical Reform* (1780), II, 101.

to look into its defects or corruptions but with due caution; that he should never dream of beginning its reformation by its subversion; that he should approach to the faults of the state as to the wounds of a father, with pious awe and trembling solicitude. By this wise prejudice we are taught to look with horror on those children of their country who are prompt rashly to hack that aged parent in pieces,[55] and put him into the kettle of magicians, in hopes that by their poisonous weeds, and wild incantations, they may regenerate the paternal constitution, and renovate their father's life.

Society is indeed a contract.[56] Subordinate contracts for objects of mere occasional interest may be dissolved at pleasure—but the state ought not to be considered as nothing better than a partnership agreement in a trade of pepper and coffee, calico or tobacco, or some other such low concern, to be taken up for a little temporary interest, and to be dissolved by the fancy of the parties. It is to be looked on with other reverence; because it is not a partnership in things subservient only to the gross animal existence of a temporary and perishable nature. It is a partnership in all science; a partnership in all art; a partnership in every virtue, and in all perfection. As the ends of such a partnership cannot be obtained in many generations, it becomes a partnership not only between those who are living, but between those who are living, those who are dead, and those who are to be born. Each contract of each particular state is but a clause in the great primaeval contract of eternal society, linking the lower with the higher natures, connecting the visible and invisible world, according to a fixed compact sanctioned by the inviolable oath which holds all physical and all moral natures, each in their appointed place. This law is not subject to the will of those, who by an obligation above them, and infinitely superior, are bound to submit their will to that law. The municipal corporations of that universal kingdom are not morally at liberty at their pleasure, and on their speculations of a contingent improvement, wholly to separate and tear asunder the bands of their subordinate community, and to dissolve it into an unsocial, uncivil, unconnected chaos of elementary principles. It is the first and supreme necessity only, a necessity that is not chosen but chooses, a necessity paramount to deliberation, that admits no discussion, and demands no evidence, which alone can justify a resort to anarchy.[57] This necessity is no exception to the rule; because this necessity itself is a part too of that moral and physical disposition of things to which man must be obedient by consent of force; but if that which is only submission to necessity should be made the object of choice, the law is broken, nature is disobeyed, and the rebellious are outlawed, cast forth, and exiled, from this world of reason, and order, and peace, and virtue, and fruitful penitence, into the antagonist world of madness, discord, vice, confusion, and unavailing sorrow. . . .

RESISTANCE AND REVOLUTION

The speculative line of demarcation, where obedience ought to end, and resistance must begin, is faint, obscure, and not easily definable. It is not a single act, or a single event, which determines it. Governments must be abused and deranged indeed, before it can be thought of; and the prospect of the future must be as bad as the experience of the past. When things are in that lamentable condition, the nature of the disease is to indicate the remedy to those whom nature has qualified to administer in extremities this critical, ambiguous, bitter potion to a distempered state. Times and occasions and provocations will teach their own lessons. The wise will determine from the gravity of the case; the irritable from sensibility to oppression; the high-minded from disdain and indignation at abusive power in unworthy hands; the brave and bold from the love of honorable danger in a generous cause: but, with or without right, a revolution will be the very last resource of the thinking and the good. . . . To make a revolution is a measure which, *prima fronte,* requires an apology. To make a revolution is to subvert the ancient state of our country; and no common reasons are called for to justify so violent a proceeding. The sense of mankind authorizes us to examine into the mode of acquiring new power, and to criticise on the use that is made of it with less awe and reverence than that which is usually conceded to a settled and recognized authority. . . .

> The subversion of a government, to deserve any praise, must be considered but as a step preparatory to the formation of something better, either in the scheme of the government itself, or in the persons who administer it, or in both. These events cannot in reason be separated. For instance, when we praise our Revolution of 1688, though the nation in that act was on the defensive, and was justified in incurring all the evils of a defensive war, we do not rest there. We always combine with the subversion of the old government the happy settlement[58] which followed. When we estimate that Revolution, we mean to comprehend in our calculation both the value of the thing parted with and the value of the thing received in exchange.
>
> The burden of proof lies heavily on those who tear to pieces the

whole frame and contexture of their country, that they could find no other way of settling a government fit to obtain its rational ends, except that which they have pursued by means unfavorable to all the present happiness of millions of people, and to the utter ruin of several hundreds of thousands. In their political arrangements, men have no right to put the well-being of the present generation wholly out of the question. Perhaps the only moral trust with any certainty in our hands is the care of our own time. With regard to futurity, we are to treat it like a ward. We are not so to attempt an improvement of his fortune as to put the capital of his estate to any hazard.

It is not worth our while to discuss, like sophisters, whether in no case some evil for the sake of some benefit is to be tolerated. Nothing universal can be rationally affirmed on any moral or any political subject. Pure metaphysical abstraction does not belong to these matters. The lines of morality are not like the ideal lines of mathematics. They are broad and deep as well as long. They admit of exceptions; they demand modifications. These exceptions and modifications are not made by the process of logic, but by the rules of prudence. Prudence is not only the first in rank of the virtues political and moral, but she is the director, the regulator, the standard of them all. Metaphysics cannot live without definition; but Prudence is cautious how she defines. Our courts cannot be more fearful in suffering fictitious cases to be brought before them for eliciting their determination on a point of law than prudent moralists are in putting extreme and hazardous cases of conscience upon emergencies not existing. Without attempting, therefore, to define what never can be defined, the case of a revolution in government, this, I think, may be safely affirmed: that a sore and pressing evil is to be removed, and that a good, great in its amount and unequivocal in its nature, must be probable almost to certainty, before the inestimable price of our own morals and the well-being of a number of our fellow-citizens is paid for a revolution. If ever we ought to be economists even to parsimony, it is in the voluntary production of evil. Every revolution contains in it something of evil.

[*An Appeal from the New to the Old Whigs* (1791), III, 15–16.]

I admit that evils may be so very great and urgent that other evils are to be submitted to for the mere hope of their removal. A war, for instance, may be necessary, and we know what are the rights of war, but before we use those rights, we ought to be clearly in the state which alone can justify them; and not, in the very fold of peace and security, by a bloody sophistry, to act towards any persons, at once as citizens and as enemies; and without the necessary formalities and evident distinctive lines of war, to exercise upon our countrymen the most dreadful of all hostilities. Strong party contentions, and a very violent opposition to our desires and opinions, are not war, nor can justify any one of its operations.

One form of government may be better than another; and this difference may be worth a struggle. I think so. I do not mean to treat any of those forms, which are often the contrivances of deep human wisdom (not the Rights of Men, as some people, in my opinion, not very wisely, talk of them) with slight or disrespect; nor do I mean to level them.

A positively vicious and abusive government ought to be changed, and if necessary, by violence, if it cannot be, (as sometimes it is the case) reformed: But when the question is concerning the more or the less *perfection* in the organization of a government, the allowance to *means* is not of so much latitude. There is, by the essential fundamental constitution of things a radical infirmity in all human contrivances, and the weakness is often so attached to the very perfection of our political mechanism, that some defect in it, something that stops short of its principle, something that controls, that mitigates, that moderates it, becomes a necessary corrective to the evils that the theoretic perfection would produce. I am pretty sure it often is so, and this truth may be exemplified abundantly.

It is true that every defect is not, of course, such a corrective as I state; but supposing it is not, an imperfect good is still a good; the defect may be tolerable, and may be removed at some future time. In that case, prudence (in all things a virtue, in politics the first of virtues) will lead us rather to acquiesce in some qualified plan that does not come up to the full perfection of the abstract idea, than to push for the more perfect, which cannot be attained without tearing to pieces the whole contexture of the commonwealth, and creating a heartache in a thousand worthy bosoms. In that case combining the means and end, the less perfect is the more desirable. The *means* to any end, being first in order, are *immediate* in their good or their evil; they are always, in a manner, *certainties*. The *end* is doubly problematical; first whether it is to be attained; then, whether supposing it obtained, we obtain the true object we sought for.*

But allow it in any degree probable, that theoretic and practical perfection may differ, that any object pure and absolute may not be so good as one lowered, mixed, and qualified, then, what we abate

---

* The world of contingency and political combination is much larger than we are apt to imagine. We never can say what may or may not happen, without a view to all the actual circumstances. Experience, upon other data than those, is of all things the most delusive. Prudence in new cases can do nothing on grounds of retrospect. A constant vigilance and attention to the train of things as they successively emerge, and to act on what they direct, are the only sure course. *Thoughts on French Affairs* (1791), III, 372.

in our demand in favor of moderation and justice and tenderness to individuals, would be neither more nor less than a real improvement which a wise legislator would make if he had no collateral motive whatsoever, and only looked in the formation of his scheme, to its own independent ends and purposes. Would it then be right to make way, through temerity and crime, to a form of things, which when obtained, evident reason, perhaps imperious necessity would compel us to alter, with the disgrace of inconsistency in our conduct, and of want of foresight in our designs?

Believe me, Sir, in all changes in the state, moderation is a virtue not only amiable but powerful. It is a disposing, arranging, conciliating, cementing virtue. In the formation of new constitutions it is in its province: great powers reside in those who can make great changes. Their own moderation is their only check; and if this virtue is not paramount in their minds, their acts will taste more of their power than of their wisdom or their benevolence. Whatever they do will be in extremes; it will be crude, harsh, precipitate. It will be submitted to with grudging and reluctance; revenge will be smothered and hoarded; and the duration of schemes made in that temper will be as precarious as their establishment was odious. This virtue of moderation (which times and situations will clearly distinguish from the counterfeits of pusillanimity and indecision) is the virtue only of superior minds. It requires a deep courage, and full of [ref]lection, to be temperate, when the voice of multitudes (the speci[ous] [m]imic of fame and reputation) passes judgment against you; [the] impetuous desires of an unthinking public will endure no course but what conducts to splendid and perilous extremes. Then to dare to be fearful, when all about you are full of presumption and confidence, and when those who are bold at the hazard of others, would punish your caution as disaffection, is to show a mind prepared for its trial; it discovers in the midst of general levity, a self possessing and collected character which sooner or later bids fair to attract every thing to it, as to a center. If however the tempest should prove to be so very violent that it would make public prudence itself unseasonable, and therefore little less than madness for the individual and the public too, perhaps a young man could not do better than to retreat for a while into study—to leave the field to those whose duty or inclination, or the necessities of their condition, have put them in possession of it;—and wait for the settlement of such a commonwealth as an honest man may act in with satisfaction and credit. This he can never do when those who counsel the public or the prince are under terror, let the authority under which they are made to speak other than the dictates of their conscience, be never so imposing in its name and attributes. [Letter to Charles-Jean-François Depont (November 1789), *Correspondence*, VI, 47–50. Spelling and punctuation modernized.]

CONSERVATION AND CORRECTION

A state without the means of some change is without the means of its conservation. Without such means it might even risk the loss of that part of the constitution which it wished the most religiously to preserve. . . . But in this, as in most questions of state, there is a middle. There is something else than the mere alternative of absolute destruction, or unreformed existence. This is, in my opinion, a rule of profound sense, and ought never to depart from the mind of an honest reformer. I cannot conceive how any man can have brought himself to that pitch of presumption, to consider his country as nothing but *carte blanche,* upon which he may scribble whatever he pleases. A man full of warm speculative benevolence may wish his society otherwise constituted than he finds it; but a good patriot, and a true politician, always considers how he shall make the most of the existing materials of his country. A disposition to preserve, and an ability to improve, taken together, would be my standard of a statesman. Every thing else is vulgar in the conception, perilous in the execution. . . .

This is my opinion with regard to the true interest of government. But as it is the interest of government that reformation should be early,* it is the interest of the people that it should be temperate. It is their interest because a temperate reform is permanent, and because it has a principle of growth. Whenever we improve, it is right to leave room for a further improvement. It is right to consider, to look about us, to examine the effect of what we have done. Then we can proceed with confidence, because we can proceed with intelligence. Whereas in hot reformations, in what men more zealous than considerate call *making clear work,* the whole is generally so crude, so harsh, so indigested, mixed with so much imprudence and

* Early reformations are amicable arrangements with a friend in power; late reformations are terms imposed upon a conquered enemy: early reformations are made in cool blood; late reformations are made under a state of inflammation. In that state of things the people behold in government nothing that is respectable. They see the abuse, and they will see nothing else. They fall into the temper of a furious populace provoked at the disorder of a house of ill-fame; they never attempt to correct or regulate; they go to work by the shortest way: they abate the nuisance, they pull down the house. *Speech on the Plan for Economical Reform* (1780), III, 64–65.

so much injustice, so contrary to the whole course of human nature and human institutions, that the very people who are most eager for it are among the first to grow disgusted at what they have done. Then some part of the abdicated grievance is recalled from its exile in order to become a corrective of the correction. Then the abuse assumes all the credit and popularity of a reform. The very idea of purity and disinterestedness in politics falls into disrepute, and is considered as a vision of hot and inexperienced men; and thus disorders become incurable, not by the virulence of their own quality, but by the unapt and violent nature of the remedies. A great part, therefore, of my idea of reform is meant to operate gradually: some benefits will come at a nearer, some at a more remote period. We must no more make haste to be rich by parsimony than by intemperate acquisition. . . .
[*Speech on the Plan for Economical Reform* (1780), II, 65.]

Old establishments are tried by their effects. If the people are happy, united, wealthy, and powerful, we presume the rest. We conclude that to be good from whence good is derived. In old establishments various correctives have been found for their aberrations from theory. Indeed they are the results of various necessities and expediencies. They are not often constructed after any theory; theories are rather drawn from them.* In them we often see the end best obtained, where the means seem not perfectly reconcilable to what we may fancy was the original scheme. The means taught by experience may be better suited to political ends than those contrived in the original project. They again react upon the primitive constitution, and sometimes improve the design itself from which they seem to have departed. I think all this might be curiously exemplified in the British constitution. At worst, the errors and deviations of every kind in reckoning are found and computed, and the ship proceeds in her course. This is the case of old establishments; but in a new and merely theoretic system, it is expected that every contrivance shall appear, on the face of it, to answer its end, especially where the projectors are no way embarrassed with an endeavor to accommodate the new building to an old one, either in the walls or on the foundations. . . .

* I do not vilify theory and speculation: no, because that would be to vilify reason itself. . . . No, whenever I speak against theory I mean always a weak, erroneous, fallacious, unfounded, or imperfect theory; and one of the ways of discovering that it is a false theory is by comparing it with practice. This is the true touchstone of all theories which regard man and the affairs of men: Does it suit his nature in general? Does it suit his nature as modified by his habits? *Speech on Reform of Representation of the Commons in Parliament* (1782), VI, 148.

The errors and defects of old establishments are visible and palpable. It calls for little ability to point them out; and where absolute power is given, it requires but a word wholly to abolish the vice and the establishment together. The same lazy but restless disposition, which loves sloth and hates quiet, directs these politicians, when they come to work, for supplying the place of what they have destroyed. To make every thing the reverse of what they have seen is quite as easy as to destroy. No difficulties occur in what has never been tried. Criticism is almost baffled in discovering the defects of what has not existed; and eager enthusiasm and cheating hope have all the wide field of imagination in which they may expatiate with little or no opposition.

At once to preserve and to reform is quite another thing. When the useful parts of an old establishment are kept, and what is superadded is to be fitted to what is retained, a vigorous mind, steady persevering attention, various powers of comparison and combination, and the resources of an understanding fruitful in expedients are to be exercised; they are to be exercised in a continued conflict with the combined force of opposite vices—with the obstinacy that rejects all improvement, and the levity that is fatigued and disgusted with every thing of which it is in possession. But you may object—"A process of this kind is slow. It is not fit for an assembly, which glories in performing in a few months the work of ages. Such a mode of reforming, possibly might take up many years." Without question it might and it ought. It is one of the excellencies of a method in which time is among the assistants, that its operation is slow and in some cases almost imperceptible. If circumspection and caution are a part of wisdom, when we work only upon inanimate matter, surely they become a part of duty too, when the subject of our demolition and construction is not brick and timber, but sentient beings, by the sudden alteration of whose state, condition, and habits, multitudes may be rendered miserable.*

But it seems as if it were the prevalent opinion in Paris that an unfeeling heart and an undoubting confidence are the sole qualifications for a perfect legislator. Far different are my ideas of that

---

* An ignorant man, who is not fool enough to meddle with his clock, is however sufficiently confident to think he can safely take to pieces, and put together at his pleasure, a moral machine of another guise, importance, and complexity, composed of far other wheels and springs and balances, and counteracting and cooperating powers. Men little think how immorally they act in meddling with what they do not understand. E. J. Payne, *Burke: Select Works* (Oxford, Eng.: Clarendon Press, 1888–1892), II, 331n.

high office. The true law-giver ought to have an heart full of sensibility. He ought to love and respect his kind and to fear himself. It may be allowed to his temperament to catch his ultimate object with an intuitive glance; but his movements towards it ought to be deliberate. Political arrangement, as it is a work for social ends, is to be only wrought by social means. There mind must conspire with mind. Time is required to produce that union of minds which alone can produce all the good we aim at. Our patience will achieve more than our force. If I might venture to appeal to what is so much out of fashion in Paris, I mean to experience, I should tell you that in my course I have known and, according to my measure, have cooperated with great men; and I have never yet seen any plan which has not been mended by the observations of those who were much inferior in understanding to the person who took the lead in the business. By a slow but well-sustained progress, the effect of each step is watched; the good or ill success of the first gives light to us in the second; and so, from light to light, we are conducted with safety through the whole series. We see that the parts of the system do not clash. The evils latent in the most promising contrivances are provided for as they arise. One advantage is as little as possible sacrificed to another. We compensate, we reconcile, we balance. We are enabled to unite into a consistent whole the various anomalies and contending principles that are found in the minds and affairs of men. From hence arises, not an excellence in simplicity, but one far superior, an excellence in composition. Where the great interests of mankind are concerned through a long succession of generations, that succession ought to be admitted into some share in the councils which are so deeply to affect them. If justice requires this, the work itself requires the aid of more minds than one age can furnish. It is from this view of things that the best legislators have been often satisfied with the establishment of some sure, solid, and ruling principle in government; a power like that which some of the philosophers have called a plastic nature; and having fixed the principle, they have left it afterwards to its own operation. . . .

This policy appears to me to be the result of profound reflection; or rather the happy effect of following nature, which is wisdom without reflection, and above it. A spirit of innovation* is generally

* I wished to warn the people against the greatest of all evils—a blind and furious spirit of innovation, under the name of reform. *Letter to William Elliot* (1795), V, 77. It cannot at this time be too often repeated, line upon line, precept upon precept, until it comes into the currency of a proverb—*To innovate is not to reform. Letter to a Noble Lord* (1796), V, 120.

the result of a selfish temper and confined views. People will not look forward to posterity, who never look backward to their ancestors. Besides, the people of England well know that the idea of inheritance furnishes a sure principle of conservation, and a sure principle of transmission without at all excluding a principle of improvement. It leaves acquisition free; but it secures what it acquires. Whatever advantages are obtained by a state proceeding on these maxims are locked fast as in a sort of family settlement, grasped as in a kind of mortmain[59] for ever. By a constitutional policy, working after the pattern of nature, we receive, we hold, we transmit our government and our privileges in the same manner in which we enjoy and transmit our property and our lives. The institutions of policy, the goods of fortune, the gifts of Providence are handed down, to us and from us, in the same course and order. Our political system is placed in a just correspondence and symmetry with the order of the world and with the mode of existence decreed to a permanent body composed of transitory parts wherein, by the disposition of a stupendous wisdom, molding together the great mysterious incorporation of the human race, the whole, at one time, is never old or middle-aged, or young, but in a condition of unchangeable constancy, moves on through the varied tenor of perpetual decay, fall, renovation, and progression. Thus, by preserving the method of nature in the conduct of the state, in what we improve we are never wholly new; in what we retain we are never wholly obsolete. By adhering in this manner and on those principles to our forefathers, we are guided not by the superstition of antiquarians, but by the spirit of philosophic analogy.* In this choice of inheritance we have given to our frame of polity the image of a relation in blood; binding up the constitution of our country with our dearest domestic ties; adopting our fundamental laws into the bosom of our family affections; keeping inseparable, and cherishing with the warmth of all their combined and mutually reflected charities, our state, our hearths, our sepulchres, and our altars.

Through the same plan of a conformity to nature in our artificial institutions, and by calling in the aid of her unerring and powerful instincts, to fortify the fallible and feeble contrivances of our reason, we have derived several other, and those no small benefits, from considering our liberties in the light of an inheritance. Always

---

* *Cf.* These analogies between bodies natural and politic, though they may sometimes illustrate arguments, furnish no argument of themselves. *Letter to William Elliot* (1795), V, 78.

acting as if in the presence of canonized forefathers, the spirit of freedom, leading in itself to misrule and excess, is tempered with an awful gravity. This idea of a liberal descent inspires us with a sense of habitual native dignity, which presents that upstart insolence almost inevitably adhering to and disgracing those who are the first acquirers of any distinction. By this means our liberty becomes a noble freedom. It carries an imposing and majestic aspect. It has a pedigree and illustious ancestors. It has its bearings and its ensigns armorial. It has its gallery of portraits; its monumental inscriptions; its records, evidences, and titles. We procure reverence to our civil institutions on the principle upon which nature teaches us to revere individual men—on account of their age and on account of those from whom they are descended. All your sophisters cannot produce any thing better adapted to preserve a rational and manly freedom than the course that we have pursued, who have chosen our nature rather than our speculations, our breasts rather than our inventions, for the great conservatories and magazines of our rights and privileges.

You might, if you pleased, have profited of our example, and have given to your recovered freedom a correspondent dignity. Your privileges, though discontinued, were not lost to memory. Your constitution, it is true, while you were out of possession, suffered waste and dilapidation; but you possessed in some parts the walls, and in all the foundations of a noble and venerable castle. You might have repaired those walls; you might have built on those old foundations. Your constitution was suspended before it was perfected; but you had the elements of a constitution very nearly as good as could be wished. In your old states you possessed that variety of parts corresponding with the various descriptions of which your community was happily composed; you had all that combination, and all that opposition of interests, you had that action and counteraction which, in the natural and in the political world, from the reciprocal struggle of discordant powers, draws out the harmony of the universe. These opposed and conflicting interests, which you considered as so great a blemish in your old and in our present constitution, interpose a salutary check to all precipitate resolutions. They render deliberation a matter not of choice, but of necessity; they make all change a subject of *compromise,* which naturally begets moderation; they produce *temperaments,* preventing the sore evil of harsh, crude, unqualified reformations; and rendering all the headlong exertions of arbitrary power, in the few or in the many, for ever impracticable. Through that diversity of members and interests, general liberty had as many securities as there were separate views in the several orders; while by pressing down the whole by the weight of a real monarchy, the separate parts would have been prevented from warping and starting from their allotted places.

You had all these advantages in your ancient states; but you chose to act as if you had never been molded into civil society, and had every thing to begin anew. You began ill, because you began by despising every thing that belonged to you. You set up your trade without a capital. If the last generations of your country appeared without much lustre in your eyes, you might have passed them by, and derived your claims from a more early race of ancestors. Under a pious predilection for those ancestors, your imaginations would have realized in them a standard of virtue and wisdom, beyond the vulgar practice of the hour: and you would have risen with the example to whose imitation you aspired. Respecting your forefathers, you would have been taught to respect yourselves. You would not have chosen to consider the French as a people of yesterday, as a nation of low-born servile wretches until the emancipating year of 1789. In order to furnish at the expense of your honor, an excuse to your apologists here for several enormities of yours, you would not have been content to be represented as a gang of Maroon slaves,[60] suddenly broke loose from the house of bondage, and therefore to be pardoned for your abuse of the liberty to which you were not accustomed and ill fitted. Would it not, my worthy friend, have been wiser to have you thought, what I, for one, always thought you, a generous and gallant nation, long misled to your disadvantage by your high and romantic sentiments of fidelity, honor, and loyalty; that events had been unfavorable to you, but that you were not enslaved through any illiberal or servile disposition; that in your most devoted submission, you were actuated by a principle of public spirit, and that it was your country you worshipped in the person of your king? Had you made it to be understood that in the delusion of this amiable error you had gone further than your wise ancestors; that you were resolved to resume your ancient privileges, while you preserved the spirit of your ancient and your recent loyalty and honor; or, if diffident of yourselves, and not clearly discerning the almost obliterated constitution of your ancestors, you had looked to your neighbors in this land, who had kept alive the ancient principles and models of the old common law of Europe meliorated and adapted to its present state—by following wise examples you would have given new examples of wisdom to the world. You would have rendered the cause of liberty venerable in the eyes of every worthy mind in every nation. You would have shamed despotism from the earth, by showing that freedom was not only reconcilable, but as, when well disciplined it is, auxiliary to law. You would have had an unoppressive but a productive revenue. You would have had a flourishing commerce to feed it. You would have had a free constitution; a potent monarchy; a disciplined army; a reformed and venerated clergy; a mitigated but spirited nobility, to lead your virtue, not to overlay it; you would have had a liberal order of commons, to emulate and to recruit that nobility; you would have had a protected, satisfied, laborious, and obedient people, taught to seek and to recognize the happiness that is to be found by virtue in all conditions; in which consists the true moral equality of mankind, and not in that monstrous fiction, which, by inspiring false ideas and vain expectations into men destined to travel in the obscure walk of laborious life, serves only to aggravate and embitter that real inequality, which it never can remove; and which the order of civil life establishes as much for the benefit of those whom it must leave in a humble state, as those whom it is able to exalt to a condition more splendid, but not more happy. You had a smooth and easy career of felicity and glory laid open to you, beyond any thing recorded in the history of the world; but you have shown that difficulty is good for man.

Compute your gains:* see what is got by those extravagant and presumptuous speculations which have taught your leaders to despise all their predecessors, and all their contemporaries, and even to despise themselves, until the moment in which they became truly despicable. By following those false lights, France has bought undignified calamities at a higher price than any nation has purchased the most unequivocal blessings! France has bought poverty by crime! France has not sacrificed her virtue to her interest; but she has abandoned her interest, that she might prostitute her virtue. All other nations have begun the fabric of a new government, or the reformation of an old, by establishing originally, or by enforcing with greater exactness some rites or other of religion. All other people have laid the foundations of civil freedom in severer manners, and a system of a more austere and masculine morality. France, when she let loose the reins of regal authority, doubled the license of a ferocious dissoluteness in manners, and of an insolent irreligion in opinions and practices; and has extended through all ranks of life, as if she were

---

* . . . so much actual crime against so much contingent advantage. Burke, *Reflections*, p. 92.

communicating some privilege, or laying open some secluded benefit, all the unhappy corruptions that usually were the disease of wealth and power. This is one of the new principles of equality in France.

France, by the perfidy of her leaders, has utterly disgraced the tone of lenient council in the cabinets of princes, and disarmed it of its most potent topics. She has sanctified the dark suspicious maxims of tyrannous distrust; and taught kings to tremble at (what will here-after be called) the delusive plausibilities of moral politicians. Sovereigns will consider those who advise them to place an unlimited confidence in their people, as subverters of their thrones; as traitors who aim at their destruction, by leading their easy good-nature, under specious pretenses, to admit combinations of bold and faithless men into a participation of their power. This alone (if there were nothing else) is an irreparable calamity to you and to mankind. Remember that your parliament of Paris told your king, that in calling the states together, he had nothing to fear but the prodigal excess of their zeal in providing for the support of the throne. It is right that these men should hide their heads. It is right that they should bear their part in the ruin which their counsel has brought on their sovereign and their country. Such sanguine declarations tend to lull authority asleep; to encourage it rashly to engage in perilous adventures of untried policy; to neglect those provisions, preparations, and precautions, which distinguish benevolence from imbecillity; and without which no man can answer for the salutary effect of any abstract plan of government or of freedom. For want of these, they have seen the medicine of the state corrupted into its poison. They have seen the French rebel against a mild and lawful monarch with more fury, outrage, and insult than ever any people has been known to rise against the most illegal usurper, or the most sanguinary tyrant. Their resistance was made to concession; their revolt was from protection; their blow was aimed at an hand holding out graces, favors, and immunities.

This was unnatural. The rest is in order. They have found their punishment in their success. Laws overturned; tribunals subverted; industry without vigor; commerce expiring; the revenue unpaid, yet the people impoverished; a church pillaged, and a state not relieved; civil and military anarchy made the constitution of the kingdom; every thing human and divine sacrificed to the idol of public credit, and national bankruptcy the consequence; and to crown all, the paper securities of new, precarious, tottering power, the discredited paper securities of impoverished fraud, and beggared rapine, held out as a currency for the support of an empire, in lieu of the two great recognized species [gold and silver] that represent the lasting conventional credit of mankind, which disappeared and hid themselves in the earth from whence they came, when the principle of property, whose creatures and representatives they are, was systematically subverted.

Were all these dreadful things necessary? Were they the inevitable results of the desperate struggle of determined patriots, compelled to wade through blood and tumult, to the quiet shore of a tranquil and prosperous liberty? No! nothing like it. The fresh ruins of France, which shock our feelings wherever we can turn our eyes, are not the devastation of civil war; they are the sad but instructive monuments of rash and ignorant counsel in time of profound peace. They are the display of inconsiderate and presumptuous, because unresisted and irresistible, authority. The persons who have thus squandered away the precious treasure of their crimes, the persons who have made this prodigal and wild waste of public evils (the last stake reserved for the ultimate ransom of the state) have met in their progress with little, or rather with no opposition at all. Their whole march was more like a triumphal procession than the progress of a war. Their pioneers have gone before them, and demolished and laid every thing level at their feet. Not one drop of *their* blood have they shed in the cause of the country they have ruined. They have made no sacrifices to their projects of greater consequence than their shoe-buckles, while they were imprisoning their king, murdering their fellow citizens, and bathing in tears, and plunging in poverty and distress, thousands of worthy men and worthy families. Their cruelty has not even been the base result of fear. It has been the effect of their sense of perfect safety in authorizing treasons, robberies, rapes, assassinations, slaughters, and burnings throughout their harassed land. But the cause of all was plain from the beginning. . . .

But am I so unreasonable as to see nothing at all that deserves commendation in the indefatigable labors of this assembly? I do not deny that among an infinite number of acts of violence and folly, some good may have been done. They who destroy every thing certainly will remove some grievance. They who make every thing new have a chance that they may establish something beneficial. To give them credit for what they have done in virtue of the authority they have usurped, or which can excuse them in the crimes by which that authority has been acquired, it must appear, that the same things could not have been accomplished without producing such a revolution. Most assuredly they might; because almost every one of the regulations made by them, which is not very equivocal, was either in the cession of the king, voluntarily made at the meeting of the States, or in the concurrent instructions to the orders. Some usages have been abolished on just grounds; but they were such that if they had stood as they were to all eternity, they would little detract from the happiness and prosperity of any state. The improvements of the National Assembly are superficial, their errors fundamental.

Whatever they are, I wish my countrymen rather to recommend to our neighbors the example of the British constitution, than to take models from them for the improvement of our own. In the former they have got an invaluable treasure. They are not, I think, without some causes of apprehension and complaint; but these they do not owe to their constitution, but to their own conduct. I think our happy situation owing to our constitution; but owing to the whole of it, and not to any part singly; owing in a great measure to what we have left standing in our several reviews and reformations, as well as to what we have altered or super-added. Our people will find employment enough for a truly patriotic, free, and independent spirit in guarding what they possess from violation. I would not exclude alteration either; but even when I changed, it should be to preserve. I should be led to my remedy by a great grievance. In what I did, I should follow the example of our ancestors. I would make the reparation as nearly as possible in the style of the building. A politic caution, a guarded circumspection, a moral rather than a complexional timidity were among the ruling principles of our fore-fathers in their most decided conduct. Not being illuminated with the light of which the gentlemen of France tell us they have got so abundant a share, they acted under a strong impression of the ignorance and fallibility of mankind. He that had made them thus fallible, rewarded them for having in their conduct attended to their nature. Let us imitate their caution, if we wish to deserve their fortune, or to retain their bequests. Let us add, if we please, but let us preserve what they have left; and, standing on the firm ground of the British constitution, let us be satisfied to admire rather than attempt to follow in their desperate flights the aëronauts of France.[60]

I have told you candidly my sentiments. I think they are not likely to alter yours. I do not know that they ought. You are young; you cannot guide, but must follow the fortune of your country. But hereafter they may be of some use to you, in some future form which your commonwealth may take. In the present it can hardly remain;

but before its final settlement it may be obliged to pass, as one of our poets says, "through great varieties of untried being," [61] and in all its transmigrations to be purified by fire and blood.

I have little to recommend my opinions, but long observation and much impartiality. They come from one who has been no tool of power, no flatterer of greatness; and who in his last acts does not wish to belie the tenor of his life. They come from one, almost the whole of whose public exertion has been a struggle for the liberty of others; from one in whose breast no·anger durable or vehement has ever been kindled, but by what he considered as tyranny; and who snatches from his share in the endeavors which are used by good men to discredit opulent oppression, the hours he has employed on your affairs; and who in so doing persuades himself he has not departed from his usual office: they come from one who desires honors, distinctions, and emoluments but little; and who expects them not at all; who has no contempt for fame, and no fear of obloquy; who shuns contention, though he will hazard an opinion: from one who wishes to preserve consistency; but who would preserve consistency by varying his means to secure the unity of his end; and, when the equipoise of the vessel in which he sails, may be endangered by overloading it upon one side, is desirous of carrying the small weight of his reasons to that which may preserve its equipoise.

FINIS.

PART II

THOMAS PAINE ON THE RIGHTS OF MAN

The Rights of Man, abridged, arranged, and annotated with excerpts from Thomas Paine's other writings.

The Rights
of Man

AUTHOR'S PREFACE (PARTS I, II)

From the part Mr. Burke took in the American Revolution, it was natural that I should consider him a friend to mankind; and as our acquaintance commenced on that ground, it would have been more agreeable to me to have had cause to continue in that opinion, than to change it.

At the time Mr. Burke made his violent speech last winter in the English Parliament against the French Revolution and the National Assembly, I was in Paris, and had written to him but a short time before, to inform him how prosperously matters were going on. Soon after this, I saw his advertisement of the pamphlet he intended to publish.

As the attack was to be made in a language but little studied, and less understood, in France, and as everything suffers by translation, I promised some of the friends of the Revolution in that country, that whenever Mr. Burke's pamphlet came forth, I would answer it.

This appeared to me the more necessary to be done, when I saw the flagrant misrepresentations which Mr. Burke's pamphlet contains; and that while it is an outrageous abuse on the French Revolution and the principles of Liberty, it is an imposition on the rest of the world.

I am the more astonished and disappointed at this conduct of Mr. Burke, as (from the circumstance I am going to mention), I had formed other expectations.

I had seen enough of the miseries of war to wish it might never more have existence in the world, and that some other mode might be found out to settle the differences that should occasionally arise in the neighborhood of nations. This certainly might be done if courts were disposed to set honestly about it, or if countries were enlightened enough not to be made the dupes of courts.

The people of America had been bred up in the same prejudices against France, which at that time characterized the people of England; but experience and an acquaintance with the French nation have most effectually shown to the Americans the falsehood of those prejudices; and I do not believe that a more cordial and confidential intercourse exists between any two countries than between America and France. . . .

When the French Revolution broke out, it certainly afforded to Mr. Burke an opportunity of doing some good, had he been disposed to it; instead of which, no sooner did he see the old prejudices wearing away, than he immediately began sowing the seeds of a new inveteracy, as if he were afraid that England and France would cease to be enemies. . . . In his last work, his *Appeal from the New to the Old Whigs,* he has quoted about ten pages from the *Rights of Man,* and having given himself the trouble of doing this, says he "shall not attempt in the smallest degree to refute them," meaning the principles therein contained. I am enough acquainted with Mr. Burke to know that he would if he could. But instead of contesting them, he immediately after consoles himself with saying that he "has done his part." He has not done his part. He has not performed his promise of a comparison of constitutions. He started the controversy, he gave the challenge, and has fled from it; and he is now a *case in point* with his own opinion that *"the age of chivalry is gone!"* The title, as well as the substance of his last work, his *Appeal,* is his condemnation. Principles must stand on their own merits, and if they are good they certainly will. To put them under the shelter of other men's authority, as Mr. Burke has done, serves to bring them into suspicion. Mr. Burke is not very fond of dividing his honors, but in this case he is artfully dividing the disgrace.

But who are those to whom Mr. Burke has made his appeal? A

set of childish thinkers and half-way politicians born in the last century; men who went no farther with any principle than as it suited their purpose as a party; the nation was always left out of the question; and this has been the character of every party from that day to this. The nation sees nothing in such works, or such politics, worthy its attention. A little matter will move a party, but it must be something great that moves a nation.

Though I see nothing in Mr. Burke's *Appeal* worth taking much notice of, there is, however, one expression upon which I shall offer a few remarks. After quoting largely from the *Rights of Man*, and declining to contest the principles contained in that work, he says, "This will most probably be done (*if such writings shall be thought to deserve any other refutation than that of criminal justice*) [1] by others, who may think with Mr. Burke and with the same zeal." . . . Pardoning the pun, it must be *criminal* justice indeed that should condemn a work as a substitute for not being able to refute it. The greatest condemnation that could be passed upon it would be a refutation. But in proceeding by the method Mr. Burke alludes to, the condemnation would, in the final event, pass upon the criminality of the process and not upon the work, and in this case, I had rather be the author than be either the judge or the jury that should condemn it.

But to come at once to the point. I have differed from some professional gentlemen on the subject of prosecutions, and I since find they are falling into my opinion, which I will here state as fully, but as concisely as I can.

I will first put a case with respect to any law, and then compare it with a government, or with what in England is, or has been, called a constitution.

It would be an act of despotism, or what in England is called arbitrary power, to make a law to prohibit investigating the principles, good or bad, on which such a law, or any other is founded.

If a law be bad, it is one thing to oppose the practice of it, but it is quite a different thing to expose its errors, to reason on its defects, and to show cause why it should be repealed, or why another ought to be substituted in its place. I have always held it an opinion (making it also my practice) that it is better to obey a bad law, making use at the same time of every argument to show its errors and procure its repeal, than forcibly to violate it; because the precedent of breaking a bad law might weaken the force, and lead to a discretionary violation of those which are good.

The case is the same with respect to principles and forms of government, or to what are called constitutions, and the parts of which they are composed.

It is for the good of nations, and not for the emolument or aggrandizement of particular individuals, that government ought to be established, and that mankind are at the expense of supporting it. The defects of every government and constitution, both as to principle and form must, on a parity of reasoning, be as open to discussion as the defects of a law, and it is a duty which every man owes to society to point them out. When those defects, and the means of remedying them are generally seen by a nation, that nation will reform its government or its constitution in the one case, as the government repealed or reformed the law in the other.

The operation of government is restricted to the making and the administering of laws; but it is to a nation that the right of forming or reforming, generating or regenerating constitutions and governments belong; and consequently those subjects, as subjects of investigation, are always before a country *as a matter of right,* and cannot, without invading the general rights of that country, be made subjects for prosecution. On this ground I will meet Mr. Burke whenever he pleases. It is better that the whole argument should come out, than to seek to stifle it. It was himself that opened the controversy, and he ought not to desert it.

I do not believe that monarchy and aristocracy will continue seven years longer in any of the enlightened countries in Europe. If better reasons can be shown for them than against them, they will stand; if the contrary, they will not. Mankind are not now to be told they shall not think, or they shall not read; and publications that go no farther than to investigate principles of government, to invite men to reason and to reflect, and to show the errors and excellencies of different systems, have a right to appear. If they do not excite attention, they are not worth the trouble of a prosecution; and if they do, the prosecution will amount to nothing, since it cannot amount to a prohibition of reading. This would be a sentence of the public, instead of the author, and would also be the most effectual mode of making or hastening revolutions.

On all cases that apply universally to a nation, with respect to systems of government, a jury of *twelve* men is not competent to decide. Where there are no witnesses to be examined, no facts to be proved, and where the whole matter is before the whole public and the merits or demerits of it resting on their opinion; and where there is nothing to be known in a court, but what every body knows out of it, every twelve men are equally as good a jury as the other, and would most probably reverse each other's verdict; or from the variety of their opinions not be able to form one.

It is one case, whether a nation approve a work, or a plan; but it is quite another case, whether it will commit to any such jury the power of determining whether the nation have a right to, or shall reform its government, or not. I mention these cases, that Mr. Burke may see I have not written on government without reflecting on what is law, as well as on what are rights. The only effectual jury in such cases would be a convention of the whole nation fairly elected; for in all such cases the whole nation is the vicinage. If Mr. Burke will propose such a jury, I will waive all privileges of being the citizen of any other country, and, defending its principles, abide the issue, provided he will do the same; for my opinion is that his work and his principles would be condemned instead of mine. . . .

On all such subjects men have only to think, and they will neither act wrong nor be misled. To say that any people are not fit for freedom is to make poverty their choice, and to say they had rather be loaded with taxes than not. If such a case could be proved, it would equally prove that those who govern are not fit to govern them, for they are a part of the same national mass.

But admitting governments to be changed all over Europe, it certainly may be done without convulsion and revenge. It is not worth making changes or revolutions, unless it be for some great national benefit; and when this shall appear to a nation, the danger will be, as in America and France, to those who oppose; and with this reflection I close my Preface.

THOMAS PAINE.

The Rights
of Man

GOVERNMENT IS FOR THE LIVING

Among the incivilities by which nations or individuals provoke
and irritate each other, Mr. Burke's pamphlet on the French Revolution is an extraordinary instance. Neither the people of France, nor
the National Assembly, were troubling themselves about the affairs
of England, or the English Parliament; and that Mr. Burke should
commence an unprovoked attack upon them, both in Parliament
and in public, is a conduct that cannot be pardoned on the score of
manners, nor justified on that of policy. There is scarcely an epithet
of abuse to be found in the English language, with which Mr. Burke
has not loaded the French nation and the National Assembly. Every
thing which rancor, prejudice, ignorance, or knowledge could suggest, are poured forth in the copious fury of near four hundred
pages. In the strain and on the plan Mr. Burke was writing, he might
have written on to as many thousands. When the tongue or the pen
is let loose in a frenzy of passion, it is the man and not the subject
that becomes exhausted.

Hitherto Mr. Burke has been mistaken and disappointed in the
opinions he had formed of the affairs of France; but such is the ingenuity of his hope, or the malignancy of his despair, that it furnishes

him with new pretenses to go on. There was a time when it was impossible to make Mr. Burke believe there would be any revolution
in France. His opinion then was that the French had neither spirit
to undertake it, nor fortitude to support it; and now that there is
one, he seeks an escape by condemning it.

Not sufficiently content with abusing the National Assembly, a
great part of his work is taken up with abusing Dr. Price (one of the
best-hearted men that lives), and the two societies in England known
by the name of the Revolution Society, and the Society for Constitutional Information.

Dr. Price had preached a sermon on the 4th of November, 1789,
being the anniversary of what is called in England the Revolution,
which took place in 1688. Mr. Burke, speaking of this sermon, says,
"The political divine proceeds dogmatically to assert that, by the
principles of the Revolution, the people of England have acquired
three fundamental rights:

"1. To choose our own governors.
"2. To cashier them for misconduct.
"3. To frame a government for ourselves."

Dr. Price does not say that the right to do these things exists in
this or in that person, or in this or in that description of persons, but
that it exists in the *whole;* that it is a right resident in the nation.
Mr. Burke, on the contrary, denies that such a right exists in the
nation, either in whole or in part, or that it exists any where; and,
what is still more strange and marvelous, he says, "that the people of
England utterly disclaim such a right, and that they will resist the
practical assertion of it with their lives and fortunes."

That men should take up arms, and spend their lives and fortunes, *not* to maintain their rights, but to maintain they have *not*
rights, is an entirely new species of discovery, and suited to the paradoxical genius of Mr. Burke.

The method which Mr. Burke takes to prove that the people of
England had no such rights, and that such rights do not now exist in
the nation, either in whole or in part, or any where at all, is of the
same marvelous and monstrous kind with what he has already said;
for his arguments are, that the persons, or the generation of persons,
in whom they did exist, are dead, and with them the right is dead
also.

To prove this, he quotes a declaration made by Parliament
about a hundred years ago, to William and Mary, in these words:
"The Lords Spiritual and Temporal, and Commons, do, in the name
of the people aforesaid," (meaning the people of England then liv-

ing) "most humbly and faithfully *submit* themselves, their *heirs* and *posterities,* for EVER." [2] He also quotes a clause of another act of Parliament made in the same reign, the terms of which, he says, "bind us," (meaning the people of that day) "our *heirs* and our *posterity,* to *them,* their *heirs* and *posterity,* to the end of time." [3]

Mr. Burke conceives his point sufficiently established by producing these clauses, which he enforces by saying that they exclude the right of the nation for *ever*. And not yet content with making such declarations, repeated over and over again, he further says, "that if the people of England possessed such a right before the Revolution," (which he acknowledges to have been the case, not only in England but throughout Europe, at an early period,) "yet that the *English nation* did, at the time of the Revolution, most solemnly renounce and abdicate it, for themselves, and for *all their posterity, for ever.*"

As Mr. Burke occasionally applies the poison drawn from his horrid principles, not only to the English nation, but to the French Revolution and the National Assembly, and charges that august, illuminated and illuminating body of men with the epithet of *usurpers,* I shall, *sans cérémonie,* place another system of principles in opposition to his.

The English Parliament of 1688 did a certain thing, which, for themselves and their constituents, they had a right to do, and which it appeared right should be done: But, in addition to this right, which they possessed by delegation, *they set up another right by assumption,* that of binding and controlling posterity to the end of time.

The case, therefore, divides itself into two parts; the right which they possessed by delegation, and the right which they set up by assumption. The first is admitted; but with respect to the second, I reply:—

There never did, there never will, and there never can exist a parliament, or any description of men, or any generation of men, in any country, possessed of the right or the power of binding and controlling posterity to the *"end of time,"* or of commanding forever how the world shall be governed, or who shall govern it; and therefore, all such clauses, acts or declarations, by which the makers of them attempt to do what they have neither the right nor the power to do, nor the power to execute, are in themselves null and void.

Every age and generation must be as free to act for itself, *in all cases,* as the ages and generations which preceded it. The vanity and presumption of governing beyond the grave is the most ridiculous and insolent of all tyrannies.

Man has no property in man; neither has any generation a property in the generations which are to follow. The Parliament or the people of 1688, or of any other period, had no more right to dispose of the people of the present day, or to bind or to control them *in any shape whatever,* than the Parliament or the people of the present day have to dispose of, bind, or control those who are to live a hundred or a thousand years hence.

Every generation is, and must be, competent to all the purposes which its occasions require. It is the living, and not the dead, that are to be accommodated. When man ceases to be, his power and his wants cease with him; and having no longer any participation in the concerns of this world, he has no longer any authority in directing who shall be its governors, or how its government shall be organized, or how administered.

I am not contending for nor against any form of government, nor for nor against any party here or elsewhere. That which a whole nation chooses to do, it has a right to do. Mr. Burke says, No. Where then *does* the right exist? I am contending for the rights of the *living,* and against their being willed away, and controlled and contracted for, by the manuscript assumed authority of the dead; and Mr. Burke is contending for the authority of the dead over the rights and freedom of the living.

There was a time when kings disposed of their crowns by will upon their death-beds, and consigned the people, like beasts of the field, to whatever successor they appointed. This is now so exploded as scarcely to be remembered, and so monstrous as hardly to be believed. But the parliamentary clauses upon which Mr. Burke builds his political church are of the same nature.

The laws of every country must be analogous to some common principle. In England, no parent or master, nor all the authority of Parliament, omnipotent as it has called itself, can bind or control the personal freedom even of an individual beyond the age of twenty-one years. On what ground of right, then, could the Parliament of 1688, or any other parliament, bind all posterity for ever?

Those who have quitted the world, and those who are not yet arrived in it, are as remote from each other as the utmost stretch of moral imagination can conceive. What possible obligation, then, can exist between them; what rule or principle can be laid down, that two nonentities, the one out of existence, and the other not in, and who never can meet in this world, that the one should control the other to the end of time?

In England, it is said that money cannot be taken out of the pockets of the people without their consent. But who authorized, or who could authorize the Parliament of 1688 to control and take away the freedom of posterity, and limit and confine their right of acting in certain cases for ever, who were not in existence to give or to withhold their consent?

A greater absurdity cannot present itself to the understanding of man, than what Mr. Burke offers to his readers. He tells them, and he tells the world to come, that a certain body of men, who existed a hundred years ago, made a law; and that there does not now exist in the nation, nor ever will, nor ever can, a power to alter it. Under how many subtilties, or absurdities, has the divine right to govern been imposed on the credulity of mankind!

Mr. Burke has discovered a new one, and he has shortened his journey to Rome, by appealing to the power of this infallible Parliament of former days; and he produces what it has done, as of divine authority; for that power must certainly be more than human, which no human power to the end of time can alter.

But Mr. Burke has done some service, not to his cause, but to his country, by bringing those clauses into public view. They serve to demonstrate how necessary it is at all times to watch against the attempted encroachment of power, and to prevent its running to excess.

It is somewhat extraordinary that the offense for which James II was expelled, that of setting up power by *assumption,* should be reenacted, under another shape and form, by the Parliament that expelled him. It shows that the rights of man were but imperfectly understood at the Revolution; for certain it is that the right which that Parliament set up by *assumption* (for by the delegation it had it not, and could not have it, because none could give it) over the persons and freedom of posterity for ever, was the same tyrannical, unfounded kind which James attempted to set up over the Parliament and the nation, and for which he was expelled.

The only difference is (for in principle they differ not), that the one was an usurper over the living, and the other over the unborn; and as the one has no better authority to stand upon than the other, both of them must be equally null and void, and of no effect.

From what, or from whence, does Mr. Burke prove the right of any human power to bind posterity for ever? He has produced his clauses; but he must produce also his proofs that such a right existed, and show how it existed. If it ever existed, it must now exist; for whatever appertains to the nature of man cannot be annihilated by man.

It is the nature of man to die, and he will continue to die as long as he continues to be born. But Mr. Burke has set up a sort of political Adam, in whom all posterity are bound forever; he must therefore prove that his Adam possessed such a power, or such a right.

The weaker any cord is, the less it will bear to be stretched and the worse is the policy to stretch it, unless it is intended to break it. Had a person contemplated the overthrow of Mr. Burke's positions, he would have proceeded as Mr. Burke has done. He would have magnified the authorities, on purpose to have called the *right* of them into question; and the instant the question of right was started, the authorities must have been given up.

It requires but a very small glance of thought to perceive, that although laws made in one generation often continue in force through succeeding generations, yet they continue to derive their force from the consent of the living. A law not repealed continues in force, not because it *cannot* be repealed, but because it is *not* repealed; and the non-repealing passes for consent.

But Mr. Burke's clauses have not even this qualification in their favor. They become null by attempting to become immortal. The nature of them precludes consent. They destroy the right which they *might* have by grounding it on a right which they *cannot* have. Immortal power is not a human right, and therefore cannot be a right of Parliament.

The Parliament of 1688 might as well have passed an act to have authorized themselves to live for ever as to make their authority to live for ever. All therefore that can be said of them is that they are a formality of words, of as much import as if those who used them had addressed a congratulation to themselves, and in the oriental style of antiquity, had said, O Parliament, live for ever!

The circumstances of the world are continually changing, and the opinions of men change also; and as government is for the living, and not for the dead, it is the living only that has any right in it. That which may be thought right and found convenient in one age, may be thought wrong and found inconvenient in another. In such cases, who is to decide, the living, or the dead? . . .

Mr. Burke is laboring in vain to stop the progress of knowledge; and it comes with the worse grace from him, as there is a certain transaction known in the City, which renders him suspected of being a pensioner in a fictitious name.[4] This may account for some strange doctrine he has advanced in his book, which, though he points it at the Revolution Society, is effectually directed against the whole nation.

"The King of England," says he, "holds *his* crown (for it does not belong to the nation, according to Mr. Burke) in *contempt* of the choice of the Revolution Society, who have not a single vote for a king among them either *individually* or *collectively;* and His Majesty's heirs, each in their time and order, will come to the crown *with the same contempt* of their choice, with which His Majesty has succeeded to that which he now wears."

As to who is king of England or elsewhere or whether there is any at all, or whether the people choose a Cherokee chief, or a Hessian hussar for a king, is not a matter that I trouble myself about,—be that to themselves; but with respect to the doctrine, so far as it relates to the rights of men and nations, it is as abominable as any thing ever uttered in the most enslaved country under heaven.

Whether it sounds worse to my ear, by not being accustomed to hear such despotism, than it does to the ear of another person, I am not so well a judge of; but of its abominable principle, I am at no loss to judge.

It is not the Revolution Society that Mr. Burke means; it is the nation, as well in its *original* as in its *representative* character; and he has taken care to make himself understood by saying that they have not a vote either *collectively* or *individually.*

The Revolution Society is composed of citizens of all denominations, and of members of both Houses of Parliament; and consequently, if there is not a right to vote in any of the characters, there can be no right to any, either in the nation or in its Parliament. . . .

It has hitherto been the practice of the English Parliaments, to regulate what was called the succession, (taking it for granted, that the nation then continued to accord to the form of annexing a monarchical branch to its government; for without this, the Parliament could not have had the authority to have sent either to Holland or to Hanover,[5] or to impose a king upon a nation against its will). And this must be the utmost limit to which Parliament can go upon the case; but the right of the nation goes to the *whole* case, because it has the right of changing its *whole* form of government.

The right of a parliament is only a right in trust, a right by delegation, and that but of a very small part of the nation; and one of its Houses has not even this. But the right of the nation is an original right, as universal as taxation. The nation is the paymaster of every thing, and every thing must conform to its general will. . . .

When the person who at any time shall be in possession of a government, or those who stand in succession to him, shall say to a nation, I hold this power in "contempt" of you, it signifies not on what authority he pretends to say it. It is no relief, but an aggravation to a person in slavery, to reflect that he was sold by his parent; and as that which heightens the criminality of an act cannot be produced to prove the legality of it, hereditary succession cannot be established as a legal thing.

In order to arrive to a more perfect decision on this head, it will be proper to consider the generation which undertakes to establish a family with *hereditary powers,* apart and separate from the generations which are to follow; and also to consider the character in which the *first* generation acts with respect to succeeding generations.

The generation which first selects a person, and puts him at the head of its government, either with the title of king, or any other distinction, acts its *own choice,* be it wise or foolish, as a free agent for itself. The person so set up is not hereditary, but selected and appointed; and the generation who sets him up, does not live under an hereditary government, but under a government of its own choice and establishment. Were the generation who sets him up, and the person so set up, to live for ever, it never could become hereditary succession; and of consequence, hereditary succession can only follow on the death of the first parties.

As therefore hereditary succession is out of the question with respect to the *first* generation, we have now to consider the character in which *that* generation acts with respect to the commencing generation, and to all succeeding ones.

It assumes a character, to which it has neither right nor title. It changes itself from a *legislator* to a *testator,* and affects to make its will, which is to have operation after the demise of the makers, to bequeath the government; and it not only attempts to bequeath, but to establish on the succeeding generation, a new and different form of government under which itself lived.

Itself, as is already observed, lived not under an hereditary government, but under a government of its own choice and establishment; and it now attempts, by virtue of a will and testament, (which it has not authority to make), to take from the commencing generation, and all future ones, the rights and free agency by which itself acted.

But, exclusive of the right which any generation has to act collectively as a testator, the objects to which it applies itself in this case, are not within the compass of any law, or of any will or testament.

The rights of men in society are neither devisable, nor transferable, nor annihilable, but are descendible only; and it is not in the power of any generation to intercept finally and cut off the descent. If the present generation, or any other, are disposed to be slaves, it does not lessen the right of the succeeding generation to be free: wrongs cannot have a legal descent. When Mr. Burke attempts to maintain that the *English nation did at the Revolution of 1688, most solemnly renounce and abdicate their rights for themselves, and for all their posterity for ever,* he speaks a language that merits not reply, and which can only excite contempt for his prostitute principles, or pity for his ignorance.

In whatever light hereditary succession, as growing out of the will and testament of some former generation, presents itself, it is an absurdity. A cannot make a will to take from B the property of B, and give it to C; yet this is the manner in which (what is called) hereditary succession by law operates.

A certain former generation made a will to take away the rights of the commencing generation, and all future ones, and to convey those rights to a third person, who afterwards comes forward, and tells them, in Mr. Burke's language, that they have *no rights,* that their rights are already bequeathed to him, and that he will govern in *contempt* of them. From such principles, and such ignorance, Good Lord deliver the world! . . .

As almost one hundred pages of Mr. Burke's book are employed upon these clauses, it will consequently follow that if the clauses themselves, so far as they set up an *assumed, usurped* dominion over posterity for ever, are unauthoritative, and in their nature null and void; that all his voluminous inferences, and declamation drawn therefrom, or founded thereon, are null and void also: and on this ground I rest the matter.

THE NATURAL AND
THE CIVIL RIGHTS OF MAN

I have now to follow Mr. Burke through a pathless wilderness of rhapsodies, and a sort of descant upon governments, in which he asserts whatever he pleases, on the presumption of its being believed, without offering either evidence or reasons for so doing.

Before anything can be reasoned upon to a conclusion, certain facts, principles, or data, to reason from, must be established, admitted, or denied. Mr. Burke, with his usual outrage, abuses the *Declaration of the Rights of Man,* published by the National Assembly of France, as the basis on which the Constitution of France is built. This he calls "paltry and blurred sheets of paper about the rights of man."

Does Mr. Burke mean to deny that *man* has any rights? If he does, then he must mean that there are no such things as rights any where, and that he has none himself; for who is there in the world but man? But if Mr. Burke means to admit that man has rights, the question then will be, what are those rights, and how came man by them originally?

The error of those who reason by precedents drawn from antiquity, respecting the rights of man, is that they do not go far enough into antiquity. They do not go the whole way. They stop in some of the intermediate stages of a hundred or a thousand years, and produce what was then done as a rule for the present day. This is no authority at all.

If we travel still further into antiquity, we shall find a directly contrary opinion and practice prevailing; and, if antiquity is to be authority, a thousand such authorities may be produced, successively contradicting each other; but if we proceed on, we shall at last come out right; we shall come to the time when man came from the hand of his Maker. What was he then? Man. Man was his high and only title, and a higher cannot be given him. But of titles I shall speak hereafter.

We have now arrived at the origin of man, and at the origin of his rights. As to the manner in which the world has been governed from that day to this, it is no further any concern of ours than to make a proper use of the errors or the improvements which the history of it presents. Those who lived a hundred or a thousand years ago were then moderns as we are now. They had *their* ancients, and those ancients had others, and we also shall be ancients in our turn.

If the mere name of antiquity is to govern in the affairs of life, the people who are to live a hundred or a thousand years hence, may as well take us for a precedent, as we make a precedent of those who lived a hundred or a thousand years ago.

The fact is that portions of antiquity, by proving every thing, establish nothing. It is authority against authority all the way, till we come to the divine origin of the rights of man, at the Creation. Here our inquiries find a resting-place, and our reason finds a home.

If a dispute about the rights of man had arisen at a distance of a hundred years from the Creation, it is to this source of authority they must have referred, and it is to the same source of authority that we must now refer.

Though I mean not to touch upon any sectarian principle of religion, yet it may be worth observing, that the genealogy of Christ is traced to Adam. Why then not trace the rights of man to the creation of man? I will answer the question. Because there have been upstart governments, thrusting themselves between, and presumptuously working to *unmake* man.

If any generation of men ever possessed the right of dictating the mode by which the world should be governed for ever, it was the first generation that existed; and if that generation did it not, no succeeding generation can show any authority for doing it, nor can set any up.

The illuminating and divine principle of the equal rights of man (for it has its origin from the Maker of man), relates not only to the living individuals, but to generations of men succeeding each other. Every generation is equal in rights to the generations which preceded it, by the same rule that every individual is born equal in rights with his contemporary.

Every history of the Creation, and every traditionary account, whether from the lettered or unlettered world, however they may vary in their opinion or belief of certain particulars, all agree in establishing one point, *the unity of man;* by which I mean that men are all of *one degree,* and consequently that all men are born equal, and with equal natural rights, in the same manner as if posterity had been continued by *creation* instead of *generation,* the latter being only the mode by which the former is carried forward; and consequently, every child born into the world must be considered as deriving its existence from God. The world is as new to him as it was to the first man that existed, and his natural right in it is of the same kind.

The Mosaic account of the Creation, whether taken as divine authority or merely historical, is full to this point *the unity or equality of man.* The expressions admit of no controversy. "And God said, let us make man in our own image. In the image of God created he him; male and female created he them." The distinction of sexes is pointed out, but no other distinction is even implied. If this be not divine authority, it is at least historical authority, and shows that the equality of man, so far from being a modern doctrine, is the oldest upon record.

It is also to be observed that all the religions known in the world are founded, so far as they relate to man, on the *unity of man,* as being all of one degree. Whether in heaven or in hell, or in whatever state man may be supposed to exist hereafter, the good and the bad are the only distinctions. Nay, even the laws of governments are obliged to slide into this principle, by making degrees to consist in crimes and not in persons.

It is one of the greatest of all truths, and of the highest advantage to cultivate. By considering man in this light, and by instructing him to consider himself in this light, it places him in a close connection with all his duties, whether to his Creator or to the creation, of which he is a part; and it is only when he forgets his origin, or, to use a more fashionable phrase, his *birth and family,* that he becomes dissolute.

It is not among the least of the evils of the present existing governments in all parts of Europe that man, considered as man, is thrown back to a vast distance from his Maker, and the artificial chasm filled up by a succession of barriers, or a sort of turnpike gates, through which he has to pass.

I will quote Mr. Burke's catalogue of barriers that he has set up between man and his Maker. Putting himself in the character of a herald, he says—"We fear God—we look with *awe* to kings— with affection to parliaments—with duty to magistrates—with reverence to priests, and with respect to nobility." Mr. Burke has forgotten to put in *"chivalry."* He has also forgotten to put in Peter.

The duty of man is not a wilderness of turnpike gates, through which he is to pass by tickets from one to the other. It is plain and simple, and consists but of two points. His duty to God, which every man must feel; and with respect to his neighbor, to do as he would be done by. If those to whom power is delegated do well, they will be respected; if not, they will be despised; and with regard to those to whom no power is delegated, but who assume it, the rational world can know nothing of them.

Hitherto we have spoken only (and that but in part) of the natural rights of man. We have now to consider the civil rights of man, and to show how the one originates from the other. Man did not enter into society to become *worse* than he was before, nor to have fewer rights than he had before, but to have those rights better secured. His natural rights are the foundation of all his civil rights. But in order to pursue this distinction with more precision, it is necessary to make the different qualities of natural and civil rights.

A few words will explain this. Natural rights are those which appertain to man in right of his existence. Of this kind are all the intellectual rights, or rights of the mind, and also all those rights of acting as an individual for his own comfort and happiness, which are not injurious to the natural rights of others. Civil rights are those which appertain to man in right of his being a member of society.

Every civil right has for its foundation some natural right pre-existing in the individual, but to the enjoyment of which his individual power is not, in all cases, sufficiently competent. Of this kind are all those which relate to security and protection.

From this short review, it will be easy to distinguish between that class of natural rights which man retains after entering into society, and those which he throws into the common stock as a member of society.

The natural rights which he retains are all those in which the *power* to execute is as perfect in the individual as the right itself. Among this class, as is before mentioned, are all the intellectual rights, or rights of the mind: consequently, religion is one of those rights.

The natural rights which are not retained are all those in which, though the right is perfect in the individual, the power to execute them is defective. They answer not his purpose. A man, by natural right, has a right to judge in his own cause; and so far as the right of the mind is concerned, he never surrenders it: but what avails it him to judge, if he has not power to redress? He therefore deposits his right in the common stock of society, and takes the arm of society, of which he is a part, in preference and in addition to his own. Society *grants* him nothing. Every man is proprietor in society, and draws on the capital as a matter of right.

From these premises, two or three certain conclusions will follow.

First, That every civil right grows out of a natural right; or, in other words, is a natural right exchanged.

Secondly, That civil power, properly considered as such, is made up of the aggregate of that class of the natural rights of man, which becomes defective in the individual in point of power, and answers not his purpose, but when collected to a focus, becomes competent to the purpose of every one.

Thirdly, That the power produced from the aggregate of natural rights, imperfect in power in the individual, cannot be applied to invade the natural rights which are retained in the individual, and in which the power to execute is as perfect as the right itself.

We have now, in a few words, traced man from a natural individual to a member of society, and shown, or endeavored to show, the quality of the natural rights retained, and those which are exchanged for civil rights. Let us now apply those principles to governments.

In casting our eyes over the world, it is extremely easy to distinguish the governments which have arisen out of society, or out the social compact, from those which have not: but to place this in a clearer light than what a single glance may afford, it will be proper to take a review of the several sources from which the governments have arisen, and on which they have been founded.

They may be all comprehended under three heads. First, superstition. Secondly, power. Thirdly, the common interests of society, and the common rights of man.

The first was a government of priestcraft, the second of conquerors, and the third of reason.

When a set of artful men pretended, through the medium of oracles, to hold intercourse with the Deity, as familiarly as they now march up the back-stairs in European courts, the world was completely under the government of superstition. The oracles were consulted, and whatever they were made to say, became the law; and this sort of government lasted as long as this sort of superstition lasted.

After these a race of conquerors arose, whose government, like that of William the Conqueror, was founded in power, and the sword assumed the name of a sceptre. Governments thus established, last as long as the power to support them lasts; but that they might avail themselves of every engine in their favor, they united fraud to force, and set up an idol which they called *Divine Right,* and which, in imitation of the Pope, who affects to be spiritual and temporal, and in contradiction to the Founder of the Christian religion, twisted itself afterwards into an idol of another shape, called *Church and State.* The key of St. Peter and the key of the Treasury became quartered on one another, and the wondering, cheated multitude worshipped the invention.

When I contemplate the natural dignity of man; when I feel (for Nature has not been kind enough to me to blunt my feelings) for the honor and happiness of its character, I become irritated at the attempt to govern mankind by force and fraud, as if they were all knaves and fools, and can scarcely avoid disgust at those who are thus imposed upon.

We have now to review the governments which arise out of

society, in contradistinction to those which arose out of superstition and conquest.

It has been thought a considerable advance toward establishing the principles of freedom, to say, that government is a compact between those who govern and those who are governed: but this cannot be true, because it is putting the effect before the cause; for as a man must have existed before governments existed, there necessarily was a time when governments did not exist, and consequently there could originally exist no governments to form such a compact with.

The fact therefore must be that the *individuals themselves,* each in his own personal and sovereign right, *entered into a compact with each other* to produce a government: and this is the only mode in which governments have a right to arise, and the only principle on which they have a right to exist.

To possess ourselves of a clear idea of what government is, or ought to be, we must trace it to its origin. In doing this, we shall easily discover that governments must have arisen, either *out* of the people, or *over* the people. Mr. Burke has made no distinction. He investigates nothing to its source, and therefore he confounds every thing. . . .

MAN AND HIS GOVERNMENT

Notwithstanding the nonsense, for it deserves no better name, that Mr. Burke has asserted about hereditary rights, and hereditary succession, and that a nation has not a right to form a government for itself; it happened to fall in his way to give some account of what Government is. *"Government,"* says he, *"is a contrivance of human wisdom."*

Admitting that Government is a contrivance of human *wisdom,** it must necessarily follow that hereditary succession and hereditary rights (as they are called), can make no part of it, because it is impossible to make wisdom hereditary; and on the other hand, *that* cannot be a wise contrivance, which in its operation may com-

---

* Government should always be considered as a matter of convenience, not of right. *The Forester's Letters* (1776) in *The Complete Writings of Thomas Paine,* ed. Philip S. Foner (New York: The Citadel Press, 1945), II, 78. All of the quotations by Paine which follow are taken from this work.

mit the government of a nation to the wisdom of an idiot. The ground which Mr. Burke now takes is fatal to every part of his cause.

The argument changes from hereditary rights to hereditary wisdom; and the question is, Who is the wisest man? He must now show that every one in the line of hereditary succession was a Solomon, or his title is not good to be a king. What a stroke has Mr. Burke now made! To use a sailor's phrase, he has *swabbed the deck,* and scarcely left a name legible in the list of kings; and he has mowed down and thinned the House of Peers, with a scythe as formidable as Death and Time. But Mr. Burke appears to have been aware of this retort, and he has taken care to guard against it, by making government to be not only a *contrivance* of human wisdom, but a *monopoly* of wisdom. He puts the nation as fools on one side, and places his government of wisdom, all wise men of Gotham,[6] on the other side; and he then proclaims, and says, that *"men have a* RIGHT *that their* WANTS *should be provided for by this wisdom."*

Having thus made proclamation, he next proceeds to explain to them what their *wants* are, and also what their *rights* are.

In this he has succeeded dexterously, for he makes their wants to be a *want* of wisdom; but as this is but cold comfort, he then informs them that they have a *right* (not to any of the wisdom) but to be governed by it; and in order to impress them with a solemn reverence for this monopoly-government of wisdom, and of its vast capacity for all purposes, possible or impossible, right or wrong, he proceeds with astrological, mysterious importance, to tell them its powers in these words—

"The Rights of Man in government are their advantages; and these are often in balances between differences of good; and in compromises sometimes between *good* and *evil,* and sometimes between *evil* and *evil.* Political reason is a *computing principle;* adding, subtracting, multiplying, and dividing, morally and not metaphysically, or mathematically, true moral demonstrations." [6a]

As the wondering audience whom Mr. Burke supposes himself talking to may not understand all this learned jargon, I will undertake to be its interpreter. The meaning then, good people, of all this is *that government is governed by no principle whatever; that it can make evil good, or good evil, just as it pleases. In short, that government is arbitrary power. . . .* Almost everything appertaining to the circumstances of a nation has been absorbed and confounded under the general and mysterious word *government*.* Though it avoids taking to its account the errors it commits, and the mischiefs it occasions, it fails not to arrogate to itself whatever has the appearance of prosperity. It robs industry of its honors by pedantically making itself the cause of its effects and purloins from the general character of man the merits that appertain to him as a social being.

It may therefore be of use, in this day of revolutions, to discriminate between those things which are the effect of government, and those which are not. This will best be done by taking a review of society and civilization, and the consequences resulting therefrom, as things distinct from what are called governments. By beginning with this investigation, we shall be able to assign effects to their proper cause, and analyze the mass of common errors.

Great part of that order which reigns among mankind is not the effect of government. It had its origin in the principles of society and the natural constitution of man.[7] It existed prior to government, and would exist if the formality of government was abolished. The mutual dependence and reciprocal interest which man has upon man, and all parts of a civilized community upon each other, create that great chain of connection which holds it together. The landholder, the farmer, the manufacturer, the merchant, the tradesman, and every occupation prospers by the aid which each receives from the other, and from the whole. Common interest regulates their concerns and forms their laws; and the laws which common usage ordains have a greater influence than the laws of government. In fine, society performs for itself almost every thing which is ascribed to government.†

---

* Notwithstanding the mystery with which the science of government has been developed, for the purpose of enslaving, plundering and imposing upon mankind, it is of all things the least mysterious and the most easy to be understood. The meanest capacity cannot be at a loss, if it begins its inquiries at the right point. Every art and science has some point, or alphabet, at which the study of that art or science begins, and by the assistance of which the progress is facilitated. The same method ought to be observed with respect to the science of government. *Dissertation on First Principles of Government* (1795) II, 571.

† Society is produced by our wants and government by our wickedness; the former promotes our happiness *positively* by uniting our affections, the latter *negatively* by restraining our vices. The one encourages intercourse, the other creates distinctions. The first is a patron, the last a punisher. Society in every state is a blessing, but government, even in its best state, is but a necessary evil; in its worst state an intolerable one. . . . Government, like dress, is the badge

To understand the nature and quantity of government proper for man, it is necessary to attend to his character. As Nature created him for social life, she fitted him for the station she intended. In all cases she made his natural wants greater than his individual powers. No one man is capable, without the aid of society, of supplying his own wants; and those wants acting upon every individual impel the whole of them into society, as naturally as gravitation acts to a center.

But she has gone further. She has not only forced man into society, by a diversity of wants, which the reciprocal aid of each other can supply, but she has implanted in him a system of social affections,[8] which, though not necessary to his existence, are essential to his happiness. There is no period in life when this love for society ceases to act. It begins and ends with our being.

If we examine, with attention, into the composition and constitution of man, the diversity of his wants, and the diversity of talents in different men for reciprocally accommodating the wants of each other, his propensity to society, and consequently to preserve the advantages resulting from it, we shall easily discover that a great part of what is called government is mere imposition.

Government is no farther necessary than to supply the few cases to which society and civilization are not conveniently competent; and instances are not wanting to show, that every thing which government can usefully add thereto, has been performed by the common consent of society, without government. . . . *

There is a natural aptness in man, and more so in society, because it embraces a greater variety of abilities and resources, to accommodate itself to whatever situation it is in. The instant formal government is abolished, society begins to act. A general association takes place, and common interest produces common security.

So far is it from being true, as has been pretended, that the abolition of any formal government is the dissolution of society,

---

of lost innocence; the palaces of kings are built upon the ruins of the bowers of paradise. *Common Sense* (1776), I, 4–5. [Paine's emphasis]

* When I inquire of a person how much government does he require, the answer I get is that he requires very little. But let me ask the same person what amount of government he judges to be required by others, and he replies: "Oh, a very large amount, indeed!" If I continue my inquiries, I receive pretty much the same answers, and so I infer that the amount actually needed lies between these two extremes: the lesser amount each considers required for himself and the larger amount he regards as needful for his neighbor. *Answer to Four Questions on the Legislative and Executive Powers* (1792), II, 529.

that it acts by a contrary impulse, and brings the latter the closer together. All that part of its organization which it had committed to its government devolves again upon itself and acts through its medium.

When men, as well from natural instinct as from reciprocal benefits, have habituated themselves to social and civilized life, there is always enough of its principles in practice to carry them through any changes they may find necessary or convenient to make in their government. In short, man is so naturally a creature of society that it is almost impossible to put him out of it.

Formal government makes but a small part of civilized life; and when even the best that human wisdom can devise is established, it is a thing more in name and idea, than in fact. It is to the great and fundamental principles of society and civilization—to the common usage universally consented to, and mutually and reciprocally maintained—to the unceasing circulation of interest, which, passing through its million channels, invigorates the whole mass of civilized man—it is to these things, infinitely more than to any thing which even the best instituted government can perform, that the safety and prosperity of the individual and of the whole depends.

The more perfect civilization is, the less occasion has it for government, because the more does it regulate its own affairs and govern itself; but so contrary is the practice of old governments to the reason of the case, that the expenses of them increase in the proportion they ought to diminish. It is but few general laws that civilized life requires, and those of such common usefulness, that whether they are enforced by the forms of government or not, the effect will be nearly the same. If we consider what the principles are that first condense men into society, and what the motives that regulate their mutual intercourse afterwards, we shall find, by the time we arrive at what is called government, that nearly the whole of the business is performed by the natural operation of the parts upon each other.

Man, with respect to all those matters, is more a creature of consistency than he is aware, or that governments would wish him to believe. All the great laws of society are laws of nature. Those of trade and commerce, whether with respect to the intercourse of individuals, or of nations, are laws of mutual and reciprocal interest. They are followed and obeyed because it is the interest of the parties so to do, and not on account of any formal laws their governments may impose or interpose.

But how often is the natural propensity to society disturbed or destroyed by the operations of government. When the latter, instead of being engrafted on the principles of the former, assumes to exist for itself, and acts by partialities of favor and oppression, it becomes the cause of the mischiefs it ought to prevent. . . .

But as fact is superior to reasoning, the instance of America presents itself to confirm these observations. If there is a country in the world, where concord, according to common calculation, would be least expected, it is America. Made up, as it is, of people from different nations,* accustomed to different forms and habits of government, speaking different languages, and more different in their modes of worship, it would appear that the union of such a people was impracticable; but by the simple operation of constructing government on the principles of society and the rights of man, every difficulty retires, and all the parts are brought into cordial unison. There the poor are not oppressed, the rich are not privileged. Industry is not mortified by the splendid extravagance of a court rioting at its expense. Their taxes are few, because their government is just; and as there is nothing to render them wretched, there is nothing to engender riots and tumults.

A metaphysical man, like Mr. Burke,[9] would have tortured his invention to discover how such a people could be governed. He would have supposed that some must be managed by fraud, others by force, and all by some contrivance; that genius must be hired to impose upon ignorance, and show and parade to fascinate the vulgar. Lost in the abundance of his research, he would have resolved and re-resolved, and finally overlooked the plain and easy road that lay directly before him.

One of the great advantages of the American Revolution has been that it led to a discovery of the principles, and laid open the imposition, of governments. All the revolutions till then had been

---

* That part of America which is generally called New England, including New Hampshire, Massachusetts, Rhode Island, and Connecticut, is peopled chiefly by English descendants. In the State of New York, about half are Dutch, the rest English, Scotch and Irish. In New Jersey, a mixture of English and Dutch, with some Scotch and Irish. In Pennsylvania, about one-third are English, another Germans, and the remainder Scotch and Irish, with some Swedes. The states to the Southward have a greater proportion of English than the Middle States, but in all of them there is a mixture; and besides those enumerated, there are a considerable number of French, and some few of all the European nations, lying on the coast. The most numerous religious denomination is the Presbyterian; but no one sect is established above another, and all men are equally citizens. [Paine]

worked within the atmosphere of a court, and never on the great floor of a nation. The parties were always of the class of courtiers; and whatever was their rage for reformation, they carefully preserved that fraud of the profession.

In all cases they took care to represent government as a thing made up of mysteries, which only themselves understood, and they hid from the understanding of the nation, the only thing that was beneficial to know, namely, *That government is nothing more than a national association acting on the principles of society.*

Having thus endeavored to show that the social and civilized state of man is capable of performing within itself almost every thing necessary to its protection and government, it will be proper, on the other hand, to take a review of the present old governments, and examine whether their principles and practice are correspondent thereto.

GOVERNMENT BY HEREDITARY SUCCESSION

Reason and Ignorance, the opposites of each other, influence the great bulk of mankind. If either of these can be rendered sufficiently extensive in a country, the machinery of government goes easily on. Reason obeys itself; and Ignorance submits to whatever is dictated to it.

The two modes of government which prevail in the world, are, *First,* government by election and representation: *Secondly,* government by hereditary succession. The former is generally known by the name of republic; the latter by that of monarchy and aristocracy.

Those two distinct and opposite forms erect themselves on the two distinct and opposite bases of Reason and Ignorance. As the exercise of government requires talents and abilities, and as talents and abilities cannot have hereditary descent, it is evident that hereditary succession requires a belief from man to which his reason cannot subscribe, and which can only be established upon his ignorance; and the more ignorant any country is, the better it is fitted for this species of government.

On the contrary, government in a well constituted republic requires no belief from man beyond what his reason can give. He sees the *rationale* of the whole system, its origin and its operation; and as it is best supported when best understood, the human faculties act with boldness and acquire under this form of government, a gigantic manliness. . . . Government on the old system is an assumption of power for the aggrandizement of itself; on the new, a delegation of power, for the common benefit of society. The former supports itself by keeping up a system of war; the latter promotes a system of peace, as the true means of enriching a nation. The one encourages national prejudices; the other promotes universal society, as the means of universal commerce. The one measures its prosperity, by the quantity of revenue it extorts; the other proves its excellence, by the small quantity of taxes it requires. . . .

Though it might be proved that the system of government now called the NEW is the most ancient in principle of all that have existed, being founded on the original inherent Rights of Man: yet, as tyranny and the sword have suspended the exercise of those rights for many centuries past, it serves better the purpose of distinction to call it a *new,* than to claim the right of calling it the old.

The first general distinction between those two systems is that the one now called the old is *hereditary,* either in whole or in part; and the new is entirely *representative.* It rejects all hereditary government:

First, as being an imposition on mankind.

Secondly, as being inadequate to the purposes for which government is necessary.

With respect to the first of these heads. It cannot be proved by what right hereditary government could begin: neither does there exist within the compass of mortal power a right to establish it. Man has no authority over posterity in matters of personal right; and therefore, no man or body of men had or can have a right to set up hereditary government. Were even ourselves to come again into existence, instead of being succeeded by posterity, we have not now the right of taking from ourselves the rights which would then be ours. On what ground, then, do we pretend to take them from others?

All hereditary government is in its nature tyranny. An heritable crown, or an heritable throne, or by what other fanciful name such things may be called, have no other significant explanation than that mankind are heritable property. To inherit a government is to inherit the people, as if they were flocks and herds.

With respect to the second head, that of being inadequate to the purposes for which government is necessary, we have only to consider what government essentially is, and compare it with the circumstances to which hereditary succession is subject. Government ought to be a thing always in maturity. It ought to be so constructed as to be superior to all the accidents to which individual man is subject; and therefore, hereditary succession, by being *subject to them all,* is the most irregular and imperfect of all the systems of government.

We have heard the Rights of Man called a *levelling* system; but the only system to which the word *levelling* is truly applicable is the hereditary monarchical systems. It is a system of *mental levelling.* It indiscriminately admits every species of character to the same authority. Vice and virtue, ignorance and wisdom, in short, every quality, good or bad, is put on the same level. Kings succeed each other, not as rationals, but as animals. It signifies not what their mental or moral characters are.

Can we then be surprised at the abject state of the human mind in monarchical countries, when the government itself is formed on such an abject levelling system? It has no fixed character. To-day it is one thing; to-morrow it is something else. It changes with the temper of every succeeding individual, and is subject to all the varieties of each. It is government through the medium of passions and accidents.

It appears under all the various characters of childhood, decrepitude, dotage, a thing at nurse, in leading-strings, or on crutches. It reverses the wholesome order of nature. It occasionally puts children over men, and the conceits of nonage over wisdom and experience. In short, we cannot conceive a more ridiculous figure of government than hereditary succession, in all its cases, presents.

Could it be made a decree in nature, or an edict registered in heaven, and man could know it, that virtue and wisdom should invariably appertain to hereditary succession, the objections to it would be removed; but when we see that nature acts as if she disowned and sported with the hereditary system; that the mental characters of successors, in all countries, are below the average of human understanding; that one is a tyrant, another an idiot, a third insane,[10] and some all three together, it is impossible to attach confidence to it, when reason in man has power to act. . . .

Passing over, for the present, all the evils and mischiefs which monarchy has occasioned in the world, nothing can more effectually prove its uselessness in a state of *civil government* than making it hereditary. Would we make any office hereditary that required wisdom and abilities to fill it? And where wisdom and abilities are not necessary, such an office, whatever it may be, is superfluous or insignificant.

Hereditary succession is a burlesque upon monarchy. It puts

it in the most ridiculous light by presenting it as an office which any child or idiot may fill. It requires some talents to be a common mechanic; but to be a king requires only the animal figure of a man —a sort of breathing automaton. This sort of superstition may last a few years more, but it cannot long resist the awakened reason and interest of man. . . . After all, what is this metaphor, called a crown, or rather what is monarchy? Is it a thing, or is it a name, or is it a fraud? Is it a "contrivance of human wisdom," or human craft, to obtain money from a nation under specious pretenses? Is it a thing necessary to a nation? If it is, in what does that necessity consist, what service does it perform, what is its business, and what are its merits?

Does the virtue consist in the metaphor, or in the man? Does the goldsmith that makes the crown, make the virtue also? Does it operate like Fortunatus' wishing cap or Harlequin's wooden sword?[11] Does it make a man a conjuror? In fine, what is it? It appears to be a something going much out of fashion, falling into ridicule, and rejected in some countries both as unnecessary and expensive. . . .

It is easy to conceive that a band of interested men, such as placemen,[12] pensioners, lords of the bed-chamber, lords of the kitchen, lords of the necessary-house,[13] and the Lord knows what besides, can find as many reasons for monarchy as their salaries, paid at the expense of the country, amount to; but if I ask the farmer, the manufacturer, the merchant, the tradesman, and down through all the occupations of life to the common laborer, what service monarchy is to him? He can give me no answer. If I ask him what monarchy is, he believes it is something like a sinecure. . . .

Whether I have too little sense to see, or too much to be imposed upon; whether I have too much or too little pride, or of anything else, I leave out of the question; but certain it is, that what is called monarchy always appears to me a silly, contemptible thing. I compare it to something kept behind a curtain, about which there is a great deal of bustle and fuss, and a wonderful air of seeming solemnity; but when, by any accident, the curtain happens to open, and the company see what it is, they burst into laughter. . . .

We must shut our eyes against reason, we must basely degrade our understanding, not to see the folly of what is called monarchy. Nature is orderly in all her works; but this is a mode of government that counteracts nature. It turns the progress of the human faculties upside down. It subjects age to be governed by children, and wisdom by folly. On the contrary, the representative system is always parallel with the order and immutable laws of nature, and meets the reason of man in every part. For example:

In the American Federal Government, more power is delegated to the President of the United States than to any other individual member of Congress. He cannot, therefore, be elected to this office under the age of thirty-five years. By this time the judgment of man becomes matured, and he has lived long enough to be acquainted with men and things, and the country with him.

But on the monarchial plan, (exclusive of the numerous chances there are against every man born into the world, of drawing a prize in the lottery of human faculties), the next in succession, whatever he may be, is put at the head of a nation, and of a government, at the age of eighteen years.

Does this appear like an act of wisdom? Is it consistent with the proper dignity and the manly character of a nation? Where is the propriety of calling such a lad the father of the people? In all other cases, a person is a minor until the age of twenty-one years. Before this period, he is not trusted with the management of an acre of land, or with the heritable property of a flock of sheep, or a herd of swine; but, wonderful to tell! he may, at the age of eighteen years, be trusted with a nation. . . .

It can only be by blinding the understanding of man, and making him believe that government is some wonderful mysterious thing, that excessive revenues are obtained. Monarchy is well calculated to ensure this end. It is the popery of government; a thing kept up to amuse the ignorant, and quiet them into paying taxes.

GOVERNMENT BY ELECTION
AND REPRESENTATION

Having thus glanced at a few of the defects of the old, or hereditary system of government, let us compare it with the new, or representative system.

The representative system takes society and civilization for its basis; nature, reason, and experience for its guide.

Experience, in all ages, and in all countries, has demonstrated, that it is impossible to control Nature in her distribution of mental powers. She gives them as she pleases. Whatever is the rule by which she, apparently to us, scatters them among mankind, that rule remains a secret to man. It would be as ridiculous to attempt to fix the hereditaryship of human beauty, as of wisdom.

Whatever wisdom constituently is, it is like a seedless plant; it may be reared when it appears, but it cannot be voluntarily produced. There is always a sufficiency somewhere in the general mass of society for all purposes; but with respect to the parts of society, it is continually changing its place. It rises in one to-day, in another to-morrow, and has most probably visited in rotation every family of the earth, and again withdrawn.

As this is the order of nature, the order of government must necessarily follow it, or government will, as we see it does, degenerate into ignorance. The hereditary system, therefore, is as repugnant to human wisdom as to human rights, and is as absurd as it is unjust.

As the republic of letters brings forward the best literary productions by giving to genius a fair and universal chance, so the representative system of government is calculated to produce the wisest laws by collecting wisdom where it can be found. I smile to myself when I contemplate the ridiculous insignificance into which literature and all the sciences would sink were they made hereditary; and I carry the same idea into governments. An hereditary governor is as inconsistent as an hereditary author. I know not whether Homer or Euclid had sons; but I will venture an opinion that if they had, and had left their works unfinished, those sons could not have completed them.

Do we need a stronger evidence of the absurdity of hereditary government, than is seen in the descendants of those men, in any line of life, who once were famous? Is there scarcely an instance in which there is not a total reverse of character? It appears as if the tide of mental faculties flowed as far as it could in certain channels, and then forsook its course, and arose in others. How irrational then is the hereditary system which establishes channels of power, in company with which wisdom refuses to flow! By continuing this absurdity, man is perpetually in contradiction with himself; he accepts, for a king, or a chief magistrate, or a legislator, a person whom he would not elect for a constable.

It appears to general observation that revolutions create genius and talents; but those events do no more than bring them forward. There is existing in man a mass of sense lying in a dormant state, and which, unless something excites it to action, will descend with him, in that condition, to the grave. As it is to the advantage of society that the whole of its faculties should be employed, the construction of government ought to be such as to bring forward, by a quiet and regular operation, all that extent of capacity which never fails to appear in revolutions.

This cannot take place in the insipid state of hereditary government, not only because it prevents, but because it operates to benumb. When the mind of a nation is bowed down by any political superstition in its government, such as hereditary succession is, it loses a considerable portion of its powers on all other subjects and objects.

Hereditary succession requires the same obedience to ignorance as to wisdom; and when once the mind can bring itself to pay this indiscriminate reverence, it descends below the stature of mental manhood. It is fit to be great only in little things. It acts a treachery upon itself, and suffocates the sensations that urge to detection.

Though the ancient governments present to us a miserable picture of the condition of man, there is one which above all other exempts itself from the general description. I mean the democracy of the Athenians. We see more to admire, and less to condemn, in that great, extraordinary people, than in any thing which history affords.

Mr. Burke is so little acquainted with constituent principles of government, that he confounds democracy and representation together. Representation was a thing unknown in the ancient democracies. In those the mass of the people met and enacted laws (grammatically speaking) in the first person.

Simple democracy was no other than the common hall of the ancients. It signifies the *form,* as well as the public principle of the government. As these democracies increased in population, and the territory extended, the simple democratical form became unwieldy and impracticable; and as the system of representation was not known, the consequence was, they either degenerated convulsively into monarchies, or became absorbed into such as then existed.

Had the system of representation been then understood, as it now is, there is no reason to believe that those forms of government, now called monarchical and aristocratical, would ever have taken place. It was the want of some method to consolidate the parts of society after it became too populous and too extensive for the simple democratical form, and also the lax and solitary condition of shepherds and herdsmen in other parts of the world, that afforded opportunities to those unnatural modes of government to begin.

As it is necessary to clear away the rubbish of errors into which the subject of government has been thrown, I shall proceed to remark on some others.

It has always been the political craft of courtiers and court-governments to abuse something which they called republicanism;

but what republicanism was, or is, they never attempt to explain. Let us examine a little into this case.

The only forms of government are the democratical, the aristocratical, the monarchical, and what is now called the representative.[14]

What is called a *republic* is not any *particular form* of government. It is wholly characteristic of the purport, matter, or object for which government ought to be instituted, and on which it is to be employed, *res-publica,* the public affairs, or the public good; or, literally translated, the *public thing.*

It is a word of a good original, referring to what ought to be the character and business of government; and in this sense it is naturally opposed to the word *monarchy,* which has a base original signification. It means arbitrary power in an individual person, in the exercise of which, *himself,* and not the *res-publica,* is the object.

Every government that does not act on the principle of a *republic,* or in other words, that does not make the *res-publica* its whole and sole object, is not a good government. Republican government is no other than government established and conducted for the interest of the public, as well individually as collectively. It is not necessarily connected with any particular form, but it most naturally associates with the representative form, as being best calculated to secure the end for which a nation is at the expense of supporting it. . . .

Various forms of government have affected to style themselves a republic. Poland calls itself a republic, which is an hereditary aristocracy, with what is called an elective monarchy. Holland calls itself a republic which is chiefly aristocratical, with an hereditary stadtholdership.

But the government of America, which is wholly on the system of representation, is the only real republic in character and practice, that now exists. Its government has no other object than the public business of the nation, and therefore it is properly a republic; and the Americans have taken care that *this,* and no other, shall always be the object of the government, by their rejecting everything hereditary, and establishing government on the system of representation only.

Those who have said that a republic is not a *form* of government calculated for countries of great extent, mistook, in the first place, the *business* of a government for a *form* of government; for the *res-publica* equally appertains to every extent of territory and population. And, in the second place, if they meant any thing with respect to *form,* it was the simple democratical form, such as was the mode of government in the ancient democracies, in which there was no representation. The case therefore, is not, that a republic cannot be extensive, but that it cannot be extensive on the simple democratical form; and the question naturally presents itself, *What is the best form of government for conducting the* RES-PUBLICA, *or the* PUBLIC BUSINESS *of a nation, after it becomes too extensive and populous for the simple democratical form?*

It cannot be monarchy, because monarchy is subject to an objection of the same amount to which the simple democratical form was subject.

It is possible that an individual may lay down a system of principles on which government shall be constitutionally established to any extent of territory. This is no more than an operation of the mind, acting by its own powers. But the practice upon those principles, as applying to the various and numerous circumstances of a nation, its agriculture, manufacture, trade, commerce, etc., requires a knowledge of a different kind, and which can be had only from the various parts of society.

It is an assemblage of practical knowledge, which no one individual can possess; and therefore the monarchical form is as much limited, in useful practice, from the incompetency of knowledge as was the democratical form from the multiplying of population. The one degenerates, by extension, into confusion; the other, into ignorance and incapacity, of which all the great monarchies are an evidence. The monarchical form, therefore, could not be a substitute for the democratical, because it has equal inconveniences.

Much less could it when made hereditary. This is the most effectual of all forms to preclude knowledge. Neither could the high democratical mind have voluntarily yielded itself to be governed by children and idiots, and all the motley insignificance of character, which attends such a mere animal system, the disgrace and the reproach of reason and of man.

As to the aristocratical form, it has the same vices and defects with the monarchical, except that the chance of abilities is better from the proportion of numbers, but there is still no security for the right use and application of them.

Referring, then, to the original simple democracy, it affords the true data from which government on a large scale can begin. It is incapable of extension, not from its principle, but from the inconvenience of its form; and monarchy and aristocracy, from their incapacity. Retaining, then, democracy as the ground, and rejecting the corrupt systems of monarchy and aristocracy, the representative system naturally presents itself; remedying at once the defects of the simple democracy as to form, and the incapacity of the other two with respect to knowledge.

Simple democracy was society governing itself without the aid of secondary means. By ingrafting representation upon democracy, we arrive at a system of government capable of embracing and confederating all the various interests and every extent of territory and population; and that also with advantages as much superior to hereditary government, as the republic of letters is to hereditary literature.

It is on this system that the American government is founded. It is representation ingrafted upon democracy. It has fixed the form by a scale parallel in all cases to the extent of the principle. What Athens was in miniature, America will be in magnitude. The one was the wonder of the ancient world; the other is becoming the admiration and model of the present. It is the easiest of all the forms of government to be understood, and the most eligible in practice; and excludes at once the ignorance and insecurity of the hereditary mode, and the inconvenience of the simple democracy. . . .

That which is called government, or rather that which we ought to conceive government to be, is no more than some common center, in which all the parts of society unite. This cannot be accomplished by any method so conducive to the various interests of the community as by the representative system.

It concentrates the knowledge necessary to the interests of the parts and of the whole. It places government in a state of constant maturity. It is, as has been already observed, never young, never old. It is subject neither to nonage, nor dotage. It is never in the cradle, nor on crutches. It admits not of a separation between knowledge and power, and is superior, as government always ought to be, to all the accidents of individual man, and is therefore superior to what is called monarchy. . . . Like the nation itself, it possesses a perpetual stamina, as well of body as of mind, and presents itself on the open theater of the world in a fair and manly manner. Whatever are its excellencies or its defects, they are visible to all. It exists not by fraud and mystery; it deals not in cant and sophistry; but inspires a language that, passing from heart to heart, is felt and understood. . . . There is no place for mystery; nowhere for it to begin. Those who are not in the representation, know as much of the nature of business as those who are. An affectation of mysterious importance would there be scouted. Nations can have no secrets; and the secrets of courts, like those of individuals, are always their defects.

In the representative system, the reason for everything must publicly appear. Every man is a proprietor in government and considers it a necessary part of his business to understand. It concerns his interest, because it affects his property. He examines the cost, and compares it with the advantages; and above all, he does not adopt the slavish custom of following what in other governments are called LEADERS.

The government of a free country, properly speaking, is not in the persons, but in the laws. The enacting of those requires no great expense; and when they are administered, the whole of civil government is performed—the rest is all court contrivance. . . .

EQUAL RIGHTS
AND MAJORITY RULE

In contemplating government by election and representation, we amuse not ourselves in inquiring when or how, or by what right, it began. Its origin is ever in view. Man is himself the origin and the evidence of the right. It appertains to him in right of his existence, and his person is the title deed.

The true and only true basis of representative government is equality of rights. Every man has a right to one vote, and no more in the choice of representatives. The rich have no more right to exclude the poor from the right of voting, or of electing and being elected, than the poor have to exclude the rich; and wherever it is attempted, or proposed, on either side, it is a question of force and not of right. Who is he that would exclude another? That other has a right to exclude him.

That which is now called aristocracy implies an inequality of rights; but who are the persons that have a right to establish this inequality? Will the rich exclude themselves? No. Will the poor exclude themselves? No. By what right then can any be excluded? It would be a question, if any man or class of men have a right to exclude themselves; but, be this as it may, they cannot have the right to exclude another. The poor will not delegate such a right to the rich, nor the rich to the poor, and to assume it is not only to assume arbitrary power, but to assume a right to commit robbery.

Personal rights, of which the right of voting for representatives is one, are a species of property of the most sacred kind: and he that would employ his pecuniary property, or presume upon the influence it gives him, to dispossess or rob another of his property or rights, uses that pecuniary property as he would use fire-arms, and merits to have it taken from him.

Inequality of rights is created by a combination in one part of the community to exclude another part from its rights. Whenever it be made an article of a constitution, or a law, that the right of voting, or of electing and being elected, shall appertain exclusively to persons possessing a certain quantity of property, be it little or much, it is a combination of the persons possessing that quantity to exclude those who do not possess the same quantity. It is investing themselves with powers as a self-created part of society, to the exclusion of the rest.*

It is always to be taken for granted, that those who oppose an equality of rights never mean the exclusion should take place on themselves; and in this view of the case, pardoning the vanity of the thing, aristocracy is a subject of laughter. This self-soothing vanity is encouraged by another idea not less selfish, which is that the opposers conceive they are playing a safe game, in which there is a chance to gain and none to lose; that at any rate the doctrine of equality includes *them,* and that if they cannot get more rights than those whom they oppose and would exclude they shall not have less.

This opinion has already been fatal to thousands, who, not contented with *equal rights,* have sought more till they lost all, and experienced in themselves the degrading *inequality* they endeavored to fix upon others.

In any view of the case it is dangerous and impolitic, sometimes ridiculous, and always unjust to make property the criterion of the right of voting. If the sum or value of the property upon which the right is to take place be considerable it will exclude a majority of the people and unite them in a common interest against the government and against those who support it; and as the power is always with the majority, they can overturn such a government and its supporters whenever they please.

If, in order to avoid this danger, a small quantity of property be fixed, as the criterion of the right, it exhibits liberty in disgrace, by putting it in competition with accident and insignificance. When a broodmare shall fortunately produce a foal or a mule that, by being worth the sum in question, shall convey to its owner the right of voting, or by its death take it from him, in whom does the origin of

---

* Rights are permanent things, fortune is not so; therefore the uncertainty and inequality of the latter cannot become a rule to the certainty and equality of the former. Freedom and fortune have no natural relation. They are as distinct things as rest and motion. To make freedom follow fortune is to suppose her the shadow of an image on a wheel—a shade of passage—an unfixable nothing. *A Serious Address to the People of Pennsylvania on the Present State of Their Affairs* (1778), II, 285.

such a right exist? Is it in the man, or in the mule? When we consider how many ways property may be acquired without merit, and lost without crime, we ought to spurn the idea of making it a criterion of rights.*

But the offensive part of the case is that this exclusion from the right of voting implies a stigma on the moral character of the persons excluded; and this is what no part of the community has a right to pronounce upon another part. No external circumstance can justify it: wealth is no proof of moral character; nor poverty of the want of it.

On the contrary, wealth is often the presumptive evidence of dishonesty; and poverty the negative evidence of innocence. If therefore property, whether little or much, be made a criterion, the means by which that property has been acquired ought to be made a criterion also.

The only ground upon which exclusion from the right of voting is consistent with justice would be to inflict it as a punishment for a certain time upon those who should propose to take away that right from others. The right of voting for representatives is the primary right by which other rights are protected.

To take away this right is to reduce a man to slavery, for slavery consists in being subject to the will of another, and he that has not a vote in the election of representatives is in this case. The proposal therefore to disfranchise any class of men is as criminal as the proposal to take away property.

When we speak of right we ought always to unite with it the idea of duties: rights become duties by reciprocity. The right which I enjoy becomes my duty to guarantee it to another, and he to me; and those who violate the duty justly incur a forfeiture of the right.†

In a political view of the case, the strength and permanent security of government is in proportion to the number of people interested in supporting it. The true policy therefore is to interest the whole by an equality of rights, for the danger arises from exclusions. It is possible to exclude men from the right of voting, but it is impossible to exclude them from the right of rebelling against that

---

* Merit without fortune will be attended with inconvenience, and fortune without merit will be incapable of the duty. The best and safest choice is where they are handsomely united. *A Serious Address to the People of Pennsylvania* (1778), II, 286.

† Whenever I use the words *freedom* or *rights,* I desire to be understood to mean a perfect equality of them. Let the rich man enjoy his riches, and the poor man comfort himself in his poverty. But the floor of Freedom is as level as water. It *can* be no otherwise of itself and *will* be no otherwise till ruffled by a storm. It is this broad base, this universal foundation, that gives security to all and every part of society. *A Serious Address to the People of Pennsylvania* (1778), II, 286–87. [Paine's emphasis]

exclusion; and when all other rights are taken away the right of rebellion is made perfect.

While men could be persuaded they had no rights, or that rights appertained only to a certain class of men, or that government was a thing existing in right of itself, it was not difficult to govern them authoritatively. The ignorance in which they were held, and the superstition in which they were instructed, furnished the means of doing it.

But when the ignorance is gone, and the superstition with it; when they perceive the imposition that has been acted upon them; when they reflect that the cultivator and the manufacturer are the primary means of all the wealth that exists in the world, beyond what nature spontaneously produces; when they begin to feel their consequences by their usefulness, and their right as members of society, it is then no longer possible to govern them as before. The fraud once detected cannot be re-acted. To attempt it is to provoke derision, or invite destruction.

That property will ever be unequal is certain. Industry, superiority of talents, dexterity of management, extreme frugality, fortunate opportunities, or the opposite, or the means of those things, will ever produce that effect, without having recourse to the harsh, ill-sounding names of avarice and oppression; and besides this there are some men who, though they do not despise wealth, will not stoop to the drudgery or the means of acquiring it, nor will be troubled with it beyond their wants or their independence; while in others there is an avidity to obtain it by every means not punishable; it makes the sole business of their lives, and they follow it as a religion. All that is required with respect to property is to obtain it honestly, and not employ it criminally; but it is always criminally employed when it is made a criterion for exclusive rights.

In institutions that are purely pecuniary, such as that of a bank[15] or a commercial company, the rights of the members composing that company are wholly created by the property they invest therein; and no other rights are represented in the government of that company than what arise out of that property; neither has that government cognizance of *anything but property.*

But the case is totally different with respect to the institution of civil government, organized on the system of representation. Such a government has cognizance of *everything,* and of *every man* as a member of the national society, whether he has property or not; and, therefore, the principle requires that *every man,* and *every kind of right,* be represented, of which the right to acquire and to hold property is but one, and that not of the most essential kind.

The protection of a man's person is more sacred than the protection of property; and besides this, the faculty of performing any kind of work or services by which he acquires a livelihood, or maintaining his family, is of the nature of property. It is property to him; he has acquired it; and it is as much the object of his protection as exterior property, possessed without that faculty, can be the object of protection in another person.

I have always believed that the best security for property, be it much or little, is to remove from every part of the community, as far as can possibly be done, every cause of complaint, and every motive to violence; and this can only be done by an equality of rights. When rights are secure, property is secure in consequence. But when property is made a pretense for unequal or exclusive rights, it weakens the right to hold the property, and provokes indignation and tumult; for it is unnatural to believe that property can be secure under the guarantee of a society injured in its rights by the influence of that property. . . .

It is at all times necessary, and more particularly so during the progress of a revolution, and until right ideas confirm themselves by habit, that we frequently refresh our patriotism by reference to first principles. It is by tracing things to their origin that we learn to understand them: and it is by keeping that line and that origin always in view that we never forget them.

An inquiry into the origin of rights will demonstrate to us that *rights* are not *gifts* from one man to another, nor from one class of men to another; for who is he who could be the first giver, or by what principle, or on what authority, could he possess the right of giving?

A declaration of rights is not a creation of them, nor a donation of them. It is a manifest of the principle by which they exist, followed by a detail of what the rights are; for every civil right has a natural right for its foundation, and it includes the principle of a reciprocal guarantee of those rights from man to man. As, therefore, it is impossible to discover any origin of rights otherwise than in the origin of man, it consequently follows, that rights appertain to man in right of his existence only, and must therefore be equal to every man.

The principle of an *equality of rights* is clear and simple. Every man can understand it, and it is by understanding his rights that he learns his duties; for where the rights of men are equal, every man must finally see the necessity of protecting the rights of others as the most effectual security for his own.*

---

* Freedom must have all or none, and she must have them equally. As a matter of political interest only, I would defend the poor out of policy to the rich. *There* is the point at which the invasion first enters, the pass which all without distinction ought to defend, and, that being well defended and made secure, all within is at rest. *First* goes the poor, next the tradesman, then the men of middling fortunes, then those of liberal fortunes, till at last some one without any fortune at all starts up, and laying hold of the popular discontents,

But if, in the formation of a constitution, we depart from the principle of equal rights, or attempt any modification of it, we plunge into a labyrinth of difficulties from which there is no way out but by retreating. Where are we to stop? Or by what principle are we to find out the point to stop at, that shall discriminate between men of the same country, part of whom shall be free, and the rest not?

If property is to be made the criterion, it is a total departure from every moral principle of liberty, because it is attaching rights to mere matter, and making man the agent of that matter. It is, moreover, holding up property as an apple of discord,[16] and not only exciting but justifying war against it; for I maintain the principle that when property is used as an instrument to take away the rights of those who may happen not to possess property, it is used to an unlawful purpose, as firearms would be in a similar case.

In a state of nature all men are equal in rights, but they are not equal in power; the weak cannot protect themselves against the strong. This being the case, the institution of civil society is for the purpose of making an equalization of powers that shall be parallel to, and a guarantee of, the equality of rights. The laws of a country, when properly constructed, apply to this purpose.

Every man takes the arm of the law for his protection as more effectual than his own; and therefore every man has an equal right in the formation of the government, and of the laws by which he is to be governed and judged. In extensive countries and societies, such as America and France, this right in the individual can only be exercised by delegation, that is, by election and representation; and hence it is that the institution of representative government arises.

Hitherto, I have confined myself to matters of principle only. First, that hereditary government has not a right to exist; that it cannot be established on any principle of right; and that it is a violation of all principle. Secondly, that government by election and representation has its origin in the natural and eternal rights of man; for whether a man be his own lawgiver, as he would be in a state of nature; or whether he exercises his portion of legislative sovereignty in his own person, as might be the case in small democracies where all could assemble for the formation of the laws by which they were to be governed; or whether he exercises it in the choice of persons to represent him in a national assembly of representatives, the origin of the right is the same in all cases. The first, as is before observed, is defective in power; the second, is practicable only in democracies of small extent; the third, is the greatest scale upon which human government can be instituted.

---

tyrannizes over the whole, and under the pretense of relieving them. *A Serious Address to the People of Pennsylvania* (1778), II, 284. [Paine's emphasis]

Next to matters of *principle* are matters of *opinion,* and it is necessary to distinguish between the two. Whether the rights of men shall be equal is not a matter of opinion but of right, and consequently of principle; for men do not hold their rights as grants from each other, but each one in right of himself. Society is the guardian but not the giver. And as in extensive societies, such as America and France, the right of the individual in matters of government cannot be exercised but by election and representation, it consequently follows that the only system of government consistent with principle, where simple democracy is impracticable, is the representative system.

But as to the organical part, or the manner in which the several parts of government shall be arranged and composed, it is altogether *matter of opinion.* It is necessary that all the parts be conformable with the *principle of equal rights;* and so long as this principle be religiously adhered to, no very material error can take place, neither can any error continue long in that part which falls within the province of opinion.

In all matters of opinion, the social compact, or the principle by which society is held together, requires that the majority of opinions becomes the rule for the whole, and that the minority yields practical obedience thereto. This is perfectly comformable to the principle of equal rights: for, in the first place, every man has *a right to give an opinion* but no man has a right that his opinion should *govern the rest.* In the second place, it is not supposed to be known beforehand on which side of any question, whether for or against, any man's opinion will fall. He may happen to be in a majority upon some questions, and in a minority upon others; and by the same rule that he expects obedience in the one case, he must yield it in the other.

All the disorders that have arisen in France during the progress of the Revolution have had their origin, not in the *principle of equal rights,* but in the violation of that principle.* The principle of equal rights has been repeatedly violated, and that not by the majority but by the minority, and *that minority has been composed of men possessing property, as well as of men without property; property, therefore, even upon the experience already had, is no more a criterion of character than it is of rights.*

It will sometimes happen that the minority are right, and the majority are wrong, but as soon as experience proves this to be the

---

* You see what mischief ensued in France by the possession of power before they understood principles. They earned liberty in words, but not in fact. The writer of this was in France through the whole of the Revolution, and knows the truth of what he speaks; for after endeavoring to give it principle, he had nearly fallen a victim to its rage. *To the French Inhabitants of Louisiana* (1804), II, 964.

case, the minority will increase to a majority, and the error will reform itself by the tranquil operation of freedom of opinion and equality of rights. Nothing, therefore, can justify an insurrection, neither can it ever be necessary where rights are equal and opinions free. . . .

Representative government is not necessarily confined to any one particular form. The principle is the same in all the forms under which it can be arranged. The equal rights of the people is the root from which the whole springs, and the branches may be arranged as present opinion or future experience shall best direct.

[*Dissertation on First Principles of Government* (1795), II, 577–86.]

GOVERNMENT BY PRECEDENT

Almost every case must now be determined by some precedent, be that precedent good or bad, or whether it properly applies or not; and the practice has become so general as to suggest a suspicion that it proceeds from a deeper policy than at first sight appears.

Since the Revolution of America, and more so since that of France, this preaching up the doctrine of precedents, drawn from times and circumstances antecedent to those events, has been the studied practice of the English Government. The generality of those precedents are founded on principles and opinions, the reverse of what they ought to be; and the greater distance of time they are drawn from, the more they are to be suspected.

But by associating those precedents with a superstitious reverence for ancient things, as monks show relics and call them holy, the generality of mankind are deceived into the design. Governments now act as if they were afraid to awaken a single reflection in man. They are softly leading him to the sepulchre of precedents to deaden his faculties and call his attention from the scene of revolutions.

They feel that he is arriving at knowledge faster than they wish, and their policy of precedents is the barometer of their fears. This political popery, like the ecclesiastical popery of old, has had its day, and is hastening to its exit. The ragged relic and the antiquated precedent, the monk and the monarch, will molder together.

Government by precedent, without any regard to the principle of the precedent, is one of the vilest systems that can be set up. In numerous instances, the precedent ought to operate as a warning, and not as an example, and requires to be shunned instead of imitated; but instead of this, precedents are taken in the lump, and put at once for constitution and for law.

Either the doctrine of precedents is policy to keep a man in a state of ignorance, or it is a practical confession that wisdom degenerates in governments as governments increase in age, and can only hobble along by stilts and crutches of precedents.

How is it that the same persons who would proudly be thought wiser than their predecessors appear at the same time only as the ghosts of departed wisdom? How strangely is antiquity treated! To answer some purposes, it is spoken of as the times of darkness and ignorance, and to answer others, it is put for the light of the world.

If the doctrine of precedents is to be followed, the expenses of government need not continue the same. Why pay men extravagently who have but little to do? If every thing that can happen is already in precedent, legislation is at an end, and precedent, like a dictionary, determines every case. Either, therefore, government has arrived at its dotage, and requires to be renovated, or all the occasions for exercising its wisdom have occurred.

We now see all over Europe, and particularly in England, the curious phenomenon of a nation looking one way, and the Government the other—the one forward and the other backward. If governments are to go on by precedent, while nations go on by improvement, they must at last come to a final separation; and the sooner, and the more civilly they determine this point, the better it will be for them. . . .*

As to the prejudices which men have from education and habit, in favor of any particular form or system of government, those prejudices have yet to stand the test of reason and reflection. In fact, such prejudices are nothing. No man is prejudiced in favor of a thing, knowing it to be wrong. He is attached to it on the belief of its being right; and when he sees it is not so, the prejudice will be gone. We have but a defective idea what prejudice is. It might be

---

* In England the improvements in agriculture, useful arts, manufactures, and commerce have been made in opposition to the genius of its government, which is that of following precedents. It is from the enterprise and industry of the individuals and their numerouos associations in which, tritely speaking, government is neither pillow nor bolster, that these improvements have proceeded.

No man thought about the Government, or who was *in*, or who was *out*, when he was planning or executing those things, and all he had to hope, with respect to government, was that it would let him alone. Three or four very silly ministerial newspapers are continually offending against the spirit of national improvement, by ascribing it to a minister. They may with as much truth ascribe this book to a minister. [Paine] said that until men think for themselves the whole is prejudice, and *not opinion;* for that only is opinion which is the result of reason and reflection. I offer this remark that Mr. Burke may not confide too much in what has been the customary prejudices of the country.

I do not believe that the people of England have ever been fairly and candidly dealt by. They have been imposed upon by parties, and by men assuming the character of leaders. It is time that the nation should rise above those trifles. It is time to dismiss that inattention which has so long been the encouraging cause of stretching taxation to excess. It is time to dismiss all those songs and toasts which are calculated to enslave, and operate to suffocate reflection. . . .

> Among the mass of national delusions calculated to amuse and impose upon the multitude, the standing one has been that of flattering them into taxes, by calling the Government (or as they please to express it, the English Constitution) *"the envy and the admiration of the world."* Scarcely an address has been voted in which some of the speakers have not uttered this hackneyed, nonsensical falsehood.*
>
> Two revolutions have taken place, those of America and France; and both of them have rejected the unnatural compounded system of the English Government. America has declared against all hereditary government, and established the representative system of government only. France has entirely rejected the aristocratical part, and is now discovering the absurdity of the monarchical, and is approaching fast to the representative system. On what ground then, do these men continue a declaration, respecting what they call the *envy and admiration of other nations,* which the voluntary practice of such nations,

* I offer a few remarks on the so much boasted Constitution of England. That it was noble for the dark and slavish times in which it was erected, is granted. When the world was overrun with tyranny the least remove therefrom was a glorious rescue. But that it is imperfect, subject to convulsions, and incapable of producing what it seems to promise, is easily demonstrated. . . . I know it is difficult to get over local or long standing prejudices, yet if we will suffer ourselves to examine the component parts of the English Constitution, we shall find them to be the base remains of two ancient tyrannies, compounded with some new Republican materials.

First.—The remains of monarchical tyranny in the person of the king.

Secondly.—The remains of aristocratical tyranny in the persons of the peers.

Thirdly.—The new Republican materials, in the persons of the Commons, on whose virtue depends the freedom of England.

The two first, by being hereditary, are independent of the people; wherefore in a *constitutional sense* they contribute nothing toward the freedom of the state. *Common Sense* (1776), I, 6–7.

as have had the opportunity of establishing government, contradicts and falsifies? Will such men never confine themselves to truth? Will they be for ever the deceivers of the people?

But I will go further and show that were government now to begin in England, the people could not be brought to establish the same system they now submit to.

In speaking on this subject (or on any other) *on the pure ground of principle,* antiquity and precedent cease to be authority, and hoary-headed error loses its effect. The reasonableness and propriety of things must be examined abstractedly from custom and usage; and, in this point of view, the right which grows into practice today is as much a right, and as old in principle and theory, as if it had the customary sanction of a thousand ages. Principles have no connection with time, nor characters with names.*

To say that the Government of this country [England] is composed of Kings, Lords, and Commons is the mere phraseology of custom. It is composed of men; and whoever the men be to whom the government of any country be intrusted, they ought to be the best and wisest that can be found, and if they are not so, they are not fit for the station. A man derives no more excellence from the change of a name, or calling him king, or calling him lord, than I should do by changing my name from Thomas to George, or from Paine to Guelph.[17] I should not be a whit more able to write a book because my name was altered; neither would any man, now called a king or a lord, have a whit more sense than he now has, were he to call himself Thomes Paine.

As to the word "Commons," applied as it is in England, it is a term of degradation and reproach, and ought to be abolished. It is a term unknown in free countries.

But to the point. Let us suppose that government was now to begin in England, and that the plan of government, offered to the nation for its approbation or rejection, consisted of the following parts:

First—That some one individual should be taken from all the rest of the nation, and to whom all the rest should swear obedience, and never be permitted to sit down in his presence, and that they should give to him one million sterling a year. That the nation should never after have power or authority to make laws but with his express consent; and that his sons and his sons' sons, whether wise or foolish,

* Time with respect to principles is an eternal NOW: it has no operation upon them: it changes nothing of their nature and qualities. But what have we to do with a thousand years? Our lifetime is but a short portion of time, and if we find the wrong in existence as soon as we begin to live, that is the point of time at which it begins to us; and our right to resist it is the same as if it never existed before. *Dissertation on First Principles of Government* (1795), II, 574.

good men or bad, fit or unfit, should have the same power, and also the same money annually paid to them for ever.

Secondly—That there should be two houses of legislators to assist in making laws, one of which should, in the first instance, be entirely appointed by the aforesaid person, and that their sons and their sons' sons, whether wise or foolish, good men or bad, fit or unfit, should for ever after be hereditary legislators.

Thirdly—That the other house should be chosen in the same manner as the house now called the House of Commons is chosen, and should be subject to the control of the two aforesaid hereditary powers in all things.

It would be impossible to cram such a farrago of imposition and absurdity down the throat of this or any other nation that was capable of reasoning upon its rights and its interest.

They would ask, in the first place, on what ground of right, or on what principle, such irrational and preposterous distinctions could, or ought to be made; and what pretensions any man could have, or what services he could render, to entitle him to a million a year? They would go further, and revolt at the idea of consigning their children, and their children's children, to the domination of persons hereafter to be born, who might, for anything they could foresee, turn out to be knaves or fools; and they would finally discover that the project of hereditary governors and legislators *was a treasonable usurpation over the rights of posterity*. Not only the calm dictates of reason, and the force of natural affection, but the integrity of manly pride, would impel men to spurn such proposals.

From the grosser absurdities of such a scheme, they would extend their examination to the practical defects—They would soon see that it would end in tyranny accomplished by fraud. That in the operation of it, it would be two to one against them, because the two parts that were to be made hereditary would form a common interest, and stick to each other; and that themselves and representatives would become no better than hewers of wood and drawers of water[18] for the other parts of the government. Yet call one of those powers King, the other Lords, and the third the Commons, and it gives the model of what is called the English Government.

[*Letter to the Addressers on the Late Proclamation* (1792), II, 482–84.]

THE ENIGMA OF MIXED GOVERNMENTS

We have next to consider what it is that gives motion to that species of government which is called mixed government, or, as it is sometimes ludicrously styled, a government of *this, that,* and *t'other.*

The moving power of this species of government is of necessity corruption. However imperfect election and representation may be in mixed governments, they still give exercise to a greater portion of reason than is convenient to the hereditary part; and therefore it becomes necessary to buy the reason up. A mixed government is an imperfect everything, cementing and soldering the discordant parts together by corruption, to act as a whole. Mr. Burke appears highly disgusted that France, since she had resolved on a revolution, did not adopt what he calls, *"A British Constitution,"* and the regretful manner in which he expresses himself on this occasion implies a suspicion that the British Constitution needed something to keep its defects in countenance.

In mixed governments there is no responsibility: the parts cover each other till responsibility is lost; and the corruption which moves the machine contrives at the same time its own escape. When it is laid down as a maxim, that a *king can do no wrong,*[19] it places him in a state of similar security with that of idiots and persons insane, and responsibility is out of the question with respect to himself. It then descends upon the minister, who shelters himself under a majority in Parliament, which, by places, pensions, and corruption, he can always command; and that majority justifies itself by the same authority with which it protects the minister. In this rotary motion, responsibility is thrown off from the parts, and from the whole.

When there is a part in a government which can do no wrong, it implies that it does nothing and is only the machine of another power, by whose advice and direction it acts. What is supposed to be the king in mixed governments is the cabinet; and as the cabinet is always a part of the parliament, and the members justifying in one character what they advise and act in another, a mixed government becomes a continual enigma, entailing upon a country, by the quantity of corruption necessary to solder the parts, the expense of supporting all the forms of government at once, and finally resolving itself into a government by committee, in which the advisers, the actors, the approvers, the justifiers, the persons responsible, and the persons not responsible, are the same persons. . . .

Much is to be learned from the French Constitution. Conquest and tyranny transplanted themselves with William the Conqueror[20] from Normandy into England, and the country is yet disfigured with the marks. May then the example of all France contribute to regenerate the freedom which a province of it destroyed!

The French Constitution says, That to preserve the national representation from being corrupt, no member of the National Assembly shall be an officer of the government, a place-man, or a pensioner. What will Mr. Burke place against this? I will whisper his answer: *Loaves* and *Fishes*.

Ah! this government of loaves and fishes has more mischief in it than people have yet reflected on. The National Assembly has made the discovery, and it holds out the example to the world. Had governments agreed to quarrel on purpose to fleece their countries by taxes, they could not have succeeded better than they have done.

Many things in the English Government appear to me the reverse of what they ought to be, and of what they are said to be. The Parliament, imperfectly and capriciously elected as it is, is nevertheless *supposed* to hold the national purse in *trust* for the nation: but in the manner in which an English parliament is constructed, it is like a man being both mortgager and mortgagee; and in the case of misapplication of trust, it is the criminal sitting in judgment upon himself.

If those who vote the supplies are the same persons who receive the supplies when voted, and are to account for the expenditure of those supplies who voted them, it is *themselves accountable to themselves,* and the *Comedy of Errors* concludes with the *Pantomime of Hush.*[21] Neither the ministerial party, nor the opposition, will touch upon this case. The national purse is the common hack which each mounts upon. It is like what the country people call, "Ride and tie —You ride a little way, and then I." * They order these things better in France. . . .

By this pantomimical contrivance, and change of scene and character, the parts help each other out in matters which neither of them singly would assume to act. When money is to be obtained, the mass of variety apparently dissolves and a profusion of parliamentary praises passes between the parts. Each admires with astonishment the wisdom, the liberality, the disinterestedness of the other; and all of them breathe a pitying sigh at the burdens of the nation.

But in a well constituted republic, nothing of this soldering, praising, and pitying, can take place; the representation being equal

---

* It is a practice in some parts of the country, when two travellers have but one horse, which like the national purse will not carry double, that the one mounts and rides two or three miles ahead, and then ties the horse to a gate, and walks on. When the second traveller arrives, he takes the horse, rides on, and passes his companion a mile or two, and ties again; and so on—*Ride and tie.* [Paine]

throughout the country, and complete in itself, however it may be arranged into legislative and executive, they have all one and the same natural source. The parts are not foreigners to each other, like democracy, aristocracy, and monarchy. As there are no discordant distinctions, there is nothing to corrupt by compromise, nor confound by contrivance.

Public measures appeal of themselves to the understanding of the nation, and, resting on their own merits, disown any flattering application to vanity. The continual whine of lamenting the burden of taxes, however successfully it may be practised in mixed governments, is inconsistent with the sense and spirit of a republic. If taxes are necessary, they are of course advantageous; but if they require an apology, the apology itself implies an impeachment. Why then is man thus imposed upon, or why does he impose upon himself? . . .

A nation is not a body, the figure of which is to be represented by the human body; but is like a body contained within a circle, having a common center, in which every radius meets; and that center is formed by representation. To connect representation with what is called monarchy is eccentric government. Representation is of itself the delegated monarchy of a nation, and cannot debase itself by dividing it with another. . . .

When men are spoken of as kings and subjects, or when government is mentioned under the distinct or combined heads of monarchy, aristocracy, and democracy, what is it that *reasoning* man is to understand by the terms? If there really existed in the world two or more distinct and separate *elements* of human power, we should then see the several origins to which those terms would descriptively apply; but as there is but one species of man, there can be but one element of human power, and that element is man himself. Monarchy, aristocracy, and democracy, are but creatures of imagination; and a thousand such may be contrived, as well as three. . . .

ON CONSTITUTIONS

That men mean distinct and separate things when they speak of constitutions and of government, is evident; or why are those terms distinctly and separately used? A constitution is not the act of a government, but of a people constituting a government; and government without a constitution is power without a right.

All power exercised over a nation must have some beginning. It must be either delegated or assumed. There are no other sources. All delegated power is trust, and all assumed power is usurpation. . . .

A constitution is not a thing in name only, but in fact. It has not an ideal, but a real existence; and wherever it cannot be produced in a visible form, there is none. A constitution is a thing *antecedent* to a government, and a government is only a creature of a constitution. The constitution of a country is not the act of its government, but of the people constituting a government.

It is the body of elements to which you can refer and quote article by article; and which contains the principles on which the government shall be established, the manner in which it shall be organized, the powers it shall have, the mode of elections, the duration of parliaments, or by what other name such bodies may be called; the powers which the executive part of the government shall have; and, in fine, every thing that relates to the complete organization of a civil government, and the principles on which it shall act, and by which it shall be bound.

A constitution, therefore, is to a government, what the laws made afterwards by that government are to a court of judicature. The court of judicature does not make the laws, neither can it alter them; it only acts in conformity to the laws made; and the government is in like manner governed by the constitution. . . .

A constitution is the property of a nation, and not of those who exercise the government. All the constitutions of America are declared to be established on the authority of the people. In France, the word nation is used instead of the people; but in both cases, a constitution is a thing antecedent to the government, and always distinct therefrom.

In England, it is not difficult to perceive that every thing has a constitution, except the nation. Every society and association that is established, first agreed upon a number of original articles, digested into form, which are its constitution. It then appointed its officers, whose powers and authorities are described in that constitution, and the government of that society then commenced. Those officers, by whatever name they are called, have no authority to add to, alter, or abridge, the original articles. It is only to the constituting power that this right belongs.

From the want of understanding the difference between a constitution and a government, Dr. Johnson,[22] and all writers of his description, have always bewildered themselves. They could not but perceive that there must necessarily be a *controlling* power existing somewhere, and they placed this power in the discretion of the persons exercising the government, instead of placing it in a constitution formed by the nation.

When it is in a constitution, it has the nation for its support, and the natural and controlling powers are together. The laws which are enacted by governments control men only as individuals, but the nation, through its constitution, controls the whole government, and has a natural ability so to do. The final controlling power, therefore, and the original constituting power, are one and the same power. . . .

Having thus spoken of constitutions generally, as things distinct from actual governments, let us proceed to consider the parts of which a constitution is composed.

Opinions differ more on this subject than with respect to the whole. That a nation ought to have a constitution, as a rule for the conduct of its government, is a simple question to which all men, not directly courtiers, will agree. It is only on the component parts that questions and opinions multiply.

But this difficulty, like every other, will diminish when put into a train of being rightly understood. The first thing is that a nation has a right to establish a constitution.

Whether it exercises this right in the most judicious manner at first, it is quite another case. It exercises it agreeably to the judgment it possesses; and by continuing to do so, all errors will at last be exploded.

When this right is established in a nation, there is no fear that it will be employed to its own injury. A nation can have no interest in being wrong.

Though all the constitutions of America are on one general principle, yet no two of them are exactly alike in their component parts, or in the distribution of the powers which they give to the actual governments. Some are more and others less complex.

In forming a constitution, it is first necessary to consider what are the ends for which government is necessary: secondly, what are the best means, and the least expensive, for accomplishing those ends.

Government is nothing more than a national association; and the object of this association is the good of all, as well individually as collectively. Every man wishes to pursue his occupation, and enjoy the fruits of his labors, and the produce of his property, in peace and safety, and with the least possible expense. When these things are accomplished, all the objects for which government ought to be established are answered.

It has been customary to consider government under three distinct general heads: The legislative, the executive, and the judicial.

But if we permit our judgment to act unincumbered by the habit of multiplied terms, we can perceive no more than two divisions of power of which civil government is composed, namely, that of legislating or enacting laws, and that of executing or administering them. Every thing, therefore, appertaining to civil government classes itself under one or other of these two divisions.

So far as regards the execution of the laws, that which is called the judicial power is strictly and properly the executive power of every country. It is that power to which every individual has an appeal, and which causes the laws to be executed; neither have we any other clear idea with respect to the official execution of the laws. In England, and also in America and France, this power begins with the magistrate, and proceeds up through all the courts of judicature. . . .

With respect to the organization of the *legislative power,*[23] different modes have been adopted in different countries. In America it is generally composed of two houses. In France it consists of but one, but in both countries, it is wholly by representation.

The case is, that mankind (from the long tyranny of assumed power) have had so few opportunities of making the necessary trials on modes and principles of government, in order to discover the best, *that government is but now beginning to be known,* and experience is yet wanting to determine many particulars.

The objections against two houses are, first, that there is an inconsistency in any part of the whole legislature coming to a final determination by vote on any matter, while *that matter,* with respect to *that whole,* is yet only in a train of deliberation, and consequently open to new illustrations.

Secondly, That by taking the vote on each, as a separate body, it always admits of the possibility, and is often the case in practice, that the minority governs the majority, and that, in some instances, to a great degree of inconsistency.

Thirdly, That two houses arbitrarily checking or controlling each other is inconsistent; because it cannot be proved, on the principles of just representation, that either should be wiser or better than the other. They may check in the wrong as well as in the right;

and therefore, to give the power where we cannot give the wisdom to use it, nor be assured of its being rightly used, renders the hazard at least equal to the precaution.*

The objection against a single house is that it is always in a condition of committing itself too soon. But it should at the same time be remembered that when there is a constitution which defines the power and establishes the principles within which a legislature shall act, there is already a more effectual check provided, and more powerfully operating, than any other check can be. For example:

Were a bill brought into any of the American legislatures, similar to that which was passed into an act of the English Parliament, at the commencement of the reign of George I, to extend the duration of the assemblies to a longer period than they now sit, the check is in the constitution, which in effect says, *thus far shalt thou go and no further.* . . .

But as nations proceed in the great business of forming constitutions, they will examine with more precision into the nature and business of that department which is called the executive. What the legislative and judicial departments are, every one can see; but with respect to what, in Europe, is called the executive, as distinct from those two, it is either a political superfluity, or a chaos of unknown things. Some kind of official department, to which reports shall be made from different parts of the nation, or from abroad, to be laid before the national representatives, is all that is necessary; but there is no consistency in calling this the executive; neither can it be considered in any other light than as inferior to the legislature. The sovereign authority in any country is the power of making laws, and every thing else is an official department. . . .[24]

To conclude this part of the subject:—One of the greatest improvements that has been made for the perpetual security and progress of constitutional liberty is the provision which the new consti-

___

* With respect to the two Houses, of which the English Parliament is composed, they appear to be effectually influenced into one, and, as a legislature, to have no temper of its own. The minister, whoever he at any time may be, touches it as with an opium wand, and it sleeps obedience.

But if we look at the distinct abilities of the two Houses, the difference will appear so great, as to show the inconsistency of placing power where there can be no certainty of the judgment to use it. Wretched as the state of representation is in England, it is manhood compared with what is called the House of Lords; and so little is this nick-named House regarded, that the people scarcely inquire at any time what it is doing. It appears also to be most under influence, and the furthest removed from the general interest of the nation. . . . [Paine]

tutions make for occasionally revising, altering and amending them. . . .

Government is but now beginning to be known. Hitherto it has been the mere exercise of power, which forbade all effectual inquiry into rights, and grounded itself wholly on possession. While the enemy of liberty was its judge, the progress of its principles must have been small indeed.

The constitutions of America, and also that of France, have either fixed a period for their revision, or laid down the mode by which improvements shall be made.

It is perhaps impossible to establish any thing that combines principles with opinions and practice, which the progress of circumstances, through a length of years, will not in some measure derange, or render inconsistent; and therefore, to prevent inconveniences accumulating, till they discourage reformations or provoke revolutions, it is best to regulate them as they occur.

The rights of man are the rights of all generations of men, and cannot be monopolized by any.* That which is worth following will be followed for the sake of its worth; and it is in this that its security lies, and not in any conditions with which it may be incumbered. When a man leaves property to his heirs, he does not connect it with an obligation that they shall accept it. Why then should we do otherwise with respect to constitutions?

The best constitution that could now be devised, consistent with the condition of the present moment, may be far short of that excellence which a few years may afford. There is a morning of reason rising upon man, on the subject of government, that has not appeared before. As the barbarism of the present old governments expires, the moral condition of the nations, with respect to each other, will be changed.

Man will not be brought up with the savage idea of considering his species as enemies, because the accident of birth gave the individuals existence in countries distinguished by different names; and as constitutions have always some relation to external as well as

---

* A nation, though continually existing, is continually in a state of renewal and succession. It is never stationary. Every day produces new births, carries minors forward to maturity, and old persons from the stage. In this ever running flood of generations there is no part superior in authority to another. Could we conceive an idea of superiority in any, at what point in time, or in what century of the world, are we to fix it? To what cause are we to ascribe it? By what evidence are we to prove it? By what criterion are we to know it? *Dissertation on First Principles of Government* (1795), II, 575.

domestic circumstances, the means of benefiting by every change, foreign or domestic, should be a part of every constitution.

THE FRENCH AND ENGLISH
CONSTITUTIONS COMPARED

From these preliminaries I proceed to draw some comparisons. I have already spoken of the Declaration of Rights; and as I mean to be as concise as possible, I shall proceed to other parts of the French Constitution.

The Constitution of France says that every man who pays a tax of sixty sous per annum (2s. and 6d. English) is an elector. What article will Mr. Burke place against this? Can any thing be more limited, and at the same time more capricious, than what the qualifications are in England?

Limited—because not one man in a hundred (I speak much within compass) is admitted to vote: capricious—because the lowest character that can be supposed to exist, and who has not so much as the visible means of an honest livelihood, is an elector in some places while, in other places, the man who pays very large taxes, and with a known fair character, and the farmer who rents to the amount of three or four hundred pounds a year, and with a property on that farm to three or four times that amount, is not admitted to be an elector.

Every thing is out of nature, as Mr. Burke says on another occasion, in this strange chaos, and all sorts of follies are blended with all sorts of crimes. William the Conqueror and his descendants parcelled out the country in this manner, and bribed one part of it by what they called charters to hold the other parts of it the better subjected to their will. This is the reason why so many of those charters abound in Cornwall.[25]

The people were averse to the government established at the Conquest, and the towns were garrisoned and bribed to enslave the country. All the old charters are the badges of this conquest, and it is from this source that the capriciousness of election arises.

The French Constitution says that the number of representatives for any place shall be in a ratio to the number of taxable inhabitants or electors. What article will Mr. Burke place against this? The county of Yorkshire, which contains near a million souls, sends two county members; and so does the county of Rutland, which contains not a hundredth part of that number.

The town of old Sarum[26] which contains not three houses, sends two members; and the town of Manchester, which contains upward of sixty thousand souls, is not admitted to send any. Is there any principle in these things? Is there any thing by which you can trace the marks of freedom or discover those of wisdom? No wonder, then, Mr. Burke has declined the comparison, and endeavored to lead his readers from the point by a wild, unsystematical display of paradoxical rhapsodies.

The French Constitution says that the National Assembly shall be elected every two years. What article will Mr. Burke place against this? Why, that the nation has no right at all in the case: that the Government is perfectly arbitrary with respect to this point; and he can quote for his authority the precedent of a former Parliament.

The French Constitution says there shall be no game laws; that the farmer on whose land wild game shall be found (for it is by the produce of those lands they are fed) shall have a right to what he can take. That there shall be no monopolies of any kind, that all trades shall be free, and every man free to follow any occupation by which he can procure an honest livelihood, and in any place, town, or city, throughout the nation. What will Mr. Burke say to this?

In England game is made the property of those at whose expense it is not fed; with respect to monopolies, the country is cut up into monopolies. Every chartered town is an aristocratic monopoly in itself, and the qualification of electors proceeds [from] one of those chartered monopolies.[27] Is this freedom? Is this what Mr. Burke means by a constitution?

In these chartered monopolies, a man coming from another part of the country is hunted from them as if he were a foreign enemy. An Englishman is not free in his own country: Every one of those places presents a barrier in his way, and tells him he is not a freeman— that he has no rights.*

Within these monopolies are other monopolies. In a city, such for instance, as Bath, which contains between twenty and thirty thousand inhabitants, the right of electing representatives to Parliament is monopolized by about thirty-one persons. And within these monopolies are still others. A man, even of the same town, whose parents were not in circumstances to give him an occupation, is

---

* The right of every man will be the same, whether he lives in a city, a town, or a village. The custom of attaching rights to *place,* or in other words, to inanimate matter, instead of to the *person,* independently of place, is too absurd to make any part of a rational argument. *Letter to the Addressers on the Late Proclamation* (1792), II, 505. [Paine's emphasis]

debarred, in many cases, from the natural right of acquiring one, be his genius or industry what it may. . . .

As one of the Houses of the English Parliament is, in a great measure, made up by elections from these corporations; and as it is unnatural that a pure stream should flow from a foul fountain, its vices are but a continuation of the vices of its origin. A man of moral honor and good political principles cannot submit to the mean drudgery and disgraceful arts by which such elections are carried. To be a successful candidate, he must be destitute of the qualities that constitute a just legislator: and being thus disciplined to corruption by the mode of entering into Parliament, it is not to be expected that the representative should be better than the man.

Mr. Burke, in speaking of the English representation, has advanced as bold a challenge as ever was given in the days of chivalry. "Our representation," says he, "has been found *perfectly adequate to all the purposes* for which a representation of the people can be desired or devised. I defy," continues he, "the enemies of our Constitution to show the contrary." [28] This declaration from a man who has been in constant opposition to all the measures of Parliament the whole of his political life, a year or two excepted,[29] is most extraordinary, and, comparing him with himself, admits of no other alternative, than that he acted against his judgment as a member, or has declared contrary to it as an author.

But it is not in the representation only that the defects lie, and therefore I proceed in the next place to aristocracy.

What is called the House of Peers is constituted on a ground very similar to that against which there is a law in other cases. It amounts to a combination of persons in one common interest. No reason can be given why a house of legislation should be composed entirely of men whose occupation consists in letting landed property, than why it should be composed of those who hire, or of brewers, or bakers, or any other separate class of men.

Mr. Burke calls this House *"the great ground and pillar of security to the landed interest."* Let us examine this idea.

What pillar of security does the landed interest require, more than any other interest in the state, or what right has it to a distinct and separate representation from the general interest of a nation? The only use to be made of this power, (and which it has always made), is to ward off taxes from itself, and throw the burden upon such articles of consumption by which itself would be least affected. That this has been the consequence (and will always be the consequence of constructing governments on combinations), is evident, with respect to England, from the history of its taxes.

Notwithstanding taxes have increased and multiplied upon every article of common consumption, the land-tax, which more particularly affects this "pillar," has diminished. In 1788, the amount of the land-tax was £1,950,000 which is half a million less than it produced almost a hundred years ago, notwithstanding the rentals are in many instances doubled since that period.

Before the coming of the Hanoverians, the taxes were divided in nearly equal proportions between the land and articles of consumption, the land bearing rather the largest share; but since that era, nearly thirteen millions annually of new taxes have been thrown upon consumption. The consequence of which has been a constant increase in the number and wretchedness of the poor, and in the amount of the poor-rates.[29a]

Yet here again the burden does not fall in equal proportions on the aristocracy with the rest of the community. Their residences, whether in town or country, are not mixed with the habitations of the poor. They live apart from distress, and the expense of relieving it. It is in the manufacturing towns and laboring villages that those burdens press the heaviest; in many of which it is one class of poor supporting another.

Several of the most heavy and productive taxes are so contrived as to give an exemption of this pillar, thus standing in its own defense. The tax upon beer brewed for sale does not affect the aristocracy, who brew their own beer free of this duty. It falls only on those who have not conveniency or ability to brew, and who must purchase it in small quantities.

But what will mankind think of the justice of taxation, when they know, that this tax alone, from which the aristocracy are from circumstances exempt, is nearly equal to the whole of the land-tax, being in the year 1788, (and it is not less now), £1,666,152, and with its proportion of the taxes on malt and hops, it exceeds it. That a single article thus partially consumed, and that chiefly by the working part, should be subject to a tax equal to that on the whole rental of a nation, is, perhaps, a fact not to be paralleled in the history of revenues.

This is one of the consequences resulting from a house of legislation composed on the ground of a combination of common interest; for whatever their separate politics as to parties may be, in this they are united. Whether a combination acts to raise the price of an article for sale, or the rate of wages; or whether it acts to throw taxes from itself upon another class of the community, the principle and the effect are the same; and if the one be illegal, it will be difficult to show that the other ought to exist.

It is no use to say that the taxes are first proposed in the House of Commons; for as the other House has always a negative, it can always defend itself; and it would be ridiculous to suppose that its acquiescence in the measures to be proposed were not understood beforehand. Besides which, it has obtained so much influence by borough traffic, and so many of its relations and connections are distributed on both sides of the Commons, as to give it, besides an absolute negative in the House, a preponderancy in the other, in all matters of common concern.[30]

It is difficult to discover what is meant by the *landed interest,* if it does not mean a combination of aristocratical land-holders, opposing their own pecuniary interest to that of the farmer, and every branch of trade, commerce, and manufacture. In all other respects, it is the only interest that needs no partial protection. It enjoys the general protection of the world.

Every individual, high or low, is interested in the fruits of the earth; men, women, and children, of all ages and degrees, will turn out to assist the farmer, rather than a harvest should not be got in; and they will not act thus by any other property. It is the only one for which the common prayer of mankind is put up, and the only one that can never fail from the want of means. It is the interest, not of the policy, but of the existence of man, and when it ceases, he must cease to be.

No other interest in a nation stands on the same united support. Commerce, manufactures, arts, sciences and everything else, compared with this, are supported but in parts. Their prosperity or their decay has not the same universal influence. When the valleys laugh and sing, it is not the farmer only, but all creation that rejoices. It is a prosperity that excludes all envy; and this cannot be said of anything else.

Why then does Mr. Burke talk of this House of Peers, as the pillar of the landed interest? Were that pillar to sink into the earth, the same landed property would continue, and the same plowing, sowing and reaping would go on. The aristocracy are not the farmers who work the land, and raise the produce, but are the mere consumers of the rent; and when compared with the active world, are the drones, a seraglio of males, who neither collect the honey nor form the hive, but exist only for lazy enjoyment.

Mr. Burke, in his first essay, called aristocracy *"the Corinthian capital of polished society."* Toward completing the figure, he has now added the *pillar,* but still the base is wanting; and whenever a nation chooses to act a Samson, not blind, but bold, down goes the temple of Dagon, the Lords and the Philistines.

If a house of legislation is to be composed of men of one class, for the purpose of protecting a distinct interest, all the other interests should have the same. The inequality, as well as the burden of taxation, arises from admitting it in one case and not in all. Had there been a house of farmers, there had been no game laws; or a house of merchants and manufacturers, the taxes had neither been so unequal nor so excessive. It is from the power of taxation being in the hands of those who can throw so great a part of it from their own shoulders, that it has raged without a check.

Men of small or moderate estates are more injured by the taxes being thrown on articles of consumption, than they are eased by warding it from landed property, for the following reasons:

First, They consume more of the productive taxable articles, in proportion to their property, than those of large estates.

Secondly, Their residence is chiefly in towns, and their property in houses; and the increase of the poor-rates, occasioned by taxes on consumption, is in much greater proportion than the land-tax has been favored. In Birmingham, the poor-rates are not less than seven shillings in the pound. From this, as is already observed, the aristocracy are in a great measure exempt.

These are but a part of the mischiefs flowing from the wretched scheme of an house of peers.

As a combination, it can always throw a considerable portion of taxes from itself; and as an hereditary house, accountable to nobody, it resembles a rotten borough,[31] whose consent is to be courted by interest. There are but few of its members who are not in some mode or other participators, or disposers of the public money. One turns a candle-holder, or a lord in waiting; another a lord of the bed-chamber, a groom of the stole,[32] or any insignificant nominal office, to which a salary is annexed, paid out of the public taxes, and which avoids·the direct appearance of corruption. Such situations are derogatory to the character of man; and where they can be submitted to, honor cannot reside.

To all these are to be added the numerous dependents, the long list of the younger branches and distant relations, who are to be provided for at the public expense: in short, were an estimation to be made of the charge of the aristocracy to a nation, it will be found nearly equal to that of supporting the poor. The Duke of Richmond alone (and there are cases similar to his) takes away as much for himself as would maintain two thousand poor and aged persons. Is it, then, any wonder that under such a system of government, taxes and rates have multiplied to their present extent?

In stating these matters, I speak an open and disinterested language, dictated by no passion but that of humanity. To me, who have not only refused offers, because I thought them improper, but have declined rewards I might with reputation have accepted, it is no wonder that meanness and imposition appear disgusting. Independence is my happiness, and I view things as they are, without regard to place or person; my country is the world, and my religion is to do good. . . .

But to return to the matters of the Constitution—

The French Constitution says *there shall be no titles;* and of consequence, all that class of equivocal generation, which in some countries is called *"aristocracy,"* and in others *"nobility,"* is done away, and the *peer* is exalted into *man.*

Titles are but nicknames, and every nickname is a title. The thing is perfectly harmless in itself, but it marks a sort of foppery in the human character which degrades it. It renders man diminutive in things which are great, and the counterfeit of woman in things which are little. It talks about its fine blue *riband* like a girl, and shows its new *garter* like a child.[33] A certain writer, of some antiquity, says, "When I was a child, I thought as a child: but when I became a man, I put away childish things." [34]

It is, properly, from the elevated mind of France, that the folly of titles has been abolished. It has outgrown the baby-clothes of *count* and *duke,* and breeched itself in manhood. France has not levelled, it has exalted. It has put down the dwarf to set up the man. The insignificance of a senseless word like *duke, count,* or *earl,* has ceased to please. Even those who possessed them have disowned the gibberish, and, as they outgrew the rickets, have despised the rattle.

The genuine mind of man, thirsting for its native home, society, contemns the gewgaws that separate him from it. Titles are like circles drawn by the magician's wand, to contract to the sphere of man's felicity. He lives immured within the Bastille of a word, and surveys at a distance the envied life of man.

Is it then any wonder that titles should fall in France? Is it not a greater wonder they should be kept up anywhere? What are they? What is their worth, and "what is their amount?" When we think or speak of a *judge* or a *general,* we associate with it the ideas of office and character; we think of gravity in the one, and bravery in the other; but when we use a word merely as a title, no ideas associate with it.

Through all the vocabulary of Adam, there is no such an animal as a duke or a count; neither can we connect any idea to the words. Whether they mean strength or weakness, wisdom or folly, a child or a man, or a rider or a horse, is all equivocal. What respect then can be paid to that which describes nothing, and which means nothing? Imagination has given figure and character to centaurs, satyrs, and down to all the fairy tribe; but titles baffle even the powers of fancy, and are a chimerical nondescript.

But this is not all. If a whole country is disposed to hold them in contempt, all their value is gone, and none will own them. It is common opinion only that makes them any thing or nothing, or worse than nothing. There is no occasion to take titles away, for they take themselves away when society concurs to ridicule them. This species of imaginary consequence has visibly declined in every part of Europe, and it hastens to its exit as the world of reason continues to rise.*

There was a time when the lowest class of what are called nobility was more thought of than the highest is now, and when a man in armor riding through Christendom in search of adventure was more stared at than a modern duke. The world has seen this folly fall, and it has fallen by being laughed at, and the farce of titles will follow its fate.

The patriots of France have discovered in good time that rank and dignity in society must take a new ground. The old one has fallen through. It must now take the substantial ground of character, instead of the chimerical ground of titles; and they have brought their titles to the altar, and made of them a burnt offering to Reason.

If no mischief had annexed itself to the folly of titles, they

* The more aristocracy appeared, the more it was despised; there was a visible imbecility and want of intellect in the majority, a sort of *je ne sais quoi,* that while it affected to be more than citizen, was less than man. It lost ground from contempt more than from hatred; and was rather jeered at as an ass, than dreaded as a lion. This is the general character of aristocracy, or what are called nobles or nobility, or rather no-ability, in all countries. *The Rights of Man,* Part I (1791), I, 310.

would not have been worth a serious and formal destruction, such as the National Assembly have decreed them: and this makes it necessary to inquire further into the nature and character of aristocracy.

That, then, which is called aristocracy in some countries, and nobility in others, arose out of the governments founded upon conquest. It was originally a military order, for the purpose of supporting military government (for such were all governments founded in conquest); and to keep up a succession of this order for the purpose for which it was established, all the younger branches of those families were disinherited, and the law of *primogenitureship*[35] set up.

The nature and character of aristocracy shows itself to us in this law. It is a law against every law of nature, and nature herself calls for its destruction. Establish family justice, and aristocracy falls. By the aristocratical law of primogenitureship, in a family of six children, five are exposed. Aristocracy has never more than *one* child. The rest are begotten to be devoured. They are thrown to the cannibal for prey, and the natural parent prepares the unnatural repast.

As every thing which is out of nature in man, affects, more or less, the interest of society, so does this. All the children which the aristocracy disowns (which are all, except the eldest) are, in general, cast like orphans on a parish, to be provided for by the public, but at a greater charge. Unnecessary offices and places in governments and courts are created at the expense of the public, to maintain them.

With what kind of parental reflections can the father or mother contemplate their younger offspring? By nature they are children, and by marriage they are heirs; but by aristocracy they are bastards and orphans. They are the flesh and blood of their parents in one line, and nothing akin to them in the other. To restore, therefore, parents to their children, and children to their parents—relations to each other, and man to society—and to exterminate the monster, aristocracy, root and branch—the French Constitution has destroyed the law of *Primogenitureship*. Here then lies the monster; and Mr. Burke, if he pleases, may write its epitaph.

Hitherto we have considered aristocracy chiefly in one point of view. We have now to consider it in another. But whether we view it before or behind, or sideways, or any way else, domestically or publicly, it is still a monster.

In France, aristocracy has one feature less, in its countenance, than what it has in some other countries. It did not compose a body of hereditary legislators. It was not *"a corporation of aristocracy,"* for such I have heard M. de Lafayette describe an English House of Peers. Let us then examine the grounds upon which the French Constitution has resolved against having such a House in France.

Because, in the first place, as is already mentioned, aristocracy is kept up by family tyranny and injustice.

Secondly, Because there is an unusual unfitness in an aristocracy to be legislators for a nation. Their ideas of *distributive justice*[36] are corrupted at the very source. They begin life by trampling on all their younger brothers and sisters, and relations of every kind, and are taught and educated so to do. With what ideas of justice or honor can that man enter a house of legislation, who absorbs in his own person the inheritance of a whole family of children, or doles out to them some pitiful portion with the insolence of a gift?

Thirdly, Because the idea of hereditary legislators is as inconsistent as that of hereditary judges, or hereditary juries; and as absurd as an hereditary mathematician, or an hereditary wise man; and as ridiculous as an hereditary poet-laureate.

Fourthly, Because a body of men holding themselves accountable to nobody ought not to be trusted by any body.

Fifthly, Because it is continuing the uncivilized principles of the governments founded in conquest, and the base idea of man having property in man, and governing him by personal right.

Sixthly, Because aristocracy has a tendency to degenerate the human species. By the universal economy of nature it is known, and by the instance of the Jews it is proved, that the human species has a tendency to degenerate, in any small number of persons, when separated from the general stock of society, and intermarrying constantly with each other.

It defeats even its pretended end, and becomes in time the opposite of what is noble in man. Mr. Burke talks of nobility; let him show what it is. The greatest characters the world has known, have arisen on the democratic floor. Aristocracy has not been able to keep a proportionate pace with democracy.

The artificial NOBLE shrinks into a dwarf before the NOBLE of Nature; and in the few instances of those (for there are some in all countries) in whom nature, as by a miracle, has survived in aristocracy, THOSE MEN DESPISE IT. But it is time to proceed to a new subject.

THE REVOLUTION IN FRANCE

As Mr. Burke has not written on constitutions, so neither has he written on the French Revolution. He gives no account of its commencement or its progress.

He only expresses his wonder. "It looks," says he, "to me as if I were in a great crisis, not of the affairs of France alone, but of all Europe, perhaps of more than Europe. All circumstances taken together, the French Revolution is the most astonishing that has hitherto happened in the world."

As wise men are astonished at foolish things, and other people at wise ones, I know not on which ground to account for Mr. Burke's astonishment; but certain it is that he does not understand the French Revolution. It has apparently burst forth like a creation from a chaos, but it is no more than the consequence of a mental revolution previously existing in France.

The mind of the nation had changed beforehand, and the new order of things had naturally followed the new order of thoughts. I will here, as concisely as I can, trace out the growth of the French Revolution, and mark the circumstances that have contributed to produce it.

The despotism of Louis XIV, united with the gaiety of his court, and the gaudy ostentation of his character, had so humbled, and at the same time so fascinated the mind of France, that the people appear to have lost all sense of their own dignity, in contemplating that of their Grand Monarch: and the whole reign of Louis XV, remarkable only for weakness and effeminacy, made no other alteration than that of spreading a sort of lethargy over the nation, from which it showed no disposition to rise.

The only signs which appeared of the spirit of liberty during those periods are to be found in the writings of the French philosophers. Montesquieu,[37] President of the Parliament of Bordeaux, went as far as a writer under a despotic government could well proceed: and being obliged to divide himself between principle and prudence, his mind often appears under a veil, and we ought to give him credit for more than he has expressed.

Voltaire, who was both the flatterer and satirist of despotism, took another line. His forte lay in exposing and ridiculing the superstitions which priestcraft, united with statecraft, had interwoven with governments.

It was not from the purity of his principles, or his love of mankind (for satire and philanthropy are not naturally concordant), but from his strong capacity of seeing folly in its true shape, and his irresistible propensity to expose it, that he made those attacks. They were however as formidable as if the motives had been virtuous; and he merits the thanks rather than the esteem of mankind.

On the contrary, we find in the writings of Rousseau and the Abbé Raynal,[38] a loveliness of sentiment in favor of liberty, that excites respect, and elevates the human faculties; but having raised his animation, they do not direct its operations, but leave the mind in love with an object, without describing the means of possessing it.

The writings of Quesnay, Turgot, and the friends of these authors,[39] are of a serious kind; but they labored under the same disadvantage with Montesquieu; their writings abound with moral maxims of government, but are rather directed to economize and reform the administration of the government, than the government itself.

But all those writings and many others had their weight; and by the different manner in which they treated the subject of government—Montesquieu by his judgment and knowledge of laws, Voltaire by his wit, Rousseau and Raynal by their animation, and Quesnay and Turgot by their moral maxims and systems of economy, readers of every class met with something to their taste, and a spirit of political inquiry began to diffuse itself through the nation at the time the dispute between England and the then colonies of America broke out.

In the war which France afterwards engaged in, it is very well known that the nation appeared to be beforehand with the French Ministry. Each of them had its view: but those views were directed to different objects; the one sought liberty, and the other retaliation on England. The French officers and soldiers who after this went to America were eventually placed in the school of Freedom, and learned the practice as well as the principles of it by heart.

As it was impossible to separate the military events which took place in America from the principles of the American Revolution, the publication of these events in France necessarily connected themselves with the principles which produced them. Many of the facts were in themselves principles; such as the declaration of American independence, and the treaty of alliance between France and America, which recognized the natural rights of man, and justified resistance to oppression.

The then Minister of France, Count Vergennes,[40] was not the friend of America; and it is both justice and gratitude to say that it was the Queen of France who gave the cause of America a fashion at the French Court. Count Vergennes was the personal and social friend of Dr. Franklin;[41] and the Doctor had obtained, by his sensible gracefulness, a sort of influence over him; but with respect to principles, Count Vergennes was a despot.

The situation of Dr. Franklin as Minister from America to France should be taken into the chain of circumstances. The diplomatic character is of itself the narrowest sphere of society that man can act in. It forbids intercourse by a reciprocity of suspicion; and a diplomatist is a sort of unconnected atom, continually repelling and repelled. But this was not the case with Dr. Franklin. He was not the diplomatist of a court, but of a MAN. His character as a philosopher had been long established, and his circle of society in France was universal.

Count Vergennes resisted for a considerable time the publication in France of the American Constitutions, translated into the French language; but even in this he was obliged to give way to public opinion, and a sort of propriety in admitting to appear what he had undertaken to defend. The American Constitutions were to liberty, what a grammar is to language: they define its parts of speech, and practically construct them into syntax. . . .

When the war closed, a vast reinforcement to the cause of liberty spread itself over France by the return of the French officers and soldiers. A knowledge of the practice was then joined to the theory; and all that was wanting to give it a real existence was opportunity. Man cannot, properly speaking, make circumstances for his purpose, but he always has it in his power to improve them when they occur; and this was the case in France. . . .

The peculiar situation of the then Marquis de Lafayette[42] is another link in the great chain. He served in America as an American officer under a commission of Congress, and by the universality of his acquaintance, was in close friendship with the civil government of America, as well as with the military line. He spoke the language of the country, entered into the discussions on the principles of government, and was always a welcome friend at any election. . . .

While I am writing this, there are accidentally before me some proposals for a Declaration of Rights by the Marquis de Lafayette (I ask his pardon for using his former address, and do it only for distinction's sake) to the National Assembly, on the 11th of July, 1789, three days before the taking of the Bastille, and I cannot but be struck by observing how opposite the sources are from which that gentleman and Mr. Burke draw their principles.

Instead of referring to musty records and moldy parchments to prove that the rights of the living are lost, "renounced and abdicated for ever," by those who are now no more, as Mr. Burke has done, M. de Lafayette applies to the living world, and emphatically says: —"Call to mind the sentiments which nature has engraved in the heart of every citizen, and which take a new force when they are solemnly recognized by all: For a nation to love liberty, it is sufficient that she knows it; and to be free, it is sufficient that she wills it."

How dry, barren and obscure is the source from which Mr. Burke labors! and how ineffectual, though gay with flowers, are all his declamation and his argument, compared with these clear, concise, and soul-animating sentiments! Few and short as they are, they lead on to a vast field of generous and manly thinking, and do not finish, like Mr. Burke's periods, with music in the ear, and nothing in the heart.

As I have introduced M. de Lafayette, I will take the liberty of adding an anecdote respecting his farewell address to the Congress of America in 1783, and which occurred fresh to my mind, when I saw Mr. Burke's thundering attack on the French Revolution.

M. de Lafayette went to America at an early period of the war, and continued a volunteer in her service to the end. His conduct through the whole of that enterprise is one of the most extraordinary that is to be found in the history of a young man, scarcely twenty years of age.

Situated in a country that was like the lap of sensual pleasure, and with the means of enjoying it, how few are there to be found who would exchange such a scene for the woods and wilderness of America, and pass the flowery years of youth in unprofitable danger and hardship; but such is the fact.

When the war ended, and he was on the point of taking his final departure, he presented himself to Congress, and contemplating, in his affectionate farewell, the Revolution he had seen, expressed himself in these words: *"May this great monument, raised to Liberty, serve as a lesson to the oppressor, and an example to the oppressed!"*

When this address came to the hands of Dr. Franklin, who was then in France, he applied to Count Vergennes, to have it inserted in the French *Gazette,* but never could obtain his consent. The fact was, that Count Vergennes was an aristocratical despot at home, and dreaded the example of the American Revolution in France, as certain other persons now dread the example of the French Revolution in England; and Mr. Burke's tribute of fear, (for in this light his book must be considered) runs parallel with Count Vergennes' refusal. But, to return more particularly to his work—

"We have seen," says Mr. Burke, "the French rebel against a mild and lawful monarch, with more fury, outrage, and insult, than any people has been known to rise against the most illegal usurper, or the most sanguinary tyrant." This is one among a thousand other instances in which Mr. Burke shows that he is ignorant of the springs and principles of the French Revolution.

It was not against Louis XVI, but against the despotic principles of the government, that the nation revolted. These principles had not their origin in him, but in the original establishment many centuries back; and they were become too deeply rooted to be removed, and the Augean stable of parasites and plunderers too abominably filthy to be cleansed,[43] by anything short of a complete and universal revolution.

When it becomes necessary to do a thing, the whole heart and soul should go into the measure, or not attempt it. That crisis was then arrived, and there remained no choice but to act with determined vigor, or not to act at all.

The King was known to be the friend of the nation, and this circumstance was favorable to the enterprise. Perhaps no man bred up in the style of an absolute king ever possessed a heart so little disposed to the exercise of that species of power as the present King of France.

But the principles of the government itself still remained the same. The monarch and the monarchy were distinct and separate things; and it was against the established despotism of the latter, and not against the person or principles of the former, that the revolt commenced, and the Revolution has been carried.

Mr. Burke does not attend to the distinction between *men* and *principles;* and therefore, he does not see that a revolt may take place against the despotism of the latter, while there lies no charge of despotism against the former.

The natural moderation of Louis XVI contributed nothing to alter the hereditary despotism of the monarchy. All the tyrannies of the former reigns, acted under that hereditary despotism, were still liable to be revived in the hands of a successor. It was not the respite of a reign that would satisfy France, enlightened as she was then become.

A casual discontinuance of the *practice* of despotism is not a discontinuance of its *principles;* the former depends on the virtue of the individual who is in immediate possession of power; the latter, on the virtue and fortitude of the nation. In the case of Charles I and James II of England, the revolt was against the personal despotism of the men; whereas in France, it was against the hereditary despotism of the established government. But men who can consign over the rights of posterity forever on the authority of a moldy parchment, like Mr. Burke, are not qualified to judge of this Revolution. It takes in a field too vast for their views to explore, and proceeds with a mightiness of reason they cannot keep pace with.

But there are many points of view in which this Revolution may be considered. When despotism has established itself for ages in a country, as in France, it is not in the person of the king only that it resides. It has the appearance of being so in show, and in nominal authority; but it is not so in practice, and in fact. It has its standard everywhere.

Every office and department has its despotism, founded upon custom and usage. Every place has its Bastille, and every Bastille its despot. The original hereditary despotism, resident in the person of the king, divides and subdivides itself into a thousand shapes and forms, till at last the whole of it is acted by deputation.

This was the case in France; and against this species of despotism, proceeding on through an endless labyrinth of office till the source of it is scarcely perceptible, there is no mode of redress. It strengthens itself by assuming the appearance of duty, and tyrannizes under the pretense of obeying.

When a man reflects on the condition which France was in from the nature of her government, he will see other causes for revolt than those which immediately connect themselves with the person or character of Louis XVI. There were, if I may so express it, a thousand despotisms to be reformed in France, which had grown up under the hereditary despotism of the monarchy, and became so rooted as to be in a great measure independent of it. Between the monarchy, the parliament, and the church, there was a *rivalship* of despotism; besides the feudal despotism operating locally, and the ministerial despotism operating everywhere.

But Mr. Burke, by considering the King as the only possible object of a revolt, speaks as if France was a village in which every thing that passed must be known to its commanding officer, and no oppression could be acted but what he could conveniently control. Mr. Burke might have been in the Bastille his whole life, as well under Louis XVI and neither the one nor the other have known that such a man as Mr. Burke existed. The despotic principles of the government were the same in both reigns, though the dispositions of the men were as remote as tyranny and benevolence.

What Mr. Burke considers as a reproach to the French Revolution (that of bringing it forward under a reign more mild than the preceding ones), is one of its highest honors. The revolutions that have taken place in other European countries have been excited by personal hatred. The rage was against the man, and he became the victim. But, in the instance of France, we see a revolution generated in the rational contemplation of the rights of man, and distinguishing from the beginning between persons and principles.

But Mr. Burke appears to have no idea of principles, when he is contemplating governments. "Ten years ago," says he, "I could have felicitated France on her having a government, without inquiring what the nature of that government was, or how it was administered." [44]

Is this the language of a rational man? Is it the language of a heart feeling as it ought to feel for the rights and happiness of the human race? On this ground, Mr. Burke must compliment every government in the world, while the victims who suffer under them, whether sold into slavery, or tortured out of existence, are wholly forgotten.

It is power, and not principles, that Mr. Burke venerates; and under this abominable depravity, he is disqualified to judge between them. Thus much for his opinion as to the occasion of the French Revolution. I now proceed to other considerations.

I know a point in America called Point-no-Point; because as you proceed along the shore, gay and flowery as Mr. Burke's language, it continually recedes and presents itself at a distance before you; but when you have got as far as you can go, there is no point at all. Just thus it is with Mr. Burke's three hundred and fifty-six pages. It is therefore difficult to reply to him. But as the points he wishes to establish may be inferred from what he abuses, it is in his paradoxes that we must look for his arguments.

As to the tragic paintings by which Mr. Burke has outraged his own imagination, and seeks to work upon that of his readers, they are very well calculated for theatrical representation, where facts are manufactured for the sake of show, and accommodated to produce, through the weakness of sympathy, a weeping effect. But Mr. Burke should recollect that he is writing history, and not *plays;* and that his readers will expect truth, and not the spouting rant of high-toned declamation.

When we see a man dramatically lamenting in a publication

intended to be believed, that, *"The age of chivalry is gone!* that *The glory of Europe is extinguished forever!* that *The unbought grace of life* (if any one knows what it is), *the cheap defense of nations, the nurse of manly sentiment and heroic enterprise, is gone!"* and all this because the Quixotic age of chivalric nonsense is gone, what opinion can we form of his judgment, or what regard can we pay to his facts?

In the rhapsody of his imagination, he has discovered a world of wind-mills, and his sorrows are that there are no Quixotes to attack them. But if the age of aristocracy, like that of chivalry, should fall, and they had originally some connection, Mr. Burke, the trumpeter of the order, may continue his parody to the end, and finish with exclaiming, *"Othello's occupation's gone!"* [45]

Notwithstanding Mr. Burke's horrid paintings, when the French Revolution is compared with that of other countries, the astonishment will be that it is marked with so few sacrifices,[46] but this astonishment will cease when we reflect that *principles* and not *persons*, were the meditated objects of destruction. The mind of the nation was acted upon by a higher stimulus than what the consideration of persons could inspire, and sought a higher conquest than could be produced by the downfall of an enemy.

Among the few who fell, there do not appear to be any that were intentionally singled out. They all of them had their fate in the circumstances of the moment, and were not pursued with that long, cold-blooded, unabated revenge which pursued the unfortunate Scotch, in the affair of 1745.[47]

Through the whole of Mr. Burke's book I do not observe that the Bastille is mentioned more than once. . . . From his violence and his grief, his silence on some points, and his excess on others, it is difficult not to believe that Mr. Burke is sorry, extremely sorry, that arbitrary power, the power of the Pope, and the Bastille, are pulled down.

Not one glance of compassion, not one commiserating reflection, that I can find throughout his book, has he bestowed on those who lingered out the most wretched of lives, a life without hope, in the most miserable of prisons.

It is painful to behold a man employing his talents to corrupt himself. Nature has been kinder to Mr. Burke than he is to her. He is not affected by the reality of distress touching his heart, but by the showy resemblage of it striking his imagination. He pities the plumage, but forgets the dying bird.

Accustomed to kiss the aristocratical hand that has purloined him from himself, he degenerates into a composition of art, and the genuine soul of nature forsakes him. His hero or his heroine must be a tragedy-victim expiring in show, and not the real prisoner of mystery, sinking into death in the silence of a dungeon.

As Mr. Burke has passed over the whole transaction of the Bastille (and his silence is nothing in its favor), and has entertained his readers with reflections on supposed facts distorted into real falsehoods, I will give, since he has not, some account of the circumstances which preceded that transaction. They will serve to show that less mischief could scarcely have accompanied such an event, when considered with the treacherous and hostile aggravations of the enemies of the Revolution.

The mind can hardly picture to itself a more tremendous scene than which the city of Paris exhibited at the time of taking the Bastille, and for two days before and after, nor conceive the possibility of its quieting so soon. At a distance, this transaction has appeared only as an act of heroism, standing on itself; and the close political connection it had with the Revolution is lost in the brilliancy of the achievement.

But we are to consider it as the strength of the parties, brought man to man, and contending for the issue. The Bastille was to be either the prize or the prison of the assailants. The downfall of it included the idea of the downfall to despotism; and this compounded image was become as figuratively united as Bunyan's Doubting Castle and Giant Despair.[48]

The National Assembly, before and at the time of taking the Bastille, were sitting at Versailles, twelve miles distant from Paris. About a week before the rising of the Parisians and their taking the Bastille, it was discovered that a plot was forming, at the head of which was the Count d'Artois,[49] the King's youngest brother, for demolishing the National Assembly, seizing its members, and thereby crushing, by a *coup de main,* all hopes and prospects of forming a free government. For the sake of humanity, as well as of freedom, it is well this plan did not succeed. Examples are not wanting to show how dreadfully vindictive and cruel are all old governments, when they are successful against what they call a revolt. . . .

Mr. Burke has spoken a great deal about plots, but he has never once spoken of this plot against the National Assembly, and the liberties of the nation; and that he might not, he has passed over all the circumstances that might throw it in his way.

The exiles who have fled from France,[50] whose cause he so

much interests himself in, and from whom he has had his lesson, fled in consequence of a miscarriage of this plot. No plot was formed against them: they were plotting against others; and those who fell, met, not unjustly, the punishment they were preparing to execute.

But will Mr. Burke say that if this plot, contrived with the subtility of an ambuscade, had succeeded, the successful party would have restrained their wrath so soon? Let the history of all old governments answer the question.

Whom has the National Assembly brought to the scaffold? None. They were themselves the devoted victims of this plot, and they have not retaliated; why then are they charged with revenge they have not acted? In the tremendous breaking forth of a whole people, in which all degrees, tempers and characters are confounded, and delivering themselves, by a miracle of exertion, from the destruction meditated against them, is it to be expected that nothing will happen?

When men are sore with the sense of oppressions, and menaced with the prospect of new ones, is the calmness of philosophy, or the palsy of insensibility to be looked for? Mr. Burke exclaims against outrage; yet the greatest is that which he has committed. His book is a volume of outrage, not apologized for by the impulse of a moment, but cherished through a space of ten months; yet Mr. Burke had no provocation, no life, no interest at stake.

More of the citizens fell in this struggle than of their opponents; but four or five persons were seized by the populace, and instantly put to death: the Governor of the Bastille, and the Mayor of Paris, who was detected in the act of betraying them; and afterwards Foulon, one of the new Ministry, and Berthier, his son-in-law, who had accepted the office of Intendant of Paris. Their heads were stuck upon spikes, and carried about the city; and it is upon this mode of punishment that Mr. Burke builds a great part of his tragic scenes. Let us therefore examine how men came by the idea of punishing in this manner.

They learn it from the governments they live under; and retaliate the punishments they have been accustomed to behold. The head stuck upon spikes, which remained for years upon Temple Bar,[51] differed nothing in the horror of the scene from those carried about on spikes at Paris; yet this was done by the English Government.

It may perhaps be said that it signifies nothing to a man what is done to him after he is dead; but it signifies much to the living.

It either tortures their feelings, or it hardens their hearts; and in either case, it instructs them how to punish when power falls into their hands.

Lay then the axe to the root, and teach governments humanity. It is their sanguinary punishments which corrupt mankind. In England, the punishment in certain cases, is by *hanging, drawing* and *quartering;* the heart of the sufferer is cut out and held up to the view of the populace.

In France, under the former government, the punishments were not less barbarous. Who does not remember the execution of Damien,[52] torn to pieces by horses? The effect of those cruel spectacles exhibited to the populace is to destroy tenderness or excite revenge, and by the base and false idea of governing men by terror, instead of reason, they become precedents.

It is over the lowest class of mankind that government by terror is intended to operate, and it is on them that it operates to the worst effect. They have sense enough to feel they are the objects aimed at; and they inflict in their turn the examples of terror they have been instructed to practise.

There is in all European countries, a large class of people of that description which in England is called the *"mob."* * Of this class were those who committed the burning and devastations in London in 1780,[53] and of this class were those who carried the heads upon the spikes in Paris. . . .

Why then does Mr. Burke charge outrages of this kind on a whole people? As well may he charge the riots and outrages of 1780 on all the people of London, or those in Ireland on all his countrymen.

But everything we see or hear offensive to our feelings and derogatory to the human character should lead to other reflections than those of reproach. Even the beings who commit them have some claim to our consideration. How then is it that such vast classes of mankind as are distinguished by the appellation of the vulgar, or the ignorant, mob, are so numerous in all old countries? †

---

* I never did, nor never would encourage what may properly be called a mob, when any legal mode of redress can be had, but there are evils which civil government cannot reach, and which the dread of public resentment only can lessen or prevent. *A Serious Address to the People of Pennsylvania* (1778), II, 289.

† Nothing tends to a greater corruption of manners and principles than a

The instant we ask ourselves this question, reflection finds an answer. They arise, as an unavoidable consequence, out of the ill construction of all old governments in Europe, England included with the rest. It is by distortedly exalting some men, that others are distortedly debased, till the whole is out of nature.

A vast mass of mankind are degradedly thrown into the background of the human picture, to bring forward, with greater glare, the puppet-show of state and aristocracy. In the commencement of a revolution, those men are rather the followers of the *camp* than of the *standard* of liberty, and have yet to be instructed how to reverence it.

I give Mr. Burke all his theatrical exaggerations for facts, and I then ask him, if they do not establish the certainty of what I here lay down? Admitting them to be true, they show the necessity of the French Revolution, as much as any one thing he could have asserted.

These outrages are not the effect of the principles of the Revolution, but of the degraded mind that existed before the Revolution, and which the Revolution is calculated to reform. Place them then to their proper cause, and take the reproach of them to your own side.

It is to the honor of the National Assembly, and the city of Paris, that during such a tremendous scene of arms and confusion, beyond the control of all authority, that they have been able, by the influence of example and exhortation, to restrain so much. Never were more pains taken to instruct and enlighten mankind, and to make them see that their interest consisted in their virtue, and not in their revenge, than what have been displayed in the Revolution of France. . . .

The conspiracy being thus dispersed, one of the first works of the National Assembly, instead of vindictive proclamations, as has been the case with other governments, published a Declaration of the Rights of Man, as the basis on which the new Constitution was to be built, and which is here subjoined.

---

too great distress of circumstances. . . . Poverty, in defiance of principle, begets a degree of meanness that will stoop to almost anything. *The Case of the Officers of Excise* (1772), II, 8, 11.

DECLARATION OF THE RIGHTS
OF MAN AND OF CITIZENS

BY THE NATIONAL ASSEMBLY OF FRANCE

The representatives of the people of FRANCE, *formed into a* NA-
TIONAL ASSEMBLY, considering that ignorance, neglect, or contempt
of human rights, are the sole causes of public misfortunes and corruptions of government, have resolved to set forth in a solemn
declaration, these natural, imprescriptible, and unalienable rights:
that this declaration, being constantly present to the minds of the
members of the body social, they may be ever kept attentive to their
rights and their duties: that the acts of the legislative and executive
powers of government, being capable of being every moment compared with the end of political institutions, may be more respected:
and also, that the future claims of the citizens, being directed by
simple and incontestable principles, may always tend to the maintenance of the Constitution, and the general happiness.

"For these reasons the NATIONAL ASSEMBLY doth recognize and
declare, in the presence of the Supreme Being, and with the hope of
His blessing in favor, the following *sacred* rights of men and of
citizens:

"I. *Men are born, and always continue, free, and equal in
respect of their rights. Civil distinctions, therefore, can be founded
only on public utility.*

"II. *The end of all political associations is the preservation of
the natural and imprescriptible rights of man; and these rights are
liberty, property, security, and resistance of oppression.*

"III. *The nation is essentially the source of all sovereignty;
nor can any* INDIVIDUAL, *or* ANY BODY OF MEN, *be entitled to any
authority which is not expressly derived from it.*

"IV. Political liberty consists in the power of doing whatever
does not injure another. The exercise of the natural rights of every
man has no other limits than those which are necessary to secure
to every *other* man the free exercise of the same rights; and these
limits are determinable only by the law.

"V. The law ought to prohibit only actions hurtful to society.
What is not prohibited by the law, should not be hindered; nor
should any one be compelled to that which the law does not require.

"VI. The law is an expression of the will of the community.
All citizens have a right to concur, either personally, or by their
representatives, in its formation. It should be the same to all, whether

it protects or punishes; and *all being equal in its sight, are equally eligible to all honors, places, and employments, according to their different abilities, without any other distinction than that created by their virtues and talents.*

"VII. No man should be accused, arrested, or held in confinement, except in cases determined by the law, and according to the forms which it has prescribed. All who promote, solicit, execute, or cause to be executed, arbitrary orders, ought to be punished; and every citizen called upon or apprehended by virtue of the law, ought immediately to obey, and renders himself culpable by resistance.

"VIII. The law ought to impose no other penalties but such as are absolutely and evidently necessary: and no one ought to be punished, but in virtue of a law promulgated before the offense, and legally applied.

"IX. Every man being presumed innocent till he has been convicted,[54] whenever his detention becomes indispensable, all rigor to him, more than is necessary to secure his person, ought to be provided against by the law.

"X. No man ought to be molested on account of his opinions, not even on account of his *religious* opinions, provided his avowal of them does not disturb the public order established by the law.

"XI. The unrestrained communication of thoughts and opinions being one of the most precious rights of man, every citizen may speak, write, and publish freely, provided he is responsible for the abuse of this liberty in cases determined by the law.

"XII. A public force being necessary to give security to the rights of men and of citizens, that force is instituted for the benefit of the community, and not for the particular benefit of the persons with whom it is intrusted.

"XIII. A common contribution being necessary for the support of the public force, and for defraying the other expenses of government, it ought to be divided equally among the members of the community, according to their abilities.

"XIV. Every citizen has a right, either by himself or his representative, to a free voice in determining the necessity of public contributions, the appropriation of them, and their amount, mode of assessment, and duration.

"XV. Every community has a right to demand of all its agents, an account of their conduct.

"XVI. Every community in which a separation of powers and a security of rights is not provided for, wants a constitution.

"XVII. The rights to property being inviolable and sacred, no one ought to be deprived of it, except in cases of evident public necessity, legally ascertained, and on condition of a previous just indemnity."

The three first articles comprehend in general terms the whole of a Declaration of Rights: All the succeeding articles either originate from them, or follow as elucidations. . . . The three first articles are the basis of liberty, as well individual as national; nor can any country be called free, whose government does not take its beginning from the principles they contain, and continue to preserve them pure; and the whole of the Declaration of Rights is of more value to the world, and will do more good, than all the laws and statutes that have yet been promulgated.

In the declaratory exordium which prefaces the Declaration of Rights, we see the solemn and majestic spectacle of a nation opening its commission, under the auspices of its Creator, to establish a Government; a scene so new, and so transcendently unequalled by any thing in the European world, that the name of a revolution is diminutive of its character, and it rises into a regeneration of man.

What are the present governments of Europe, but a scene of iniquity and oppression? What is that of England? Do not its own inhabitants say, It is a market where every man has his price, and where corruption is common traffic, at the expense of a deluded people? No wonder, then, that the French Revolution is traduced.

Had it confined itself merely to the destruction of flagrant despotism, perhaps Mr. Burke and some others had been silent. Their cry now is, "It is gone too far": that is, it has gone too far for them.* It stares corruption in the face, and the venal tribe are all alarmed. Their fear discovers itself in their outrage, and they are but publishing the groans of a wounded vice. . . .

There is a general enigma running through the whole of Mr. Burke's book. He writes in a rage against the National Assembly; but what is he enraged about? If his assertions were as true as they are groundless, and that France, by her Revolution, had annihilated her power, and become what he calls a *chasm,* it might excite the

* Those words, "temperate and moderate," are words either of political cowardice, or of cunning, or seduction. A thing, moderately good, is not so good as it ought to be. Moderation in temper is always a virtue; but moderation in principle, is a species of vice. *Letter to the Addressers of the Late Proclamation* (1792), II, 511.

grief of a Frenchman (considering himself as a national man), and provoke his rage against the National Assembly; but why should it excite the rage of Mr. Burke?

Alas! it is not the nation of France that Mr. Burke means, but the *Court;* and every court in Europe, dreading the same fate, is in mourning. He writes neither in the character of a Frenchman nor an Englishman, but in the fawning character of that creature known in all countries, and a friend to none, a *Courtier.* Whether it be the Court of Versailles, or the Court of St. James or Carlton-House,[55] or the Court in expectation, signifies not; for the caterpillar principles of all courts and courtiers are alike. They form a common policy throughout Europe, detached and separate from the interest of nations: and while they appear to quarrel, they agree to plunder. Nothing can be more terrible to a court or a courtier than the Revolution of France. That which is a blessing to nations is bitterness to them; and as their existence depends on the duplicity of a country, they tremble at the approach of principles, and dread the precedent that threatens their overflow. . . .

But from such opposition, the French Revolution, instead of suffering, receives an homage. The more it is struck, the more sparks it will emit; and the fear is, it will not be struck enough. It has nothing to dread from attacks: Truth has given it an establishment; and Time will record it with a name as lasting as his own.

Having now traced the progress of the French Revolution through most of its principal stages, from its commencement, to the taking of the Bastille, and its establishment by the Declaration of Rights, I will close the subject with the energetic apostrophe of M. de Lafayette—*May this great monument, raised to Liberty, serve as a lesson to the oppressor, and an example to the oppressed!*

MR. BURKE'S POLITICAL CHURCH

Throughout this work, various and numerous as the subjects are, which I have taken up and investigated, there is only a single paragraph upon religion, *viz. "that every religion is good that teaches man to be good."*

I have carefully avoided to enlarge upon the subject, because I am inclined to believe that what is called the present Ministry wish to see contentions about religion kept up, to prevent the nation turning its attention to subjects of government. It is as if they were to say, *"look that way, or any way but this."*

But as religion is very improperly made a political machine, and the reality of it is thereby destroyed, I will conclude this work with stating in what light religion appears to me.*

If we suppose a large family of children, who, on any particular day, or particular occasion, make it a custom to present to their parents some token of their affection and gratitude, each of them would make a different offering, and most probably in a different manner.

Some would pay their congratulations in themes of verse and prose, by some little devices, as their genius dictated, or according to what they thought would please; and, perhaps, the least of all, not able to do any of those things, would ramble into the garden, or the field, and gather what it thought the prettiest flower it could find, though, perhaps, it might be but a simple weed. The parents would be more gratified by such a variety than if the whole of them had acted on a concerted plan, and each had made exactly the same offering.

This would have the cold appearance of contrivance, or the harsh one of control. But of all unwelcome things, nothing would more afflict the parent than to know that the whole of them had afterwards gotten together by the ears, boys and girls, fighting, reviling, and abusing each other about which was the best or the worst present.

Why may we not suppose that the great Father of all is pleased with variety of devotion; and that the greatest offense we can act is that by which we seek to torment and render each other miserable?

---

* There is a single idea, which, if it strikes rightly upon the mind, either in a legal or a religious sense, will prevent any man, or any body of men, or any government, from going wrong on the subject of religion; which is, that before any human institutions of government were known in the world, there existed, if I may so express it, a compact between God and man, from the beginning of time; and that as the relation and condition which man in his *individual person* stands in toward his Maker cannot be changed, or any ways altered by any human laws or human authority, that religious devotion, which is a part of this compact, cannot so much as be made a subject of human laws; and that all laws must conform themselves to this prior existing compact, and not assume to make the compact conform to the laws, which, besides being human, are subsequent thereto. The first act of man, when he looked around and saw himself a creature which he did not make, and a world furnished for his reception, must have been devotion; and devotion must ever continue sacred to every individual man, *as it appears right to him;* and governments do mischief by interfering. [Paine]

For my own part I am fully satisfied that what I am now doing, with an endeavor to conciliate mankind, to render their condition happy, to unite nations that have hitherto been enemies, and to extirpate the horrid practice of war and break the chains of slavery and oppression, is acceptable in His sight, and being the best service I can perform I act it cheerfully. . . .

With respect to what are called denominations of religion, if every one is left to judge of his own religion, there is no such thing as a religion that is wrong; but if they are to judge of each other's religion, there is no such thing as a religion that is right; and therefore all the world is right, or all the world is wrong.

But with respect to religion itself, without regard to names, and as directing itself from the universal family of mankind to the divine object of all adoration, *it is man bringing to his Maker the fruits of his heart;* and though these fruits may differ from each other like the fruits of the earth, the grateful tribute of every one is accepted.

A bishop of Durham, or a bishop of Winchester, or the archbishop who heads the dukes, will not refuse a tithe-sheaf of wheat, because it is not a cock of hay; nor a cock of hay, because it is not a sheaf of wheat; nor a pig, because it is neither the one nor the other: but these same persons, under the figure of an established church, will not permit their Maker to receive the various tithes of man's devotion.

One of the continual choruses of Mr. Burke's book, is "church and state." He does not mean some one particular church, or some one particular state, but any church and state; and he uses the term as a general figure to hold forth the political doctrine of always uniting the church with the state in every country, and he censures the National Assembly for not having done this in France. Let us bestow a few thoughts on this subject.

All religions are in their nature mild and benign, and united with principles of morality. They could not have made proselytes at first by professing anything that was vicious, cruel, persecuting or immoral. Like every thing else, they had their beginning; and they proceeded by persuasion, exhortation, and example. How then is it that they lose their native mildness, and become morose and intolerant?

It proceeds from the connection which Mr. Burke recommends. By engendering the church with the state, a sort of mule-animal, capable only of destroying, and not of breeding up, is produced,

called, *The Church established by Law*. It is a stranger, even from
its birth to any parent mother on which it is begotten, and whom in
time it kicks out and destroys.

The Inquisition in Spain does not proceed from the religion
originally professed, but from this mule-animal, engendered between the church and the state. The burnings in Smithfield [56] proceeded from the same heterogeneous production; and it was the
regeneration of this strange animal in England afterwards, that
renewed rancor and irreligion among the inhabitants, and that
drove the people called Quakers and Dissenters to America.

Persecution is not an original feature in *any* religion; but it is
always the strongly marked feature of all law-religions, or religions
established by law. Take away the law-establishment, and every
religion reassumes its original benignity. In America, a Catholic
priest is a good citizen, a good character, and a good neighbor; an
Episcopal minister is of the same description: and this proceeds,
independently of the men, from there being no law-establishment
in America.

If also we view this matter in a temporal sense, we shall see the
ill effects it has had on the prosperity of nations. The union of
church and state has impoverished Spain. The revoking the edict
of Nantes[57] drove the silk manufacture from France into England;
and church and state are now driving the cotton manufacture from
England to America and France.

Let then Mr. Burke continue to preach his anti-political doctrine of Church and State. It will do some good. The National
Assembly will not follow his advice, but will benefit by his folly.
It was by observing the ill effects of it in England that America has
been warned against it; and it is by experiencing them in France,
that the National Assembly have abolished it, and, like America,
have established UNIVERSAL RIGHT OF CONSCIENCE, AND UNIVERSAL
RIGHT OF CITIZENSHIP. . . .

Toleration is not the *opposite* of intoleration, but is the *counterfeit* of it. Both are despotisms. The one assumes to itself the right
of withholding liberty of conscience, and the other granting it. The
one is the Pope, armed with fire and faggot, and the other is the
Pope selling or granting indulgences. The former is church and
state, and the latter is church and traffic.

But toleration may be viewed in a much stronger light. Man
worships not himself, but his Maker: and the liberty of conscience
which he claims is not for the service of himself but of his God.
In this case, therefore, we must necessarily have the associated idea

of two beings: the *mortal* who renders the worship, and the *immortal being* who is worshipped.

Toleration therefore, places itself not between man and man, nor between church and church, nor between one denomination of religion and another, but between God and man, between the being who worships and the *being* who is worshipped; and by the same act of assumed authority by which it tolerates man to pay his worship, it presumptuously and blasphemously sets up itself to tolerate the Almighty to receive it.

Were a bill brought into Parliament entitled, "An *act* to tolerate or grant liberty to the Almighty to receive the worship of a Jew or a Turk," or "to prohibit the Almighty from receiving it," all men would startle, and call it blasphemy. There would be an uproar. The presumption of toleration in religious matters would then present itself unmasked; but the presumption is not the less because the name of "Man" only appears to those laws, for the associated idea of the *worshipper* and the *worshipped* cannot be separated.

Who, then, art thou, vain dust and ashes! by whatever name thou are called, whether a king, a bishop, a church or a state, a parliament or any thing else, that obtrudest thine insignificance between the soul of man and his Maker? Mind thine own concerns. If he believes not as thou believest, it is a proof that thou believest not as he believeth, and there is no earthly power can determine between you.

WAR AND PEACE

The obscurity in which the origin of all the present old governments is buried, implies the iniquity and disgrace with which they began. The origin of the present governments of America and France will ever be remembered, because it is honorable to record it; but with respect to the rest, even flattery has consigned them to the tomb of time, without an inscription.

It could have been no difficult thing in the early and solitary ages of the world, while the chief employment of men was that of attending flocks and herds, for a banditti of ruffians to overrun a country, and lay it under contributions. Their power being thus established, the chief of the band contrived to lose the name of robber in that of monarch; and hence the origin of monarchy and kings.

The origin of the government of England, so far as relates to what is called its line of monarchy, being one of the latest, is perhaps the best recorded. The hatred which the Norman invasion and tyranny begat, must have been deeply rooted in the nation to have outlived the contrivance to obliterate it. Though not a courtier will talk of the curfew-bell, not a village in England has forgotten it.

Those bands of robbers having parcelled out the world and divided it into dominions, began, as is naturally the case, to quarrel with each other. What at first was obtained by violence was considered by others as lawful to be taken, and a second plunderer succeeded the first. They alternately invaded the dominions which each had assigned to himself, and the brutality with which they treated each other explains the original character of monarchy. It was ruffian torturing ruffian.

The conqueror considered the conquered, not as his prisoner, but as his property. He led him in triumph, rattling in chains, and doomed him, at pleasure, to slavery or death. As time obliterated the history of their beginning, their successors assumed new appearances, to cut off the entail of their disgrace, but their principles and objects remained the same. What at first was plunder, assumed the softer name of revenue; and the power originally usurped, they affected to inherit.

From such beginning of governments, what could be expected, but a continual system of war and extortion? It has established itself into a trade. The vice is not peculiar to one more than to another, but is the common principle of all. There does not exist within such government sufficient stamina whereon to ingraft reformation; and the shortest, easiest, and most effectual remedy, is to begin anew.

What scenes of horror, what perfection of iniquity, present themselves in contemplating the character, and reviewing the history of such governments! If we would delineate human nature with a baseness of heart and hypocrisy of countenance, that reflection would shudder at and humanity disown, it is kings, courts, and cabinets, that must sit for the portrait. Man, naturally as he is, with all his faults about him, is not up to the character.

Can we possibly suppose that if governments had originated in a right principle, and had not an interest in pursuing a wrong one, that the world could have been in the wretched and quarrelsome condition we have seen it? What inducement has the farmer, while following the plough, to lay aside his peaceful pursuit, and go to war with the farmer of another country? Or what inducement has the manufacturer? What is dominion to them, or to any class of men in a nation? Does it add an acre to any man's estate, or raise its value? Are not conquest and defeat each of the same price, and taxes the never failing consequence? Though this reasoning may be good to a nation, it is not so to a government. War is the faro-table of governments, and nations the dupes of the games.

If there is any thing to wonder at in this miserable scene of governments, more than might be expected, it is the progress which the peaceful arts of agriculture, manufacture and commerce have made, beneath such a long accumulating load of discouragement and oppression. It serves to show that instinct in animals does not act with stronger impulse, than the principles of society and civilization operate in man. Under all discouragements, he pursues his object, and yields to nothing but impossibilities. . . . It shows that man, were he not corrupted by governments, is naturally the friend of man, and that human nature is not of itself vicious. . . .

It is attributed to Henry IV of France, a man of an enlarged and benevolent heart, that he proposed, about the year 1610, a plan of abolishing war in Europe. The plan consisted in constituting an European Congress, or as the French authors style it, a Pacific Republic, by appointing delegates from the several nations, who were to act as a court of arbitration in any disputes that might arise between nation and nation. Had such a plan been adopted at the time it was proposed, the taxes of England and France, as two of the parties, would have been at least ten millions sterling annually to each nation less than they were at the commencement of the French Revolution.

To conceive a cause why such a plan has not been adopted (and that instead of a congress for the purpose of *preventing* war, it has been called only to *terminate* a war, after fruitless expense of several years), it will be necessary to consider the interest of governments as a distinct interest to that of nations.

Whatever is the cause of taxes to a nation becomes also the means of revenue to a government. Every war terminates with an addition of taxes, and consequently with an addition of revenue; and in any event of war, in the manner they are now commenced and concluded, the power and interest of governments are increased.

War, therefore, from its productiveness, as it easily furnishes the pretence of necessity for taxes and appointments to places and offices, becomes a principal part of the system of old governments; and to establish any mode to abolish war, however advantageous it might be to nations, would be to take from such government the

most lucrative of its branches. The frivolous matters upon which
war is made, show the disposition and avidity of governments to
uphold the system of war, and betray the motives upon which they
act.

Why are not republics plunged into war, but because the nature
of their government does not admit of an interest distinct from that
of the nation? Even Holland, though an ill-constructed republic,
and with a commerce extending over the world, existed nearly a
century without war: and the instant the form of government was
changed in France, the republican principles of peace and domestic
prosperity and economy arose with the new Government; and the
same consequences would follow the same causes in other nations.

As war is the system of government on the old construction, the
animosity which nations reciprocally entertain is nothing more than
what the policy of their governments excites, to keep up the spirit
of the system. Each government accuses the other of perfidy, intrigue,
and ambition, as a means of heating the imagination of their respective nations, and increasing them to hostilities. Man is not the enemy
of man, but through the medium of a false system of government.
Instead, therefore, of exclaiming against the ambition of kings, the
exclamation should be directed against the principle of such governments; and instead of seeking to reform the individual, the wisdom
of a nation should apply itself to reform the system.

THE POOR AND THEIR RELIEF

Having in all the preceding parts of this work endeavored to establish a system of principles as a basis on which governments ought
to be erected, I shall proceed in this to the ways and means of rendering them into practice. But in order to introduce this part of the
subject with more propriety and stronger effect, some preliminary
observations, deducible from or connected with those principles, are
necessary.

Whatever the form or constitution of government may be,
it ought to have no other object than the *general* happiness. When,
instead of this, it operates to create and increase wretchedness in
any of the parts of society, it is on a wrong system, and reformation
is necessary.

Customary language has classed the condition of man under
the two descriptions of civilized and uncivilized life. To the one it
has ascribed felicity and affluence; to the other hardship and want.
But, however our imagination may be impressed by painting and

comparison, it is nevertheless true that a great portion of mankind in what are called civilized countries are in a state of poverty and wretchedness, far below the condition of an Indian. I speak not of one country, but of all. It is so in England, it is so all over Europe.* Let us inquire into the cause.

It lies not in any natural defect in the principles of civilization, but in preventing those principles having. an universal operation; the consequence of which is a perpetual system of war and expense, that drains the country, and defeats the general felicity of which civilization is capable.

All the European governments (France now excepted) are constructed not on the principle of universal civilization, but on the reverse of it. So far as those governments relate to each other, they are in the same condition as we conceive of savage, uncivilized life; they put themselves beyond the law as well of God as of man, and are, with respect to principle and reciprocal conduct, like so many individuals in a state of nature.

The inhabitants of every country, under the civilization of laws, easily associate together, but governments being yet in an uncivilized state, and almost continually at war, they pervert the abundance which civilized life produces to carry on the uncivilized part to a greater extent.

By thus ingrafting the barbarism of government upon the internal civilization of a country, it draws from the latter, and more especially from the poor, a great portion of those earnings which should be applied to their own subsistence and comfort. Apart from all reflections of morality and philosophy it is a melancholy fact that more than one-fourth of the labor of mankind is annually consumed by this barbarous system. What has served to continue this evil is the pecuniary advantage which all the governments of Europe have found in keeping up this state of uncivilization. It affords to them pretenses for power and revenue, for which there would be neither occasion nor apology, if the circle of civilization were rendered complete.

Civil government alone, or the government of laws, is not productive of pretenses for many taxes; it operates at home, directly

* The great mass of the poor in all countries are become an hereditary race, and it is next to impossible for them to get out of that state of themselves. It ought also to be observed that this mass increases in all countries that are called civilized. More persons fall annually into it than get out of it. *Agrarian Justice* (1795–96), I, 619.

under the eye of the country, and precludes the possibility of much imposition. But when the scene is laid in the uncivilized contention of governments, the field of pretenses is enlarged, and the country, being no longer a judge, is open to every imposition which governments please to act.

Not a thirtieth, scarcely a fortieth, part of the taxes which are raised in England are either occasioned by, or applied to, the purposes of civil government. It is not difficult to see that the whole which the actual government does in this respect is to enact laws, and that the country administers and executes them, at its own expense, by means of magistrates, juries, sessions, and assize, over and above the taxes which it pays.

In this view of the case, we have two distinct characters of government: the one, the civil government, or the government of laws, which operates at home; the other, the court or cabinet government, which operates abroad, on the rude plan of uncivilized life; the one attended with little charge, the other with boundless extravagance; and so distinct are the two, that if the latter were to sink, as it were, by a sudden opening of the earth, and totally disappear, the former would not be deranged. It would still proceed, because it is the common interest of the nation that it should, and all the means are in practice.

Revolutions, then, have for their object a change in the moral condition of governments, and with this change the burden of public taxes will lessen, and civilization will be left to the enjoyment of that abundance of which it is now deprived. . . .*

No question has arisen within the records of history that pressed with the importance of the present. It is not whether this or that party shall be in or out, or Whig or Tory, or high or low shall prevail; but whether man shall inherit his rights, and universal civilization take place? Whether the fruits of his labor shall be enjoyed by himself, or consumed by the profligacy of governments? Whether robbery shall be banished from courts, and wretchedness from countries?

When, in countries that are called civilized, we see age going to the work-house, and youth to the gallows, something must be wrong

---

* A revolution in the state of civilization is the necessary companion of revolutions in the system of government. If a revolution in any country be from bad to good, or from good to bad, the state of what is called civilization in that country, must be made conformable thereto, to give that revolution effect. *Agrarian Justice* (1795–96), I, 621.

in the system of government. It would seem, by the exterior appearance of such countries, that all was happiness; but there lies hidden from the eye of common observation, a mass of wretchedness that has scarcely any other chance than to expire in poverty or infamy. Its entrance into life is marked with the presage of its fate; and until this is remedied, it is in vain to punish.

Civil government does not consist in executions; but in making that provision for the instruction of youth, and the support of age, as to exclude, as much as possible, profligacy from the one, and despair from the other. Instead of this, the resources of a country are lavished upon kings, upon courts, upon hirelings, impostors, and prostitutes; and even the poor themselves, with all their wants upon them, are compelled to support the fraud that oppresses them.

Why is it that scarcely any are executed but the poor? The fact is a proof, among other things, of a wretchedness in their condition. Bred up without morals, and cast upon the world without a prospect, they are the exposed sacrifice of vice and legal barbarity. . . . No wonder that jails are crowded, and taxes and poor-rates increased. Under such systems, nothing is to be looked for but what has already happened; and as to reformation, whenever it comes, it must be from the nation, and not from the government. . . . The millions that are superfluously wasted upon governments are more than sufficient to reform those evils, and to benefit the condition of every man in the nation, not included within the purlieus of a court. . . .

It is now very probable that the English Government (I do not mean the nation) is unfriendly to the French Revolution. Whatever serves to expose the intrigue and lessen the influence of courts, by lessening taxation, will be unwelcome to those who feed upon the spoil. While the clamor of French intrigue, arbitrary power, popery, and wooden shoes, could be kept up, the nations were easily allured and alarmed into taxes. Those days are now past; deception, it is to be hoped, has reaped its last harvest, and better times are in prospect for both countries, and for the world. . . .

Of all nations in Europe, there is none so much interested in the French Revolution as England. Enemies for ages, and that at a vast expense and without any national object, the opportunity now presents itself of amicably closing the scene, and joining their efforts to reform the rest of Europe.

By doing this, they will not only prevent the further effusion of blood, and increase of taxes, but be in a condition of getting rid of a considerable part of their present burdens, as has been already stated. Long experience, however, has shown that reforms of this kind are not those which old governments wish to promote, and therefore, it is to nations, and not to such governments, that these matters present themselves. . . .

That France as a nation and a national government would prefer an alliance with England is a matter of certainty. Nations, like individuals, who have long been enemies, without knowing each other, or knowing why, become better friends when they discover the errors and impositions under which they had acted.

Admitting, therefore, the probability of such a connection, I will state some matters by which such an alliance, together with that of Holland, might render service, not only to the parties immediately concerned, but to all parts of Europe.

It is, I think quite certain, that if the fleets of England, France and Holland were confederated, they could propose, with effect, a limitation to, and a general dismantling of, all the navies in Europe, to a certain proportion to be agreed upon. . . . If men will permit themselves to think, as rational beings ought to think, nothing can appear more ridiculous and absurd, exclusive of all moral reflections, than to be at the expense of building navies, filling them with men, and then hauling them into the ocean, to try which can sink each other fastest.

Peace, which costs nothing, is attended with infinitely more advantage than any victory with all its expense. . . . The same fleets and armies will no longer be necessary to either, and the reduction can be made ship for ship on each side. But to accomplish these objects, the governments must necessarily be fitted to a common correspondent principle. Confidence can never take place while a hostile disposition remains in either, or where mystery and secrecy on one side is opposed to candor and openness on the other.

These matters admitted, the national expenses might be put back, *for the sake of a precedent,* to what they were at some period when France and England were not enemies. . . . Taking therefore, one million and a half as a sufficient peace establishment for all the honest purposes of government, which is three thousand pounds more than the peace establishment in the profligate and prodigal times of Charles II (notwithstanding, as has been already observed, the pay and salaries of the army, navy, and revenue-officers, continue the same as at that period), there will remain a surplus of upwards of six millions out of the present current expenses. The question then will be how to dispose of this surplus. . . .

In the present state of things, a laboring man, with a wife and two or three children, does not pay less than between seven and eight pounds a year in taxes. He is not sensible of this, because it is disguised to him in the articles which he buys, and he thinks only of their dearness; but as the taxes take from him, at least, a fourth part of his yearly earnings, he is consequently disabled from providing for a family, especially if himself, or any of them, are afflicted with sickness.

The first step, therefore, of practical relief would be to abolish the poor-rates entirely, and, in lieu thereof, to make a remission of taxes to the poor to double the amount of the present poor-rates, *viz.,* four millions annually out of the surplus taxes. By this measure, the poor would be benefited two millions, and the housekeepers two millions. This alone would be equal to a reduction of one hundred and twenty millions of the national debt, and consequently equal to the whole expense of the American War.

It will then remain to be considered, which is the most effectual mode of distributing the remission of four millions.

It is easily seen that the poor are generally composed of large families of children, and old people unable to labor. If these two classes are provided for, the remedy will so far reach to the full extent of the case, that what remains will be incidental, and, in a great measure, fall within the compass of benefit clubs,[58] which, though of humble invention, merit to be ranked among the best of modern institutions.

Admitting England to contain seven millions of souls; if one-fifth thereof are of that class of poor which need support, the number will be one million four hundred thousand. Of this number, one hundred and forty thousand will be aged poor, as will be hereafter shown, and for which a distinct provision will be proposed.

There will then remain one million two hundred and sixty thousand, which, at five souls to each family, amount to two hundred and fifty-two thousand families, rendered poor from the expense of children and the weight of taxes. . . . It is certain that if the children are provided for, the parents are relieved of consequence, because it is from the expense of bringing up children that their poverty arises.

Having thus ascertained the greatest number that can be supposed to need support on account of young families, I proceed to the mode of relief, or distribution, which is,

To pay as a remission of taxes to every poor family, out of the surplus taxes and in room of poor-rates, four pounds a year for every child under fourteen years of age; enjoining the parents of such children to send them to school, to learn reading, writing, and common arithmetic; the ministers of every parish, of every denomination, to certify jointly to an office, for this purpose, that the duty is performed. The amount of this expense will be:

> For six hundred and thirty thousand children
> at four pounds each per annum   £2,520,000

By adopting this method, not only the poverty of the parents will be relieved, but ignorance will be banished from the rising generation, and the number of poor will hereafter become less, because their abilities, by the aid of education, will be greater. Many a youth, with a good natural genius, who is apprenticed to a mechanical trade, such as a carpenter, joiner, millwright, blacksmith, etc., is prevented getting forward the whole of his life, from the want of a little common education when a boy.

I now proceed to the case of the aged.

I divide age into two classes. First, the approach of old age, beginning at fifty. Secondly, old age commencing at sixty.

At fifty, though the mental faculties of man are in full vigor, and his judgment better than at any preceding date, the bodily powers are on the decline. He cannot bear the same quantity of fatigue as at an earlier period. He begins to earn less, and is less capable of enduring the wind and weather; and in those retired employments where much sight is required, he fails apace, and feels himself like an old horse, beginning to be turned adrift.

At sixty, his labor ought to be over, at least from direct necessity. It is painful to see old age working itself to death, in what are called civilized countries, for its daily bread. . . .

The persons to be provided for out of this gross number will be husbandmen, common laborers, journeymen of every trade and their wives, sailors, and disbanded soldiers, wornout servants of both sexes, and poor widows.

There will also be a considerable number of middling tradesmen, who, having lived decently in the former part of life, begin, as age approaches, to lose their business, and at last fall into decay.

Besides these, there will be constantly thrown off from the revolutions of that wheel, which no man can stop, nor regulate, a number from every class of life connected with commerce and adventure. . . .

To pay to every such person of the age of fifty years, and until he shall arrive at the age of sixty, the sum of six pounds per annum out of the surplus taxes; and ten pounds per annum during life, after the age of sixty. The expense of which will be:

Seventy thousand persons at ten pounds per annum	£420,000
Seventy thousand persons at ten pounds per annum	700,000
	£1,120,000

This support, as already remarked, is not of the nature of charity, but of a right. Every person in England, male or female, pays on an average of taxes, two pounds eight shillings and sixpence per annum from the day of his (or her) birth; and if the expense of collection be added, he pays two pounds, eleven shillings and sixpence; consequently, at the end of fifty years, he has paid one hundred and twenty-eight pounds fifteen shillings; and at sixty, one hundred and fifty-four pounds ten shillings.

Converting, therefore, his (or her) individual tax into a tontine, the money he shall receive after fifty years is but little more than the legal interest of the net money he has paid; the rest is made up from those whose circumstances do not require them to draw such support, and the capital in both cases defrays the expenses of government. . . .

After all the above cases are provided for, there will still be a number of families who, though not properly of the class of poor, yet find it difficult to give education to their children, and such children, under such a case, would be in a worse condition than if their parents were actually poor. A nation under a well regulated government should permit none to remain uninstructed. It is monarchial and aristocratical governments, only, that require ignorance for their support.

Suppose then four hundred thousand children to be in this condition, which is a greater number than ought to be supposed. After the provisions already made, the method will be:

To allow for each of those children ten shillings a year for the expense of schooling, for six years each, which will give them six months schooling each year, and half a crown a year for paper and spelling books.

The expense of this will be annually £250,000.

There will then remain one hundred and ten thousand pounds.

Notwithstanding the great modes of relief which the best instituted and best principled government may devise, there will still be a number of smaller cases, which it is good policy as well as beneficence in a nation to consider.

Were twenty shillings to be given to every woman immediately on the birth of a child, who should make the demand, and none will make it whose circumstances do not require it, it might relieve a great deal of instant distress.

There are about two hundred thousand births yearly in England; and if claimed by one-fourth,

The amount would be	£50,000
And twenty shillings to every new married couple who should claim in like manner.	
This would not exceed the sum of	£20,000

Also twenty thousand pounds to be appropriated to defray the funeral expenses of persons, who, traveling for work, may die at a distance from their friends. By relieving parishes from this charge, the sick stranger will be better treated.

I shall finish this part of my subject with a plan adapted to the particular condition of a metropolis, such as London.

Cases are continually occurring in a metropolis different from those which occur in the country, and for which a different, or rather an additional mode of relief is necessary. In the country, even in large towns, people have a knowledge of each other and distress never rises to that extreme height it sometimes does in a metropolis. There is no such thing in the country as persons, in the literal sense of the word, starved to death, or dying with cold from the want of a lodging. Yet such cases, and others equally as miserable, happen in London.

Many a youth comes up to London full of expectations, and little or no money, and unless he gets employment he is already half undone; and boys bred up in London without any means of a livelihood, and, as it often happens, of dissolute parents, are in a still worse condition, and servants long out of place are not much better off. In short, a world of little cases is continually arising, which busy or affluent life knows not of, to open the first door to distress. Hunger is not among the postponable wants, and a day, even a few hours, in such a condition, is often the crisis of a life of ruin.

These circumstances, which are the general cause of the little thefts and pilferings that lead to greater, may be prevented. There yet remain twenty thousand pounds out of the four millions of surplus taxes, which, with another fund hereafter to be mentioned, amounting to about twenty thousand pounds more, cannot be better applied than to this purpose. The plan then will be:

First, To erect two or more buildings, or take some already erected, capable of containing at least six thousand persons, and to have in each of these places as many kinds of employment as can be contrived, so that every person who shall come, may find something which he or she can do.

Secondly, To receive all who shall come, without inquiring who or what they are. The only condition to be, that for so much or so many hours work, each person shall receive so many meals of wholesome food, and a warm lodging, at least as good as a barrack. That a certain portion of what each person's work shall be worth shall be reserved, and given to him, or her, on their going away; and that each person shall stay as long, or as short time, or come as often as he chooses, on these conditions.

If each person stayed three months, it would assist by rotation twenty-four thousand persons annually, though the real number, at all times, would be but six thousand. By establishing an asylum of this kind, such persons to whom temporary distresses occur would have an opportunity to recruit themselves, and be enabled to look out for better employment. . . .

By the operation of this plan, the poor laws, those instruments of civil torture, will be superseded, and the wasteful expense of litigation prevented. The hearts of the humane will not be shocked by ragged and hungry children, and persons of seventy and eighty years of age begging for bread. The dying poor will not be dragged from place to place to breathe their last, as a reprisal of parish upon parish.

Widows will have maintenance for their children, and will not be carted away, on the death of their husbands, like culprits and criminals; and children will no longer be considered as increasing the distress of their parents. The haunts of the wretched will be known, because it will be to their advantage; and the number of petty crimes, the offspring of distress and poverty, will be lessened. The poor, as well as the rich, will then be interested in the support of government, and the cause and apprehension of riots and tumults will cease. . . .

The plan is easy of practice. It does not embarrass trade by a sudden interruption in the order of taxes, but effects the relief by changing the application of them; and the money necessary for the purpose can be drawn from the excise collections, which are made eight times a year in every market town in England. . . .

When taxes are proposed, the country is amused by the plausible language of taxing luxuries. One thing is called a luxury at one time, and something else at another; but the real luxury does not consist in the article, but in the means of procuring it, and this is always kept out of sight.

I know not why any plant or herb of the field should be a greater luxury in one country than in another, but an overgrown estate in either is a luxury at all times, and, as such, is the proper object of taxation. It is, therefore, right to take those kind, tax-making gentlemen upon their own word, and argue on the principle themselves have laid down, that of *taxing luxuries*. If they or their champion, Mr. Burke, who, I fear, is growing out of date like the man in armor, can prove that an estate of twenty, thirty, or forty thousand pounds a year is not a luxury, I will give up the argument.

Admitting that any annual sum, say for instance, one thousand pounds, is necessary or sufficient for the support of a family, consequently the second thousand is of the nature of a luxury, the third still more so, and by proceeding on, we shall at last arrive at a sum that may not improperly be called a prohibitable luxury. It would be impolitic to set bounds to property acquired by industry, and therefore it is right to place the prohibition beyond the probable acquisition to which industry can extend; but there ought to be a limit to property, or the accumulation of it by bequest. . . .

It would be attended with no good consequences to inquire how such vast estates as thirty, forty, or fifty thousand a year could commence, and that at a time when commerce and manufactures were not in a state to admit of such acquisitions. Let it be sufficient to remedy the evil by putting them in a condition of descending again to the community by the quiet means of apportioning them among all the heirs and heiresses of those families. This will be the more necessary, because hitherto the aristocracy have quartered their younger children and connections upon the public, in useless posts, places and offices, which, when abolished, will leave them destitute, unless the law of primogeniture be also abolished or superseded.

A progressive tax will, in a great measure, effect this object, and that as a matter of interest to the parties most immediately concerned, as will be seen by the following table, which shows the net produce upon every estate, after subtracting the tax.

By this it will appear that after an estate exceeds thirteen or fourteen thousand a year, the remainder produces but little profit to the holder, and consequently, will either pass to the younger children or to other kindred.

NO. OF THOUSANDS PER ANNUM	TOTAL TAX SUBTRACTED	NET PRODUCE
£ 1000	£ 21	£ 979
2000	59	1941
3000	109	2891
4000	184	3816
5000	284	4716
6000	434	5566
7000	634	6366
8000	880	7120
9000	1180	7820
10,000	1530	8480
11,000	1930	9070
12,000	2380	9620
13,000	2880	10,120
14,000	3430	10,670
15,000	4030	10,970
16,000	4680	11,320
17,000	5380	11,620
18,000	6130	11,870
19,000	6930	12,170
20,000	7780	12,220
21,000	8680	12,320
22,000	9630	12,370
23,000	10,630	12,370

N.B. The odd shillings are dropped in this table.

According to this table, an estate cannot produce more than £12,370 clear of the land tax and the progressive tax, and therefore the dividing such estates will follow as a matter of family interest. An estate of £23,000 a year, divided into five estates of four thousand each and one of three, will be charged only £1,129, which is but five per cent, but if held by any one possessor, will be charged £10,630.

Although an inquiry into the origin of those estates be unnecessary, the continuation of them in their present state is another subject. It is a matter of national concern. As hereditary estates, the law has created the evil, and it ought also to provide the remedy. Primogeniture ought to be abolished, not only because it is unnatural and unjust, but because the country suffers by its operation.

By cutting off (as before observed) the younger children from their proper portion of inheritance, the public is loaded with the expense of maintaining them; and the freedom of elections violated by the overbearing influence which this unjust monopoly of family property produces. Nor is this all. It occasions a waste of national property. A considerable part of the land of the country is rendered unproductive by the great extent of parks and chases which this law serves to keep up, and this at a time when the annual production of grain is not equal to the national consumption.

In short the evils of the aristocratical system are so great and numerous, and so inconsistent with every thing that is just, wise, natural, and beneficent, that when they are considered, there ought not to be a doubt that many, who are now classed under that description, will wish to see such a system abolished.

What pleasure can they derive from contemplating the exposed condition and almost certain beggary of their younger offspring? Every aristocratical family has an appendage of family beggars hanging round it, which, in a few ages, or a few generations, are shook off, and console themselves with telling their tale in almshouses, work-houses and prisons. This is the natural consequence of aristocracy. The peer and the beggar are often of the same family. One extreme produces the other; to make one rich many must be made poor; neither can the system be supported by other means.

There are two classes of people to whom the laws of England are particularly hostile, and those the most helpless: younger children and the poor. Of the former I have just spoken; of the latter I shall mention one instance out of the many that might be produced, and with which I shall close this subject.

Several laws are in existence for regulating and limiting workmen's wages. Why not leave them as free to make their own bargains, as the law-makers are to let their farms and houses? Personal labor is all the property they have. Why is that little, and the little freedom they enjoy, to be infringed? But the injustice will appear stronger, if we consider the operation and effect of such laws. When wages are fixed by what is called a law, the legal wages remain stationary, while every thing else is in progression; and as those who make that law still continue to lay on new taxes by other laws, they increase the expense of living by one law, and take away the means by another.

But if these gentlemen law-makers and tax-makers thought it right to limit the poor pittance which personal labor can produce, and on which a whole family is to be supported, they certainly must feel themselves happily indulged in a limitation on their own part of not less than twelve thousand a year, and that of property they never acquired (nor probably any of their ancestors), and of which they have made so ill a use. . . .

Whatever the reforms in the taxes may be, they ought to be made in the current expenses of government, and not in the part applied to the interest of the national debt. By remitting the taxes of the poor, *they* will be totally relieved and all discontent will be taken away; and by striking off such of the taxes as are already mentioned, the nation will more than recover the whole expense of the mad American War.

There will then remain only the national debt as a subject of discontent, and in order to remove, or rather prevent this, it would be good policy in the stockholders themselves to consider it as property, subject like all other property, to bear some portion of the taxes. It would give to it both popularity and security, and, as a great part of its present inconvenience is balanced by the capital which it keeps alive, a measure of this kind would so far add to that balance as to silence objections.

This may be done by such gradual means as to accomplish all that is necessary with the greatest ease and convenience.

Instead of taxing the capital, the best method would be to tax the interest by some progressive ratio, and to lessen the public taxes in the same proportion as the interest diminished. . . .

Never did so great an opportunity offer itself to England, and to all Europe, as is produced by the two revolutions of America and France. By the former, freedom has a national champion in the Western world; and by the latter, in Europe. When another nation shall join France, despotism and bad government will scarcely dare to appear. To use a trite expression, the iron is becoming hot all over Europe. The insulted German and the enslaved Spaniard, the Russ and the Pole are beginning to think. The present age will hereafter merit to be called the Age of Reason, and the present generation will appear to the future as the Adam of a new world.*

When all the governments of Europe shall be established on the representative system, nations will become acquainted, and the animosities and prejudices fomented by the intrigues and artifice of courts will cease. The oppressed soldier will become a free man; and the tortured sailor, no longer dragged through the streets like a felon, will pursue his mercantile voyage in safety. It would be better

---

* From what we now see, nothing of reform on the political world ought to be held improbable. It is an age of revolutions, in which every thing may be looked for. *The Rights of Man*, I, 344.

that nations should continue the pay of their soldiers during their lives, and give them their discharge and restore them to freedom and their friends, and cease recruiting, than retain such multitudes at the same expense, in a condition useless to society and to themselves.

As soldiers have hitherto been treated in most countries, they might be said to be without a friend. Shunned by the citizen on an apprehension of their being enemies to liberty, and too often insulted by those who commanded them, their condition was a double oppression. But where genuine principles of liberty pervade a people, everything is restored to order; and the soldier, civilly treated, returns the civility.

REVOLUTION AND THE RIGHTS OF MAN

The fraud, hypocrisy, and imposition of governments are now beginning to be too well understood to promise them any longer career. The farce of monarchy and aristocracy, in all countries, is following that of chivalry, and Mr. Burke is dressing for the funeral. Let it then pass quietly to the tomb of all other follies, and the mourners be comforted. . . .

Conquest and tyranny, at some early period, dispossessed man of his rights, and he is now recovering them. And as the tide of all human affairs has its ebb and flow in directions contrary to each other, so also is it in this. Government founded on a *moral theory, on a system of universal peace, on the indefeasible, hereditary rights of man,* is now revolving from West to East, by a stronger impulse than the government of the sword revolved from East to West. It interests not particular individuals, but nations, in its progress, and promises a new era to the human race. . . .

Whether the forms and maxims of governments which are still in practice were adapted to the condition of the world at the period they were established is not in this case the question. The older they are, the less correspondence can they have with the present state of things. Time, and change of circumstances and opinions, have the same progressive effect in rendering modes of government obsolete, as they have upon customs and manners. Agriculture, commerce, manufactures, and the tranquil arts, by which the prosperity of nations is best promoted, require a different system of government, and a different species of knowledge to direct its operations, than what might have been required in the former condition of the world. . . .

What is government more than the management of the affairs of a nation? It is not, and from its nature cannot be, the property of any particular man or family, but of the whole community, at whose expense it is supported; and though by force or contrivance it has been usurped into an inheritance, the usurpation cannot alter the right of things. Sovereignty, as a matter of right, appertains to the nation only, and not to any individual; and a nation has at all times an inherent indefeasible right to abolish any form of government it finds inconvenient, and establish such as accords with its interest, disposition, and happiness. The romantic and barbarous distinction of [making] men into king and subjects, though it may suit the condition of courtiers, cannot that of citizens; and is exploded by the principle upon which governments are now founded. Every citizen is a member of the sovereignty, and, as such, can acknowledge no personal subjection; and his obedience can be only to the laws. . . .

If systems of government can be introduced, less expensive, and more productive of general happiness, than those which have existed, all attempts to oppose their progress will in the end be fruitless. Reason, like time, will make its own way, and prejudice will fall in a combat with interest.* If universal peace, civilization, and commerce, are ever to be the happy lot of man, it cannot be accomplished but by a revolution in the system of governments. All the monarchial governments are military. War is their trade, plunder and revenue their objects. While such governments continue, peace has not the absolute security of a day. . . .

When it shall be said in any country in the world, "My poor are happy; neither ignorance nor distress is to be found among them; my jails are empty of prisoners, my streets of beggars; the aged are not in want, the taxes are not oppressive; the rational world is my friend, because I am a friend of its happiness":—when these things can be said, then may that country boast of its constitution and its government. Within the space of a few years we have seen two revolutions, those of America and France. In the former, the contest was long and the conflict severe; in the latter, the nation acted with such a consolidated impulse that having no foreign enemy to contend with, the revolution was complete in power the moment it appeared.

From both those instances it is evident that the greatest force

---

* Time makes more converts than reason. Introduction to *Common Sense* (1776), I, 3.

that can be brought into the field of revolutions are reason and common interest. Where these can have the opportunity of acting, opposition dies with fear, or crumbles away by conviction. It is a great standing which they have now universally obtained; and we may hereafter hope to see revolutions, or changes in governments, produced with the same quiet operation by which any measure, determinable by reason and discussion, is accomplished.

When a nation changes its opinion and habits of thinking, it is no longer to be governed as before; but it would not only be wrong, but bad policy, to attempt by force what ought to be accomplished by reason. Rebellion consists in forcibly opposing the general will of a nation, whether by a party or by a government. There ought, therefore, to be in every nation a method of occasionally ascertaining the state of public opinion with respect to government. . . .

If it prefer a bad or defective government to a reform, or choose to pay ten times more taxes than there is any occasion for, it has a right to do so; and so long as the majority do not impose conditions on the minority different from what they impose upon themselves, though there may be much error, there is no injustice.* Neither will the error continue long. Reason and discussion will soon bring things right, however wrong they may begin.

By such a process no tumult is to be apprehended. The poor in all countries are naturally both peaceable and grateful in all reforms in which their interest and happiness are included. It is only by neglecting and rejecting them that they become tumultuous. . . .

In contemplating revolutions, it is easy to perceive that they may arise from two distinct causes: the one, to avoid or get rid of some calamity, the other, to obtain some great and positive good; and the two may be distinguished by the names of active and passive revolutions. In those which proceed from the former cause, the temper becomes incensed and soured; and the redress, obtained by danger, is too often sullied by revenge.

But in those which proceed from the latter, the heart, rather animated than agitated, enters serenely upon the subject. Reason and discussion, persuasion and conviction, become the weapons in the contest, and it is only when those are attempted to be suppressed that recourse is had to violence.

When men unite in agreeing that a *thing is good,* could it be

---

* It is only by each nation reforming its own, that the whole can be improved, and the full benefit of reformation enjoyed. Only partial advantages can flow from partial reforms. *The Rights of Man,* I, 404.

obtained, such as relief from a burden of taxes and the extinction of corruption, the object is more than half accomplished. What they approve as the end, they will promote in the means. . . .

If, therefore, the good to be obtained be worthy of a passive, rational and costless revolution, it would be bad policy to prefer waiting for a calamity that should force a violent one. I have no idea, considering the reforms which are now passing and spreading throughout Europe, that England will permit herself to be the last; and where the occasion and the opportunity quietly offer, it is better than to wait for a turbulent necessity. It may be considered as an honor to the animal faculties of man to obtain redress by courage and danger, but it is far greater honor to the rational faculties to accomplish the same object by reason, accommodation, and general consent. . . .

What were formerly called revolutions were little more than a change of persons, or an alteration of local circumstances. They rose and fell like things of course, and had nothing in their existence or their fate that could influence beyond the spot that produced them. But what we now see in the world, from the revolutions of America and France, is a renovation of the natural order of things, a system of principles as universal as truth and the existence of man, and combining moral with political happiness and national prosperity:

"I. *Men are born and always continue free and equal in respect to their rights. Civil distinctions, therefore, can be founded only on public utility.*

"II. *The end of all political associations is the preservation of the natural and imprescriptible rights of man; and these rights are liberty, property, security, and resistance of oppression.*

"III. *The Nation is essentially the source of all Sovereignty; nor can any individual or any body of men be entitled to any authority which is not expressly derived from it.*"

In these principles, there is nothing to throw a nation into confusion by inflaming ambition. They are calculated to call forth wisdom and abilities, and to exercise them for the public good, and not for the emolument or aggrandizement of particular descriptions of men or families. Monarchial sovereignty, the enemy of mankind, and the source of misery, is abolished; and sovereignty itself is restored to its natural and original place, the nation. Were this the case throughout Europe, the cause of wars would be taken away. . . .

Some gentlemen have affected to call the principles upon which this work and the former part of the *Rights of Man* are founded "a new fangled doctrine." The question is not whether these principles are new or old, but whether they are right or wrong. Suppose the former, I will show their effect by a figure easily understood.

It is now toward the middle of February. Were I to take a turn into the country, the trees would present a leafless, wintery appearance. As people are apt to pluck twigs as they go along, I perhaps might do the same, and by chance might observe that a *single bud* on that twig has begun to swell. I should reason very unnaturally, or rather not reason at all, to suppose *this* was the *only bud* in England which had this appearance.

Instead of deciding thus, I should instantly conclude that the same appearance was beginning, or about to begin, everywhere; and though the vegetable sleep will continue longer on some trees and plants than on others, and though some of them may not *blossom* for two or three years, all will be in leaf in the summer, except those which are *rotten*. What pace the political summer may keep with the natural, no human foresight can determine. It is, however, not difficult to perceive that the spring is begun.

Thus wishing, as I sincerely do, freedom and happiness to all nations, I close the SECOND PART.

EDITOR'S
NOTES

Editor's Preface

1 Thomas W. Copeland, *Our Eminent Friend Edmund Burke* (New Haven: Yale University Press, 1949), p. 148.
2 James T. Boulton, *The Language of Politics in the Age of Wilkes and Burke* (London: Routledge & Kegan-Paul, 1963), chs. VI–VII.
3 *Letter to the Sheriffs of Bristol* (1777), in *Burke: Selected Writings and Speeches on America,* ed. Thomas H. D. Mahoney (New York: Bobbs-Merrill, 1964), p. 287. Unless otherwise indicated, all quotations from Burke's public papers dealing with America have been taken from this source.
4 *An Appeal from the New to the Old Whigs* (1791), in Bohn's Standard Library Edition of *The Works of Edmund Burke* (London: George Bell & Sons, 1901), III, p. 87. Unless otherwise indicated, all quotations from Burke's papers have been taken from this edition.
5 *Thoughts on the Cause of the Present Discontents* (1770), I, 337.
6 *The Rights of Man* (Part I) [1791], I, 327. Two years earlier he had written, "I defend the cause of the poor, of the manufacturers, of the tradesmen, of the farmers, and of all those on whom the real burden of taxation falls—but, above all, I defend the cause of humanity." *Prospects on the Rubicon* (1787), in *The Complete Writings of Thomas Paine,* ed. Philip S. Foner (New York: Citadel Press, 1945), II, 632. Unless otherwise indicated, all quotations by Paine have been taken from this work.
7 *Reflections on the Revolution in France* (1790), ed. Thomas H. D.

Mahoney (New York: Bobbs-Merrill, 1955), p. 163. All citations from Burke's *Reflections* refer to this edition.

8 *The Rights of Man* (Part I) [1791], I, 317–18.

9 *The Rights of Man* (Part I) [1791], I, 282, 318, 272, 322.

10 Boulton, p. 110.

11 *Reflections*, p. 104.

Prelude
to the
Great Debate

1 *The Rights of Man,* Part I (1792) in Philip S. Foner, *The Complete Writings of Thomas Paine* (New York: Citadel Press, 1945), I, 344. Unless otherwise indicated, all citations to Paine's works refer to this source.

2 *Reflections on the Revolution in France* (1790), ed. Thomas H. D. Mahoney (Indianapolis: Bobbs-Merrill, 1955). All quotations from Burke's *Reflections* are taken from this source.

3 *The Rights of Man* (Part II), I, 354.

4 Arnold J. Toynbee, *The Continuing Effect of the American Revolution* (Colonial Williamsburg, Virginia: 1961), pp. 8–20. See also Richard B. Morris, *The American Revolution Reconsidered* (New York: Harper & Row, 1967) for a similar position. This view, it should be noted, has been sharply challenged by Hannah Arendt: "It was the French and not the American Revolution that set the world on fire. . . . The sad truth of the matter is that the French Revolution, which ended in disaster, has made world history, while the American Revolution, so triumphantly successful, has remained an event of little more than local importance." *On Revolution* (New York: Viking Press, 1963), p. 49.

5 The word "revolution," as Hannah Arendt has pointed out, was origi-

nally an astronomical term which was first used metaphorically in the political realm to suggest that the affairs of men, like the sun, moon, and stars, always revolved back to some pre-established point. A revolution, in short, meant originally a restoration to a preordained order, which is quite the opposite to its meaning today. Both Burke and Paine, each in his own way, were influenced by the old usage. Thus, to Burke, though not to Paine, the Whig Revolution of 1688 was truly a revolution. To Paine the American and French Revolutions were "counter-revolutions" because men were trying to recover rights and liberties which they once allegedly enjoyed at some earlier period. Arendt, pp. 35–38.

6 *The Case of the Officers of Excise* (1772), II, 8, 11. The most recent and reliable biography of Paine is Alfred Owen Aldridge's *Man of Reason: The Life of Thomas Paine* (Philadelphia: J. B. Lippincott Co., 1959) on which much of the following account of Paine's early career is based.

7 *African Slavery in America* (1775), II, 17–18.

8 *A Serious Thought* (1775), II, 20. In 1775 Paine also joined the first anti-slavery society organized in America, and five years later, as clerk of the Pennsylvania Assembly, he wrote the preamble to the first legislative enactment to call for the gradual emancipation of slaves in America. Foner, II, 15, 21.

9 Aldridge, p. 42.

10 *Common Sense* (1776), I, 29, 25, 6–7, 9.

11 *Common Sense,* I, 18–24 *passim.*

12 *American Crisis* I (1776), I, 50.

13 *American Crisis* IV (1777), I, 102.

14 *American Crisis* V (1778), I, 104, 108, 114.

15 *American Crisis* II (1777), I, 67–68, 70.

16 *American Crisis* II (1777), I, 63.

17 *American Crisis* III (1777), I, 76, 77, 90. The emphasis is Paine's,

18 *American Crisis* III (1777), I, 99, 100. The oath which was actually adopted went well beyond a declaration of one's own loyalty. Anyone who signed, as did Paine in July, 1778, promised to report the activities of any suspicious characters or persons believed hostile to the American cause. In doing so, he was urged not to be "misled" into supposing that his testimony against "such offenders" was either "officious" or "dishonorable." In other words, to inform on one's neighbors and associates was to be considered respectable. See Aldridge, p. 60.

19 American historians still debate the extent to which the American Revolution was truly a revolution in the social sense. "To some extent, and for some purposes," Henry S. Commager and Richard S. Morris declare, "the Revolution was a class conflict, a war, if not between the 'haves' and 'have nots,' then between the 'ins' and the outs.'" Yet even they caution that "there are so many exceptions [to the class pattern] that the generalization is not very helpful." Commager and Morris, *The Spirit of 'Seventy-Six* (New York: Harper & Row, 1957), pp. 325, 326. John R. Alden, on the other hand, insists that the Tory exiles differed from the Patriots in "ancestry, wealth, class, breeding, or education" only in "minor degree." Yet, as he concedes, "On balance, men who sought to rise in the world were more likely to be Patriots; on the other hand, those who had much to lose would tend to be Loyalists." John R. Alden, *A History of the American Revolution* (New York: Alfred A. Knopf, 1959), pp. 496, 497. See also J. Franklin Jameson, *The American Revolution Considered as a Social Movement* (Princeton: Princeton University Press, 1926), pp. 21–27.

20 *American Crisis* VII (1778), I, 150, 141, 145.

21 *American Crisis* VIII (1780), I, 159–60, 161, 155.

22 *American Crisis* I (1776), I, 50.

23 *American Crisis* VII (1778), I, 151.

24 *American Crisis* VIII (1780), I, 163.

25 *Speech on Conciliation with America* (1775) in Thomas H. D. Mahoney, ed., *Edmund Burke: Selected Writings and Speeches on America* (Indianapolis: Bobbs-Merrill, 1964), p. 117. Unless otherwise indicated, all citations to Burke's works on America refer to this source.

26 *Speech on Conciliation with America* (1775), p. 131.

27 *Observations on a Late Publication entitled "The Present State of the Nation"* (1769), pp. 42, 41, 47, 46.

28 *Observations on . . . "The Present State of the Nation,"* pp. 21, 53.

29 *Speech on American Taxation* (1774), p. 113.

30 *Observations on . . . "The Present State of the Nation,"* p. 49.

31 Bernard Bailyn, *The Ideological Origins of the American Revolution* (Cambridge: Harvard University Press, 1967), pp. 158–59.

32 Gerald W. Chapman, *Edmund Burke: The Practical Imagination* (Cambridge: Harvard University Press, 1967), p. 253.

33 Under a law enacted under the reign of Henry VIII which was revived in 1769.

[34] Ernest Barker, *Essays on Government,* 2nd ed. (Oxford: Clarendon Press, 1951), p. 171.

[35] Thomas W. Copeland, *Our Eminent Friend: Edmund Burke* (New Haven: Yale University Press, 1949), pp. 62–63.

[36] Mahoney, p. xv. Burke's career as provincial agent is carefully analyzed in Ross J. S. Hoffman, *Edmund Burke, New York Agent with his letters to the New York Assembly* (Philadelphia: American Philosophical Society, 1956).

[37] Ernest Barker's essay on "Burke and His Bristol Constituency, 1774–1780," in his *Essays on Government,* pp. 154–204, is still the most insightful account of the Bristol phase of Burke's parliamentary career.

[38] *Speech to the Electors of Bristol* (1774), I, 447.

[39] *Speech on Conciliation with America* (1775), pp. 172, 148–49, 136, 137, 131–32.

[40] *Speech on Conciliation with America* (1775), pp. 140, 142–43, 144–45, 130–31.

[41] *Speech on Conciliation with America* (1775), pp. 147, 161.

[42] Mahoney, p. 110.

[43] *Speech on Conciliation with America* (1775), pp. 172–73, 183. In his speech on American taxation, Burke had spoken of "the mischief of not having large and liberal ideas in the management of great affairs." Mahoney, p. 64.

[44] *Speech on American Taxation* (1774), p. 76.

[45] *Speech on Conciliation with America* (1775), pp. 182–83.

[46] The speech is summarized in the *Parliamentary History,* Vol. xviii, pp. 963–82 and reprinted in Mahoney, pp. 187–206. The portions excerpted may be found at pp. 196, 199, 203, 199–200 in Mahoney.

[47] *Letter to the Marquess of Rockingham* (January 6, 1777), pp. 207–215.

[48] After provoking armed resistance by seizing the colonial arsenal and dissolving the colonial assembly, Governor Dunmore was forced to flee for safety. From the English warship on which he took refuge, he then invoked martial law, declared all able-bodied men who did not resort to His Majesty's standard to be traitors, and promised freedom to their indentured servants and African slaves if they joined His 'Majesty's troops "as soon as may be." Hundreds of slaves and servants responded to his call "only later to be deserted by Dunmore when he had no further use for them." Many of the fugitives were shot on sight, some were hanged, and still others sold to planters in the West Indies.

"Those who had not borne arms were pardoned, though no doubt they were brutally lashed and otherwise seriously punished on being returned to their masters." See George F. Willison, *Patrick Henry and His World* (New York: Doubleday & Co., 1969), pp. 289–90, 293, 293n. All in all, Burke's indignation seems one-sided, if not misplaced.

49 *Address to the King* (1777), pp. 221, 223–24, 225.

50 *Address to the King* (1777), pp. 218–20, 228–29.

51 *Address to the King* (1777), pp. 229–31.

52 A *bill of pains and penalties* was originally used by Parliament to punish those who had placed themselves beyond the jurisdiction of the common law courts by fleeing the realm. Later it was employed, in the form of a bill of attainder, to convict any person of treason or other high crime whenever the evidence against him seemed insufficient to convict in the regular courts. Bills of attainder or of other "pains and penalties" have been outlawed in the United States since 1789 (U.S. Constitution, Art. I, secs. 9, 10) and in Great Britain since 1870 as to all penalties except forfeiture of property in the case of fugitives from justice (33 & 34 Victoria, ch. 23).

53 *Address to the King* (1777), pp. 211–13.

54 *Address to the British Colonists in North America* (1777), pp. 237–38, 236, 234.

55 *Address to the British Colonists in North America* (1777), pp. 239–42.

56 Carl B. Cone, *Burke and the Nature of Politics* (Lexington, Ky.: University of Kentucky Press, 1957), pp. 291–92.

57 *Letter to the Sheriffs of Bristol* (1777), pp. 253–54.

58 *Letter to the Sheriffs of Bristol* (1777), pp. 261, 282–83.

59 *Letter to the Sheriffs of Bristol* (1777), pp. 246–54.

60 "[T]o tax and to please, no more than to love and to be wise, is not given to men." *Speech on American Taxation* (1774), p. 106.

61 *Letter to the Sheriffs of Bristol* (1777), pp. 272–76.

62 Much later, after his return to America, Thomas Paine was to write: "To know if any theory or position be true or rational in practise, the method is to carry it to its greatest extent; if it not be true upon the whole, or be absurd, it is so in all its parts, however small." *Constitutional Reform: to the Citizens of Pennsylvania on the Proposal for Calling a Convention* (1805), II, 1002.

63 *Letter to the Sheriffs of Bristol* (1777), p. 277.

[64] *Letter to the Sheriffs of Bristol* (1777), pp. 257–60.

[65] *Letter to the Sheriffs of Bristol* (1777), pp. 265–68.

[66] *Letter to the Sheriffs of Bristol* (1777), p. 271.

[67] *The Rights of Man* (Part II), I, 366.

[68] *Letter to the Sheriffs of Bristol* (1777), p. 259.

[69] *Letter to the Abbé Raynal* (1782), II, 233. The emphasis is Paine's.

[70] Aldridge, p. 68.

[71] Foner, I, 132.

[72] Foner, II, 175 (July 31, 1779).

[73] Aldridge, p. 63. The following summary of Paine's involvement in the Deane affair is based largely on Aldridge's account, pp. 64–77.

[74] To his later embarrassment, Paine had once reproached Deane for his indiscreet disclosures involving Arthur Lee. "[I]t is the business of a foreign minister to learn other men's secrets and keep their own." *Public Letter to Silas Deane, Esq're,* (December 15, 1778), II, 104.

[75] *Open Letter to Messrs. Deane, Jay, and Gerard* (September 14, 1779), II, 183–85.

[76] *Third Letter on Peace and the Newfoundland Fisheries* (July 21, 1779), II, 204. Almost as if to prove Paine's point that Gérard interested himself—and allowed others to involve him—in matters which were none of his business, Joseph Reed, president of Pennsylvania's executive council, saw fit to ask Gérard's advice whether Paine should be given a pension for his past services to the Revolution. Gérard's response was that "if you believe you are able to guide his pen for public welfare and utility, which perhaps will not be difficult for your zeal, your talent, and your superior enlightenment, I shall be the first to applaud the success of an attempt in which I have failed." Aldridge, p. 79.

[77] Aldridge, pp. 85–89.

[78] Foner, II, 187.

[79] In 1842 Congress, still unaware of Deane's treason, voted his heirs $37,-000 in belated restitution of his losses during the Revolution. "As it was then impossible to repay him what was due," Carl Van Doren observed, "so it was impossible to punish him for the treachery about which Congress did not know." See his *Secret History of the American Revolution* (New York: Viking Press, 141), p. 432.

[80] Aldridge, pp. 90, 93.

[81] Foner, I, 213, 215.

82 Aldridge, p. 94.

83 *Letter to the Abbé Raynal* (1782), II, 217–18, 238–39.

84 *Letter to the Abbé Raynal* (1782), II, 240, 242–43.

85 See Darrel Abel, "The Significance of the Letter to the Abbé Raynal on the Progress of Thomas Paine's Thought," *Pennsylvania Magazine of History and Biography,* LXVI (April 1942), 176–90.

86 Aldridge, pp. 96–97.

87 Foner, I, 237–38.

88 Foner, I, xxiii.

89 Aldridge, pp. 103–104.

90 This discovery led him later to reject the claims of revealed religions in *The Age of Reason,* Part I of which is at least in part a treatise on astronomy. See Ralph C. Roper, "Thomas Paine: Scientist-Religionist," *The Scientific Monthly* (LVIII, February 1944), 101–111. Paine himself explained what an orrery is: "It is a machinery of clockwork, representing the universe in miniature, and in which the revolution of the earth round itself and round the sun, the revolution of the moon round the earth, the revolution of the planets round the sun, their relative distances from the sun, as the center of the whole system, their relative distances from each other and their different magnitudes are represented as they really exist in what we call the heavens." *The Age of Reason,* I, 498n.

91 Later, Paine gave all of his papers and experiments on steam propulsion to Robert Fulton. Sir Richard Phillips, who assisted Fulton in his steamboat experiments on the Thames, and Fitch himself "admitted Paine's priority in the application of steam to navigation." Roper, "Thomas Paine: Scientist-Religionist," p. 111. See also Aldridge, pp. 56, 108.

92 Aldridge, pp. 108, 109.

93 Aldridge, pp. 118–120.

94 *Ibid.*

95 *Prospects on the Rubicon* (1787), II, 624, 650, 634.

96 Aldridge, pp. 121–24.

97 Foner, I, 8.

98 To Thomas Walker, Esqr. (February 26, 1789), II, 1280, 1279.

99 Aldridge, p. 124.

100 Foner, II, 1265–66.

101 Foner, II, 1271, 1283.

102 *Second Letter to Rhode Island* (December 28, 1782), II, 345.

103 Mahoney, p. 262.

104 *The Correspondence of Edmund Burke,* (Cambridge, Eng.: Cambridge University Press, 1963), IV, 363n, 383–397, 418–19. Source cited hereafter as *Correspondence.*

105 Barker, pp. 206–207.

106 Copeland, pp. 165–66.

107 Burke's first extended political treatise, *A Vindication of Natural Society* (1756) was a satirical attack on the *Idea of a Patriot King* expounded by Henry St. John, the first Viscount Bolingbroke. In governing his subjects, Bolingbroke had said, the wise and patriotic sovereign would make no distinction between their rights and his own except to treat the former as a trust and the latter as absolute property. If George III had been trained in this philosophy, as it has been claimed, he lacked either the intellect to understand it or the generosity needed to apply it. This "wretched monarch," as John Morley described him, "tried to play the good despot over the vast empire of Britain, with a capacity barely over the mark of a village constable." From this experience Morley drew this Burkean conclusion: "There is nothing more fatal, either in private life or in the larger affairs of state, than for an incompetent man to grasp a principle of action that is too big for him." John Morley, *Edmund Burke* (New York: Alfred A. Knopf, 1924), pp. 9–10.

108 *Speech on the Plan for Economical Reform* (1780), in *The Works of Edmund Burke* (London: George Ball & Sons, 1901), II, 106–07. All quotations from Burke's public writings except his *Reflections* and his speeches on America have been taken from this source.

109 *Thoughts on French Affairs* (1791), II, 38.

110 According to Burke's first biographer, Robert Bisset, Paine was "frequently a visitor" at Burke's estate during the fall of 1787, but he cites no evidence at all to support the claim. Indeed, Paine himself stated that he did not "put" the letter from the Cardinal's secretary "into the hands of Mr. Burke" until "almost three years" prior to the time he wrote his preface to Part I of the English edition of *The Rights of Man.* If, as seems likely, he wrote that preface shortly before his work was published in February, 1791, and if he was correct in his recollection, the time of that meeting was the summer of 1788 during his *second* visit to England. This raises at least the possibility that Burke and Paine may not have met at all during Paine's first visit to England. It seems much more likely, however, as Professor Copeland concludes,

that Paine did call on Burke in the fall of 1787 but that "he acted the part of an inventor looking for patronage rather than a political missionary bringing new ideas from France." In that case, Paine may simply have waited until his return to England in the summer of 1788 before delivering the letter from the Cardinal's secretary. See Copeland, p. 155 and Foner, I, 246.

111 To Dr. French Laurence (August 18, 1788), *Correspondence*, V, 412.

112 To Sir Gilbert Elliot (September 3, 1788), *Correspondence*, V, 415.

113 Copeland, p. 160, quoting a letter to Jefferson (January 15, 1789), published there for the first time.

114 To Thomas Jefferson (February 26, 1789), II, 1283.

115 In the controversy over the Deane affair Morris had sided with Deane. During the debate in the Congress over Paine's involvement, he called Paine a "mere adventurer *from England,* without fortune, without family or connexions, ignorant even of grammar," who should never have been appointed to high office. Later in France he told Lafayette that although Paine "has an excellent Pen to write, he has but an indifferent Head to think." Privately, in his diary, his language was even stronger: Paine, he thought, was "a little mad," "inflated to the Eyes and big with a Litter of Revolution," and "drunk with Self Conceit." It is not surprising that he seems to have made little effort to win Paine's release when, later, he was imprisoned during the Revolution. The reason, he explained to Jefferson, then Secretary of State, was that Paine was safer in prison than out while the Terror lasted, adding, "for in the best of times he has a larger share of every other sense than common sense, and lately the intemperate use of ardent spirits has, I am told, considerably impaired the small stock he originally possessed." Aldridge, pp. 69, 126, 147, 211–214.

116 Copeland, p. 161.

117 *The Rights of Man* (Part II), I, 453.

118 Aldridge, p. 125.

119 Thomas Paine to Edmund Burke (January 17, 1790), *Correspondence*, VI, 69.

120 *Ibid.,* 71–72.

121 The complete text of Jefferson's letter to Paine, dated July 11, 1789, was first published in Copeland, pp. 186–89.

122 Thomas Paine to Edmund Burke (January 17, 1790), *Correspondence*, VI, 71–72. Burke was alarmed by Paine's confident claim that the revolution in France was but a forerunner of others to come, but he had

only scorn for the scheme by which France was divided into "eighty-three parts [departments] latitudinally," as Paine put it, "and longitudinally." It was sheer folly, he believed, to create entirely new subdivisions within a country on a principle which required "no better apparatus" than the surveyor's chain, sight, and theodolite and "the arithmetic of an exciseman." "No man ever was attached by a sense of pride, partiality, or real affection," he was soon to write, "to a description of square measurement. . . . We begin our public affections in our families. No cold relation is a zealous citizen. We pass on to our neighborhoods and our habitual provincial connections. . . . To be attached to the subdivision, to love the little platoon we belong to in society, is the first principle (the germ as it were) of public affections. It is the first link in the series by which we proceed towards a love to our country and to mankind." *Reflections on the Revolution in France* (1790), 202, 215, 231, 53.

123 This, on the assumption that Professor Copeland is correct in his surmise that the exchange described below took place by letter—and not face-to-face—early in 1790 during Paine's second extended visit to France and not much earlier, as Burke's first biographers had reported. Cf. Robert Bisset, *Life of Edmund Burke*, 2nd ed. (London: George Cawthorn, 1800), II, 284–88, and George Croly, *Life of Edmund Burke* (Edinburgh: W. Blackwood & Sons, 1840), I, 298–300. See Copeland, pp. 171–72.

124 Paine himself seems to have spelled his name variously early in his career. Although the name was spelled "Paine" in the church register of his parents' marriage, it was spelled "Payne" in the record of his sister's birth. On both occasions when he was married, the name was recorded "Pain" in the church register; and this spelling was used when he was first mentioned in the Pennsylvania press. With the publication of *Common Sense* and consistently thereafter he called himself Paine. Aldridge, p. 19.

125 Mrs. Aubrey LeBlond, *Charlotte Sophie, Countess Bentinck* (London: Hutchinson & Co., 1912), I, 163.

126 Croly, I, 298.

127 Bisset, II, 285.

128 Bisset, II, 285–86.

129 Croly, I, 298–99.

130 LeBlond, I, 163.

131 To Thomas Jefferson (September 9, 1788), II, 1270.

132 *The Rights of Man*, Part I, Preface to the French edition, I, 249.

133 To the Earl of Charlemont (August 9, 1789), *Correspondence*, VI, 10.

134 To Charles-Jean François Dèpont (November, 1789), *Correspondence*, VI, 42–46, 49.

135 *Ibid.*, pp. 41, 45–46, 50.

136 *Speech in the Debate on the Army Estimates* (February 9, 1790), III, 269–81. See also *Correspondence*, VI, 81–82, editors' note.

137 Copeland, pp. 172–74.

138 *Ibid.*, pp. 41, 45–46, 50. Depont was not at all pleased to have had the *Reflections* addressed to him even anonymously. After their translation and publication in France he wrote Burke in some anguish:
When I took the liberty, last year, of asking your opinion on the political events in France, I had certainly no idea that my letter would lead to the publication of the work you have so kindly sent me. I will even confess that I should never have made the request, had I been able to foresee its effect; and that if I had at that time known your opinions, far from begging you to express them, I should have besought you not to make them public. James T. Boulton, *The Language of Politics in the Age of Wilkes and Burke* (London: Routledge & Kegan-Paul, 1963), pp. 75–76, 81, 94–95.

139 Aldridge, pp. 126–127.

140 *Letter to the Addressers of the Late Proclamation* (1792), II, 497–98. The "late proclamation" was issued on May 21, 1792 against all "wicked seditious writings printed, published and industriously dispersed." Paine himself was prosecuted for sedition after publication of Part II of *The Rights of Man* and found guilty *in absentia* after he left England to represent Pas de Calais in the French National Convention.

141 To Thomas Christie (April 16, 1790), II, 1301–02. Foner attributes the letter to an "anonymous" correspondent, but it is clearly addressed to Christie.

142 Copeland, p. 148.

143 See Peter Viereck, *Conservatism from John Adams to Churchill* (Princeton: D. Van Nostrand Co., 1956), p. 13.

The Consecrated State
of Edmund Burke

1 *Dear Sir:* Burke addressed these *Reflections* to "a very young gentleman
at Paris" whose name he never publicly disclosed. For many years it was
mistakenly assumed that the correspondent was Pierre-Gaëton Dupont,
the French lawyer who translated the work in the first of its foreign editions. Now it is known that he was Charles-Jean-François Depont, an
even younger French lawyer who had once visited Burke at Beaconsfield.
See pp. 63–64, 66.

2 *Our revolution,* to Englishmen generally and especially to Whigs of all
persuasion, was the Glorious Revolution of 1688 by which James II was
deposed, after he had fled the country, for having violated the fundamental laws of the realm.

3 *The Society for Promoting Constitutional Information* was founded in
1780 to promote parliamentary reform and included among its members
a number of prominent Whig peers and members of Parliament. By
1792 it had come to support the French Revolution as well.

4 *The Revolution Society* of London was merely one of a number of local
societies of that name which were founded to commemorate the English
Revolution of 1688. Unlike the Constitutional Society, its membership
was largely non-conformist opposed, at least in theory, to the Established
(Anglican) Church.

5 *Dissenters* were those Protestants who separated themselves from the
communion of the Established (Anglican) Church. The dissenters who

not only dissented from the national church but were opposed on principle to any established church were sometimes called "non-conformists."

6 *The Metaphysic Knight of the Sorrowful Countenanace* is, of course, Don Quixote, one of whose idiosyncrasies, was to free criminals on the basis of their abstract right to liberty. Like many other writers of the day, Burke used the term "metaphysic" to describe ideas which were considered to be overly subtle or abstract. Paine, indeed, applied the term to Burke himself. See p. 185.

7 *Dr. Richard Price* (1723–1791) was a Unitarian minister and political economist of some repute who, though not as well known, was even more sympathetic to American independence than Burke himself. He was identified with the Shelburne faction of the Whig party, to which Burke and the other Rockingham Whigs were strongly opposed. When Burke wrote his *Reflections,* the Shelburne Whigs, minus their leader, were in power under William Pitt (the Younger), perhaps England's greatest prime minister. Burke may very well have feared, therefore, that the French revolutionists might assume that Dr. Price's views reflected the sympathies of the English government. This may help to explain why Burke, ordinarily a generous and considerate man, attacked Price, who was then an old man and in failing health, with such virulence. See E. J. Payne, *Burke: Select Works* (Oxford, Eng.: Clarendon Press, 1888–1892), II, 301–302n.

8 *Privilegium non transit in exemplum:* "A privilege does not establish a precedent," is an adage of Roman Law.

9 The three laws cited here, established many of the rights of Englishmen in which Burke took great pride, but, as he failed to point out, each had to be imposed upon a reluctant king. Under the *statutum de tallagio non concedendo* proclaimed in 1297, but not effective until 1340, English kings lost their feudal right to tax their domain (demesne lands) and towns without the consent of the peers, knights, burgesses, "and other free men." Burke considered this act to be "the foundation of the unity and happiness of England since that time." *Second Speech on Conciliation with America* (1775), the official summary of which is reprinted in *Edmund Burke: Selected Writings and Speeches on America,* ed. Thomas H. D. Mahoney (Indianapolis: Bobbs-Merrill, 1964), p. 197. Under the *Petition of Right,* which Parliament compelled King Charles I to sign in 1628, no tax of any kind was henceforth to be levied without the consent of Parliament, and no free man was to be detained or imprisoned or troops billeted in private homes or martial law declared contrary to the laws of the land. By the *Habeas Corpus Act,* to which Charles II gave his reluctant consent in 1679, any person accused of crime must be brought before a judge within a specified time to determine whether he is being lawfully detained. If not, he is entitled to be released with or without bail.

10 *The abdication of King James* was used by the Whigs to justify his deposition. As Burke noted in a footnote: "That King James the second, having endeavoured to *subvert the constitution* of the kingdom, by breaking the *original contract* between king and people, and by the advice of Jesuits, and other wicked persons, having violated the *fundamental* laws, and *having withdrawn himself out of the kingdom,* hath *abdicated* the government, and the throne is thereby *vacant.*" This "declaration" was part of the original Declaration of Rights in which Parliament in 1689 laid down the conditions under which William and Mary were offered the throne.

11 This statue is the famous Bill of Rights of 1689, one of the great charters of English liberty. It incorporates, in slightly amended form, the Declaration of Rights.

12 Act of Settlement (1701). This statute was especially important to Whigs, because it established a new and original contract from which the Germanic princes of the House of Hanover derived their right to rule.

13 *Justicia of Aragon* was the chief magistrate of the medieval Spanish kingdom of Aragon whose process for a time not even the king could obstruct. In the fourteenth century, no other country in Europe, according to the English constitutional historian Henry Hallam, "could boast . . . a more effective barrier against oppression." See his *State of Europe during the Middle Ages* (1818), Chapter IV.

14 *Sir Edward Coke* (1552–1634), though best known as a judge for his able and courageous advocacy of the common law, later, as a member of Parliament, defended its prerogatives with equal zeal and helped to frame and to pass the Petition of Right in 1628.

15 *Sir William Blackstone* (1723–1780) was the English jurist whose *Commentaries on the Laws of England* were perhaps as influential in America as in his own country.

16 *John Selden* (1584–1654) distinguished himself as a scholar and jurist before his election to Parliament where he took such a prominent part in opposing Charles I that he and two of his colleagues were imprisoned in the Tower of London. Though a staunch Puritan, he was no fanatic, and he disapproved of King Charles' execution.

17 *Abbé Sieyès* (Emmanuel Joseph Sieyès, 1748–1836) was the leading ideologist of the second, bourgeois stage of the French Revolution. Though born into a prosperous bourgeois family of noble origins and trained as a priest, he sided with the middle class who comprised the Third Estate against the two privileged orders. The central theme in his many writings and speeches was the cause of democratic nationalism. "The nation is prior to everything," he proclaimed. "It is the source of everything. Its will is always legal; indeed it is the law itself." As a member of the

Directory, he helped bring Napoleon to power. His most famous work, *What is the Third Estate?* (1789), proved to be so successful as a "recipe for popular revolution" everywhere, Professor Peter Campbell has claimed, that "it challenges comparison with the *Communist Manifesto* and with Lenin's *What is to be done?*" See his introduction to Sieyès, *What is the Third Estate?* trans. J. Blondel (New York: Frederick A. Praeger, 1964), pp. 4, 10, 25. Paine's chapter "On the Old and New Systems of Government" (Part II, *The Rights of Man*) was addressed to Sieyès rather than to Burke.

18 It is not surprising that Burke should hold Rousseau, Voltaire, Helvé-tius, and what he called "the rest of that infamous gang" ultimately responsible for almost everything he feared and despised in the French Revolution, though none of the three whom he named lived to see it.

Claude Adrien *Helvétius* (1715–1771) is best known for his hedo-nistic, utilitarian philosophy. Insisting that man was a mere animal guided solely by self-interest, he believed that it was futile—or worse—to rely on morals to thwart sensual gratification. From the premise that all knowledge originates in sensation, he concluded that men were equal in talent at birth and unequal in later years only because they did not receive the same education.

Voltaire (1694–1778), the great French satirist, was regarded by Burke and other conservatives as an enemy of religion and of established order. Actually, he is best described, as is Tom Paine, as a free-thinker, and not an atheist.

It was Jean Jacques *Rousseau* (1712–1778), however, who appeared to Burke to be the real prophet of the French Revolution. "Everybody knows that there is a great dispute amongst their leaders, which of them is the best resemblance of Rousseau. In truth, they all resemble him. His blood they transfuse into their minds and into their manners. Him they study; him they meditate; him they turn over in all the time they can spare from the laborious mischief of the day or the debauches of the night." It was not only Rousseau's "mischievous" influence which Burke deplored but the example of his life. As self-revealed in his famous *Confessions,* Rousseau was "a wild, ferocious, low-minded, hard-hearted father, of fine general feelings, a lover of his kind, but a hater of his kindred." Yet for all of his moral defects and mental quirks, Rousseau was "a writer of great force and vivacity" and "a moralist, or he is nothing," though a moralist, to be sure, whose own character was badly flawed. Even his monumental vanity, Burke was willing to concede, may have been made worse by the madness which from time to time plagued the last ten or fifteen years of his life. *Letter to a Member of the National Assembly* (1791).

19 *Prejudices,* to Burke, were the "untaught feelings" which men hold *in favor of* the institutions under which they have lived for many years. Their antiquity was in itself proof of their "latent wisdom" and of their

superiority to "naked reason." The only prejudices which Burke scorned were those which men hold without sufficient practical experience.

20 *Janissaries* (or Janizaries) were the elite corps of the Turkish army during most of the Ottoman Empire. So fanatical and disciplined were they that for more than four centuries (1400–1826) they were the terror of Europe—and of the Sultans whom they were supposed to protect. Their closest counterpart was the praetorian guard during the Roman Empire. The "images of Asiatic despotism and voluptuousness" appear to have made a strong impression in the West. In *The Federalist,* No. 67, Alexander Hamilton referred to them in a sentence which Burke himself might have penned: "We have been taught to tremble at the terrific visages of murdering janizaries, and to blush at the unveiled mysteries of a future seraglio."

21 *Euripus* is the strait between the island of Euboea and the Greek mainland feared by the ancients because of its mysteriously swift current.

22 *Sophisters,* a variant of sophists, meant those who reason adroitly and speciously rather than soundly. Even the original class of teachers who bore that name in ancient Greece incurred some distrust because they were professionals who accepted pay. See, for example, *The Republic of Plato,* trans. and ed. Allan Bloom (New York: Basic Books, 1968), Book VI, 492a–493d.

23 The *confiscation* of church property voted by the National Assembly on November 2, 1789, did not seem as "dishonest, perfidious, and cruel" to many in both France and England as it did to Burke. Although the state, to be sure, did appropriate the church's lands, it also assumed the church's financial obligations including the salaries of all churchmen. Though they became in fact salaried civil servants, many of the clergy later took an oath to support the new system. The non-juring priests who refused the oath continued to receive a pension but they were replaced in office and forbidden to receive a stipend. The response of the Vatican, though somewhat belated, was severe. In the spring of 1791, Pope Pius VI condemned not only the church policies of the National Assembly but even the Declaration of the Rights of Man and of the Citizen. See Georges Lefebvre, *The French Revolution From Its Origins to 1793* (New York: Columbia University Press, 1962), pp. 159–161, 166–171.

24 The courtyard of the *Palais Royale,* surrounded as it was by restaurants and shops, had become a favorite meeting place in Paris where orators harangued crowds and organized demonstrations.

25 The *Jacobins,* who took their name from the old Dominican monastery of St. Jacques where they met, were but one of the political clubs supporting the Revolution. At first the club restricted its membership to

those serving in the National Assembly, and it favored moderate, reformist policies. In time, however, it fell under the domination of the most militantly radical wing of the Revolution which was later largely responsible for the Reign of Terror. To Burke and other conservatives Jacobinism represented all of the social and political doctrines which they despised in Revolutionary France and feared in their own country.

25a *troublous storms that toss* . . . Edmund Spenser, *Faerie Queene*, II, c. 7, st. 14.

26 In the original text Burke added a footnote of his own about the *Cardinal of Lorraine*: "This is on a supposition of the truth of this story; but he was not in France at the time. One name serves as well as another." During the infamous St. Bartholomew's Day Massacre (1572) some 25,000–50,000 French Protestants or Huguenots were slain on the order of King Charles IX. It was disingenuous of Burke, nevertheless, to suggest that the Cardinal of Lorraine was blameless He introduced the Inquisition to France, and he was the most powerful and zealous prelate in France.

27 *The stipend of an exciseman* is one of two slighting references to the rather lowly position which Tom Paine held as a young man in England. The other, equally invidious, is to the "arithmetic of an exciseman" cited in note 122 on pp. 279–80. It is possible, perhaps even likely, that Burke, whose memory for detail was prodigious, intended these as a bankhanded swipe at Paine.

28 The *sort of education* . . . described here by Burke is a fair description of the philosophy for which Helvétius was best known. See footnote 18.

29 The *Long Parliament* was so-called because technically it remained in session for twenty years (1640–60). It was during this period that the English Civil War broke out, King Charles I was deposed and beheaded, and a Commonwealth established under Oliver Cromwell and his Bible-reading Puritan army. The most severe measure taken against the Church of England, to which Burke belonged, was not the limited expropriation of some of its property, but its disestablishment in favor of a Puritan state church embracing the three major Puritan groups— the Independents, Presbyterians, and Baptists.

30 *One of the greatest of their own lawyers:* Jean Domat (1625–1696) was a French jurist who regarded the laws and customs of a nation as the reflex of its political history.

31 *Munera Terrae:* "The gifts of the earth" (Horace, *Odes,* xiv); i.e., the transient, as opposed to the eternal.

32 The *old fanatics of single arbitrary power* included Peter Heylyn (1600–1662), an English clergyman who defended the Stuarts' despotism, and Sir Robert Filmer (d. 1653), who upheld the divine right of kings.

33 *A democracy has many striking points of resemblance with a tyranny:* "Both show a similar temper; both behave like despots to the better class of citizens; the decrees of the one are like the edicts of the other; the popular leader in the one is the same as, or at any rate like, the flatterer in the other; and in either case the influence of favorites predominates—that of the flatterer in tyrannies, and that of the popular leaders in democracies of this variety." *The Politics of Aristotle,* Ernest Barker, ed. (New York: Oxford University Press, 1962), Book IV, Ch. iv, sec. 28. It was a matter of some pride to Burke that he was still able to quote this passage in Greek after so many years. It should be noted, however, that Aristotle saw this resemblance only between tyranny and *one* type of democracy, i.e., a polity under the sway of demagogues in which popular decrees, not the laws, were sovereign. He even denied that such a system, under which everything was managed by decrees, was a democracy "in any real sense." *Ibid.,* IV, iv, 31.

34 Henry St. John, the first Viscount *Bolingbroke* (1678–1751), was an English statesman, whose writings, especially his *Idea of a Patriot King,* presented the Tory cause in its most favorable light. For this reason, one suspects, Burke found it hard to praise him: "Who now reads Bolingbroke?" he asked contemptuously in a passage from the *Reflections* not included here. Still, Bolingbroke was too considerable a figure to ignore. His openly stated preference for "natural" religion led Burke to write *A Vindication of Natural Society* (1756), which many readers failed to recognize as the satire it was intended to be. See also note 107, p. 278.

35 *States-General* was the name given in prerevolutionary France to the general assemblies representing the three estates or orders—clergy, nobility, and the bourgeoisie—which were convoked by the king at his pleasure. That which met in 1789 was only the second called in 200 years. As in Great Britain the commons—the Third Estate—met separately from the clergy and the nobility, but they lacked the legal authority and the proud tradition of the House of Commons. Nevertheless, it was the bourgeoisie, assisted by many parish priests and a few nobles, who precipitated the French Revolution by integrating the three orders into a single *National Assembly.* With this step France broke sharply with its feudal past and the Revolution entered its bourgeois stage.

36 *Tahmas Kouli Khan* (1688–1747), also known as Nadir Shah, was the Turkish adventurer who, after seizing the throne of Persia in 1736, waged aggressive war against its neighbors in the next decade. His exploits, which ended disastrously for Persia, were well known in Burke's day.

37 The adversaries whose *good nature* Burke did not dispute were those in his own country and especially of his own party, including its then

290 Burke and Paine

leader Charles James Fox (1749–1806), who were inclined at first to look favorably on the French Revolution. He was not willing to make allowances even for the moderate wing of the revolutionary party in France.

38 The *queen of France*, to whom Burke referred, was, of course, Marie Antoinette (1755–1793), eleventh daughter of the Holy Roman Emperor, Francis I, and Maria Theresa. From the time of her marriage to Louis XVI in 1770 until her death, she was distrusted and disliked by many of her French subjects, all the more because she was Austrian. Her frivolity, extravagance, and inclination to meddle in affairs of state, though no doubt exaggerated by her enemies, served to weaken the moral authority of the monarchy and to add to its financial woes. Even while she was imprisoned, she managed to take part in a series of intrigues to free the royal family and to stir up a counterrevolutionary coalition among the other European powers. Her dignity and courage during her confinement, trial, and execution did much to rehabilitate her reputation.

This "apostrophe" to the Queen may well be the most celebrated of the many memorable passages in Burke's *Reflections*. To some of his contemporaries the whole passage seemed affected and overwrought; even Burke's good friend, Philip Francis, dismissed it as "pure foppery." Burke himself insisted that the sentiments which he expressed were not only true but deeply felt; his "tears," he said, "wetted" the paper when he wrote the lines. James T. Boulton has called the passage "the centerpiece of the *Reflections*," because, more successfully than any other, it illustrates the fusion of thought and emotion "which distinguishes almost all of Burke's work." See Boulton, *The Language of Politics in the Age of Wilkes and Burke* (London: Routledge & Kegan-Paul, 1963), pp. 98, 255.

39 *The groves of their academy* is a reference to the public groves in ancient Athens in which Plato and other philosophers taught.

39a *Non satis est pulchra esse poemata, dulcia sunto:* "It is not enough that poems be beautiful, they must be tender as well." Horace, *Ars Poetica*, 99.

40 *Swinish multitude.* No remark of Burke aroused more resentment than this allusion to the pearls thrown before swine in *St. Matthew*, VII; 6. It became for a time a watchword among the friends of the Revolution in England and America and inspired, among many other tracts, *An Address to the Hon. Edmund Burke from the Swinish Multitude* (1793).

41 *Officious* is used here to mean "ready to serve," not in the modern sense of meddlesome or overbearing.

41a *Omnes boni nobilitati semper favemus:* "All we who are good citizens always favour noble birth." Cicero, *Pro Sestio,* ix. 21. (Tr. R. Gardner)

42 *Sortition or rotation.* Sortition was the scheme proposed in 1782 by one of Burke's colleagues in Parliament to have the ministry chosen by lot each year from 30 selected members of the House of Lords and 100 from the House of Commons. Much earlier, during the Puritan Revolution, James Harrington (1611–1677) proposed a bicameral legislature for his *Commonwealth of Oceana* in which one-third of the members of the upper house—the senate—would be replaced at each election at which members of the lower house were elected. Thus, barring reappointment, there would be a complete *rotation* of the senate membership after three elections. Though never applied to the British Parliament, this scheme was adopted in somewhat modified form in the United States Senate.

43 *third of the legislature.* In Burke's day the monarch, the Peers, and the Commons each had to give its assent to legislation. Though today the monarch's assent is purely a formality, statutes are still enacted, technically, by the King's most excellent majesty" (or the "Queen's most gracious majesty") with the advice and consent of the lords and commons in Parliament assembled.

44 *Ostracism* was the practice in ancient Athens and a few other Greek city-states by which any citizen could be banished for ten years by vote of the popular assembly and senate. It was not necessary that he be found guilty of some crime; it was enough that his ambition and influence were believed to pose a threat to the state.

45 *all the charities of all:* Cicero, *De Officiis* i. 17.

46 *told by the head,* i.e., counted as individuals. In Burke's day and for some time thereafter even members of the House of Commons were understood to represent the landed or mercantile interests of their constituency rather than its individual voters.

47 *lamppost for its second.* . . . : a grim allusion to the practice by which Parisian mobs lynched enemies of the Revolution on the lampposts (lanterne) which lighted the streets.

48 *incoherent republics.* One of the first actions taken by the National Assembly was to decentralize the administration of France. The nation was divided into 83 departments, the departments into districts, the districts into cantons, and each canton contained a number of communes or municipalities. For a time each municipality enjoyed the right to tax imports and exports, maintain public order, requisition troops, and proclaim martial law. In Paris alone the government was divided among 60 departments, each of which considered itself to be a city-state on the ancient Greek model. It was to these "incoherent republics" that Burke referred. Under Napoleon the municipalities, Paris included, lost almost all of their power of self-government and the administration became highly centralized.

⁴⁹ *The troll of their categorical table . . . eight heads more . . .* Here Burke is suggesting that the French "sophisters" did not understand their own metaphysics. According to Aristotle, all objects can be categorized on the basis of ten irreducible characteristics—substance and quantity, which are most apparent, and *eight heads more*—quality, relation, space, time, situation, condition, action, and passion (i.e. being acted on).

⁵⁰ *dullish sluggish race . . . mediocrity of freedom.* Elsewhere Burke offered his "praises of the British government, loaded with all its encumbrances; clogged with its peers and its beef; its parsons and its pudding; its commons and its beer; and its dull slavish liberty of going about just as one pleases. . . ." *Letter to William Elliot* (1795), VI, 69.

⁵¹ *member of Bristol.* Bristol was the second of the three constituencies which Burke represented in his own independent way during the 28 years he was a member of the House of Commons. It was then a busy seaport with a prosperous trade with North America and the West Indies, and, in Burke's words, "the second city of the Kingdom." He declined his party's nomination for a second term in the face of almost certain defeat because of his unpopular stands favoring free trade with Ireland and independence for America. See Ernest Barker, "Burke and his Bristol Constituency," *Essays in Government* (London: Oxford University Press, 1951), pp. 154–201.

⁵² *portions with jointures.* Here Burke anticipates, as elsewhere he deplores, the breakup of many of the great landed estates because there was no son to succeed to ownership under the law of *primogeniture.* Then it became lawful for only a part (*portion*) of the estate to pass to an heir or, under *jointure,* for the whole of it to go to the wife if she outlived her husband.

⁵³ *charges of election.* . . . The cost of conducting a campaign was particularly high in the larger constituencies like London, Bristol, Westminster, and Liverpool, because "there the voters expected to be wooed with beef, ale, and cash by the gentlemen of England." Burke had no money of his own for this purpose, so the charges of his first election in Bristol were borne by a small group of wealthy merchants. In the other two constituencies which he represented (Wendover and Malton) there was no need to campaign because both were pocket boroughs controlled by the Rockingham Whig families with which Burke was associated. See notes 26 and 27, p. 301.

⁵⁴ *Lucan* (A.D. 39–65), a Latin poet, whose republican sympathies led him to oppose the Emperor Nero and plot his assassination. Pierre *Corneille* (1606–1684), the leading French dramatic poet of his day, whose "fine raptures" in praise of liberty were much more muted.

⁵⁵ *hack that aged parent in pieces* . . . : a legendary allusion to the daughters of King Pelias of Thessaly, who chopped their father in pieces and boiled him in a cauldron at the behest of the sorceress Medea.

⁵⁶ *Society is indeed a contract.* Interestingly, Burke's view of the social contract is closer to Rousseau, "this insane Socrates of the National Assembly," than to his own countryman and fellow Whig, John Locke, in at least one respect: in order that man in an "uncivil state" might secure "*some* liberty," he made "a surrender in trust of the *whole* of it." In other respects, too, as Alfred Cobban has pointed out, there is a "remarkable similarity" between Burke and Rousseau. "Both were realists or naturalists in politics, both were in the forefront of the romantic movement, both prophets of the reborn spirit of mysticism. And Burke, like Rousseau, was, whether he wished it or not, inevitably forced back on natural rights and apriorism. He is constantly concerned with the rights of men and so of Man." Alfred Cobban, *Edmund Burke and the Revolt Against the Eighteenth Century,* 2nd ed. (London: George Allen & Unwin, Ltd., 1960), p. 45.

⁵⁷ *resort to anarchy.* Yet even Burke had found anarchy to be "tolerable" on one occasion. In 1774, when resistance to the Crown was especially strong in Massachusetts, its "ancient government" was abrogated in the belief that "the first feeling, if not the very prospect of anarchy, would instantly enforce a complete submission." Instead, "a new, strange, unexpected face of things appeared. . . . A vast province has now subsisted, and subsisted in a considerable degree of health and vigor, for near a twelve-month, without governor, without public council, without judges, without executive magistrates." He concluded that "Obedience is what makes government, and not the names by which it is called. . . ." *Speech on Conciliation with America* (1775), 139.

⁵⁸ *The happy settlement* which followed the Revolution of 1688 established the right of Parliament to depose a king and to bind his successor to adhere to the Church of England and to govern according to acts of Parliament. It established, in short, a limited, constitutional monarchy in place of the arbitrary rule of the Stuarts.

⁵⁹ *kind of mortmain:* comparable to the status of land and other real property which under feudal law could not be sold.

⁶⁰ *Maroon slaves:* the fugitive African slaves living in the wilder parts of the West Indies.

⁶¹ Joseph Addison, *Cato,* V, I, II.

Thomas Paine
on the Rights of Man

1 The *criminal justice* which Burke suggests here that Paine deserved was a prosecution for seditious libel. Whether at Burke's prompting or not, this was the course of action taken by the Pitt Ministry. In December, 1792, Paine was tried in absentia (he was then in France serving as an elected member of the National Convention) and found guilty by an English jury. This much was to have been expected, given the strictness of the English libel law at the time, but not the extraordinary lengths to which the government went to stir up popular feeling against Paine. Once the author was dealt with, the printers and booksellers who handled *The Rights of Man* were proceeded against on the same charge. Despite the government's efforts to suppress the work, *The Rights of Man* reached an enormous public—far greater than Burke's *Reflections*. Between four and five hundred thousand copies of Part I were sold in England, Scotland, and Ireland alone, by Paine's own account, and Part II enjoyed an even greater success. According to Philip Foner, "close to a million and a half copies [were] published in England during the author's lifetime." *The Complete Writings of Thomas Paine,* ed. Philip S. Foner (New York: The Citadel Press, 1945), II, 910; I, 345. Unless otherwise noted, all quotations from Paine's writings are from this edition.

2 Bill of Rights, 1 William and Mary, sess. 2, c. 2 (1689).

3 Act of Settlement, 12 & 13 William III, c. 2 (1701). Actually, Paine is quoting Burke's paraphrase of the statute, not the act itself.

4 Paine's insinuation that Burke was a *pensioner in a fictitious name* was untrue but it proved to be prophetic in part. In 1794 Burke did accept a pension from the King, but only near the end of a long parliamentary career in which he, like other members, had received no compensation from the government. There was nothing unlawful about the pension because it was paid openly out of the public treasury. Under an act of Parliament which Burke himself had sponsored in 1782, only secret pensions had been outlawed. The King continued to have the power to grant pensions out of the civil list from which the expenses of the royal household were paid, so there was no need to refer the matter to Parliament for its approval. Nevertheless, Burke was openly attacked on the floor of the House by members of the Whig Opposition, and he was moved to reply in his famous *Letter to a Noble Lord.* "What I have obtained was the fruit of no bargain; the production of no intrigue; the result of no compromise; the effect of no solicitation. . . . I was not made for a minion or a tool. . . . At every step of my progress in life, (for in every step was I traversed and opposed,) and at every turnpike I met, I was obliged to show my passport, again and again to prove my sole title to the honour of being useful to my country. . . ." V, 112, 125.

5 *send either to Holland or to Hanover.* In 1688 Parliament offered the throne to William of Orange, Stadtholder of Holland, and his wife Mary, thereby deposing Mary's father, James II, for his subversion of the British Constitution. In 1701 Parliament provided that the throne would pass to Sophia, Elector of Hanover and her heirs, upon the death of Queen Anne, who had succeeded William and Mary. Sophia died before Anne, however, and her son George became the first of the Hanoverian kings of England (1714–1727).

6 *wisemen of Gotham.* Gotham was an English village whose inhabitants were proverbially known for their foolishness.

6a *"true moral demonstrations":* Here Burke has been misquoted slightly and harmlessly; he had, in fact, written "true moral *denominations.*" A much less trivial and excusable misquotation is cited in note 44, p. 306.

7 *the natural constitution of man.* Unlike Paine, who attributed man's capacity for order to his natural goodness, Burke was inclined to credit God: "[I] do not like to compliment the contrivances of men with what is due in a great degree to the bounty of Providence." Burke, *Reflections,* p. 148.

8 *social affections.* A term which is still to be found in America's three oldest state constitutions—Massachusetts (1780), New Hampshire (1784),

and Vermont (1790). There the "social affections" are identified as "justice, moderation, temperance, industry, and frugality" and declared to be "indispensably necessary to preserve the blessings of liberty and good government."

9 *A metaphysical man, like Mr. Burke.* Here Paine is repaying Burke in his own coin. Not much significance should be read into the term in either case, since it was used by both men in a pejorative sense.

10 *a third insane.* It is almost certain that Paine is alluding here to King George III, who had suffered at least two attacks of mental illness by 1789 and would suffer two more before he became permanently deranged during the last nine years of his life (1811–1820).

11 *Fortunatus' wishing cap or Harlequin's wooden sword.* Fortunatus and Harlequin were two stock figures in the folk theater in Paine's day. Fortunatus and his son possessed two gifts which were the envy of Everyman—an inexhaustible purse of gold and a wishing cap, which in the end proved ruinous. Harlequin, in the English tradition, was the pantomimist, half hero and half buffoon, who had exchanged his gift of speech for a magic wand in the form of a wooden sword which he used to protect his mistress, Columbine, against the Clown and Pantaloon.

12 *Placemen* were those members of Parliament whose independence of the Crown had been compromised by accepting a place or office at its hands. Even when the office was not a sinecure, as was sometimes the case, placemen were expected to support the King and his ministers. Their frantic, last-minute efforts in the House to muster a majority for the government led Burke to compare them scornfully to the "whippers-in" of the hounds at a fox hunt, and the term "whip" has survived to this day, despite its derogatory origin, as an essential element of the party leadership in English and American legislatures. As late as 1741 more than one-third of the Members of Parliament—200 out of 528—held places under the Crown; by 1790 the number had declined, but it was still high. From time to time members of the House were forbidden to hold any other civil office of profit, but as often, the ban was soon repealed. Otherwise, the British cabinet system could not have evolved, because it requires the executive power of the realm to be placed in the hands of the leaders of the party controlling the House of Commons. Placemen present no problem in the United States where the legislative and executive branches are constitutionally separate and independent. Thus, members of Congress are barred from holding any civil office under the United States (U.S. Constitution, Art. I, Sec. 6), and similar restrictions apply to state legislators under their own state constitution.

13 *lords of the necessary house.* It seems hardly necessary to point out, except perhaps to American readers, that there was no such office, but

one quite like it did exist—the *grooms of the stole* to which Paine later alludes. That worthy originally served the King's stole chamber or privy although by Paine's day his duties were broadened to include the entire royal household. See footnote 32.

14 *The only forms of government.* . . . The distinction which Paine makes here between monarchical, aristocratic, and democratic governments was well known to the ancient Greeks, but their classification, in some respects, was more sophisticated than his. Aristotle, for example, distinguished in theory between the *"true* forms of government"— monarchy, aristocracy, and polity or polyarchy—which govern in the interest of all citizens, and their respective "perversions"—tyranny, oligarchy, and democracy—in which the rulers govern in their own interest. In practice, however, he found that few governments were pure in their form, and that most tended to be either oligarchic or democratic, depending on whether they were controlled by the relatively few who were rich or the many who were poor. Aristotle's own preference, among those forms which he thought men were most likely to attain, was for a polity or constitutional government, which combined aristocratic and democratic elements under the rule of the middle class. Burke's bias was clearly in favor of a polity in which the aristocratic clearly outweighed the democratic elements. See Aristotle, *Politics,* Bk. III, Chs. 7–8; Bk. IV, chs. 7–9.

15 *institutions that are purely pecuniary, such as that of a bank.* Paine was much more solicitous about vested property rights than might have been suspected from someone of his populist sympathies. In 1786 he took part in the bitter struggle in Pennsylvania between the wealthy merchants in Philadelphia and the back-country farmers over the Bank of North America. The bank had been founded five years earlier to provide credit to the Continental Army at a time when the state governments seemed unable or unwilling to do so themselves. In the hard times which followed the Revolution the frontier communities, then heavily in debt to Philadelphia merchants and bankers, looked to the state capitol for relief. A number of state legislators responded by introducing bills to increase the amount of paper money in circulation. At the same time they proposed to repeal the charter of the bank for fear that it would refuse to accept the paper money as legal tender. Paine threw himself into the fray with his usual zeal, denouncing the legislature for its "ingratitude" and its "rash, injudicious, and violent proceedings" for even considering such a "bare-faced act of injustice." In any event, he argued, legal tender laws violated the personal and property rights guaranteed by the Pennsylvania constitution. "In this pledge and compact lies the foundation of the republic; and the security to the rich and the consolation to the poor is, that what each man has is his own; that no despotic sovereign can take it from him, and that the common cementing principle which holds all the parts of a

republic together, secures him likewise from the despotism of numbers: for despotism may be more effectually acted by many over a few, than by one man over all." *Dissertations on Government* (1786), II, 373–74, 397, 409.

Actually, as Philip S. Foner has pointed out, Paine had special reason to support the Bank because it was "the offspring of [an] institution he had helped found in 1780 and to which he had contributed his own money. . . . Nor should it be overlooked that Paine's views were widely shared by the city mechanics in Philadelphia who did not favor the further issuance of paper money, fearing its inflationary effects on their living standards." *Ibid.*, 368. The fact remains, however, that in this controversy Paine took an essentially conservative position and used arguments which even Burke would have approved.

16 The original *apple of discord*, in Euripides' version of the Greek myth, was the device by which Eris, the goddess of discord, gained revenge on the other gods for slighting her. Since it was a golden apple inscribed "For the Fairest," each of the goddesses on Olympus wanted it for herself, but wisely Zeus refused to act as judge. At his suggestion, the choice was then referred to Paris, son of Priam, King of Troy, who awarded the apple to Aphrodite, goddess of love, less for her own beauty than for the promise of the love of one ever fairer. That beauty, of course, was Helen, wife of Menelaus, King of Sparta. Her abduction by Paris led to the Trojan War.

17 *Guelph* was the original family name of the German princes who ruled both Hanover, one of the German states, and Great Britain itself after the accession of George I. "George Guelph," therefore, was George III, whom earlier, during the American Revolution, Paine had called the "Royal Brute of Great Britain" and "the hardened, sullen-tempered Pharaoh of England."

18 *hewers of wood and drawers of water: Joshua* 9:21.

19 *That a king can do no wrong* is still a maxim of English law, but the immunity which it confers is not as sweeping as it implies. The rule simply means that the king—or whoever else may be the sovereign— may not be sued without his consent for any wrongful acts or failure to act on the part of his servants. In this way the king was able to disassociate himself from the misdeeds of anyone acting or failing to act in his name. At no time, however, did the rule suggest that the king was above the law. King John was merely the first of several English Kings who were made to feel the "bridle of the law." In Bracton's famous phrase, "the king is under no man, but he is under God and the Law."

20 *Conquest and tyranny transplanted themselves with William the Conqueror,* who elsewhere in *The Rights of Man* is described as "the son of a prostitute and the plunderer of the English nation." Here Paine is expressing what Christopher Hill has called the "Norman Yoke" in-

terpretation of English political history, i.e., the view that the Norman
conquerors destroyed the freedom and representative government which
they found in Anglo-Saxon England and established an oppressive
monarchy and feudal order of their own. See Christopher Hill, *Puritan-
ism and Revolution* (London: Secker and Warburg, 1958), pp. 99–109.
This theory, though greatly exaggerated, helped to keep alive popular
resentment against the Norman and Plantagenet kings.

21 *Comedy of Errors . . . Pantomime of Hush.* Two other examples, as
Boulton notes, of the effective use Paine made of theatrical terms which
Englishmen could understand without further explanation. See James
T. Boulton, *The Language of Politics in the Age of Wilkes and Burke*
(London: Routledge & Kegan-Paul, 1963), p. 141.

22 *Dr. Johnson* was, of course, Samuel Johnson, the great English critic,
essayist, and lexicographer whose life was immortalized by James Boswell. Although a staunch Tory ("Sire," he once said to some unfortunate, "I perceive that you are a vile Whig"), he was Burke's close friend
and warm admirer.

23 *The organization of the legislative power,* Paine concluded, "is altogether a matter of opinion," and his own opinion underwent several
changes as to whether two legislative chambers were better than one. In
1777 he had nothing but praise for the Pennsylvania constitution which
created a single legislative Assembly. Yet by 1786 he was convinced that
a "single house" is as much subject to "haste, rashness and passion" as
a single person "when party operates to produce party laws." The cause
of his disenchantment was the Assembly's repeal of the Bank of North
America's charter. See footnote 15. In 1792 he unveiled a scheme in
Part II of *The Rights of Man* which he believed would "remove the
objection against a single House (that of acting with too quick an impulse) and at the same . . . avoid the inconsistencies, in some cases
absurdities, arising from the two Houses." His proposal was to elect but
one body of representatives but divide them, by lot, into two or three
parts or sections. Every bill would be debated in each section with the
other section(s) in attendance, after which the entire body would assemble for a general debate and vote. Yet by 1795 his disillusionment with
a single legislature was complete, confirmed at first hand by his three
years' service in the French National Assembly which he had seen
degenerate into an instrument first of the Terror and then of Reaction.
He no longer thought it wise "that the whole [representation] should sit
together and debate at once." "[W]hen the whole legislature is crowded
into one body, it is an individual in mass" and "subject to the precipi-
tancy and passion of an individual." *Dissertation on First Principles of
Government* (1795), II, 585.

24 *The sovereign authority . . . is the power of making laws. . . .* Here
Paine is expressing a Whig view of legislative power which his adopted

country, America, had already abandoned in its then new Constitution. Perhaps the classic statement is by John Locke: "there can be but one supreme power, which is the legislative, to which all the rest are and must be subordinate. . . ." *Second Treatise on Civil Government,* Ch. XIII. Yet Paine, like Locke, recognized that there may be occasions when the executive must be entrusted with great discretion. "There is a species of sovereign powers in a single person," Paine wrote in 1786, "which is very proper when applied to a commander-in-chief over an army, so far as it relates to the military government of an army, and the condition and purpose of an army constitutes the reason why it is so." *Dissertations on Government,* II, 371.

25 *The reason why so many of those charters abound in Cornwall* is that the Tudor and Stuart kings, *not* their Norman predecessors, sought to pack the House of Commons by granting new charters to towns in Cornwall where their influence was strongest. In the century and a half which spanned the reigns of Henry VIII and Charles II (1510–1660) no less than 180 members were added to the House by royal charter alone.

26 *Old Sarum* was one of a number of "pocket boroughs," called that because they belonged to some landed noble as much as the watch he carried in his pocket. Although it was little more than an open field, Old Sarum had the same representation as the largest towns—two members—and half that of London itself. As in the other pocket boroughs, the two members from Old Sarum were hand-picked by the proprietor to serve his interests.

27 *Chartered monopolies.* During Paine's lifetime—and Burke's—417 of the 513 English seats in the House of Commons were elected by boroughs, the rest by counties. The county franchise was uniform; freeholders owning or leasing land yielding 40 shillings or more each year were allowed to vote. The borough franchise, on the other hand, varied greatly from town to town depending on its charter. In twelve boroughs almost every resident was qualified to vote, and in 80 others, everyone who had inherited or been granted the formal status of freemen. Elsewhere the borough franchise was greatly restricted. In some 40 boroughs only those who paid the ancient parish tax could vote, and in the 40 *burgage* boroughs, voting was restricted to landowners whose property was specified in the borough charter. In the so-called *corporation* boroughs, also about 40 in number, members of Parliament were named by the borough council or corporation. In 1760 only 85,000 Englishmen were elegible to vote for the borough members, who constituted nearly three-fourths of all House seats, and some 15,000 of this number elected over half of the borough members. See Colin Rhys Lovell, *English Constitutional and Legal History* (New York: Oxford University Press, 1962), pp. 235–36, 428–31.

28 *"Our representation,"* says [Burke], *"has been found perfectly adequate*

*to all the purposes for which a representation of the people can be
desired or devised. I defy . . . the enemies of our Constitution to
show the contrary."* The most persuasive testimony that Paine was right
and Burke wrong about the adequacy of parliamentary representation
came from two men who were in no sense enemies of the British Constitution—the William Pitts', father and son. In 1766 the elder Pitt—
Lord Chatham—denounced the borough representation as "the rotten
part of our constitution. It cannot continue a century; if it does not drop,
it must be amputated." The indictment of the younger Pitt was no less
severe: "This House is not representative of the people of Great Britain,
it is the representative of nominal [pocket] boroughs of ruined and
exterminated towns, of noble families, of wealthy individuals, of foreign
potentates." See Thomas Pitt Taswell-Langmead, *English Constitutional
History,* 10th ed. (1946), pp. 637, 631. The most that can be said in
support of Burke's position is that some few members of Parliament,
like Burke himself, retained their independence of the Crown, and
some of the larger constituencies respected independence unless it
threatened their vital interests and that some corruption was inevitable
and perhaps even necessary for cabinet government to develop in the
absence of strong, disciplined political parties. So Professor L. B. Na-
mier argues in his study of the *Structure of Politics at the Accession of
George III* (London: The Macmillan Co., 1928), I, 262–265.

29 *a man who has been in constant opposition to all the measures of
Parliament the whole of his political life, a year or two excepted.* In
the nearly thirty years that Burke served in Parliament, his "party"—
the Rockingham (later the Portland) Whigs—controlled or shared control of the British government for only two short periods. Burke himself held just two offices, neither of the first rank; in 1782–83, he was
the Paymaster General and a member of the Privy Council. Several
explanations have been advanced as to why Burke never held higher
office. One is that his aristocratic friends and patrons overlooked his
great talents because of his modest background; another is that, as he
realized himself, temperamentally he was not suited to high executive
office. Actually, as Carl B. Cone argues, Burke preferred the paymaster-
ship because it gave him the best opportunity to promote his economical reforms. See his *Burke and the Nature of Politics* (Lexington, Ky.:
University of Kentucky Press, 1957–64), II, 4, 8–9, 19.

29a *poor-rates . . .* the local tax or assessment levied on householders for
the relief or support of the poor in England until the modern welfare
state.

30 [The House of Lords] *has obtained so much influence by borough
traffic . . . as to give it, . . . a preponderancy in the other. . . .*
Here Paine was unquestionably on solid ground. Many of the peers
who constituted the House of Lords were landed proprietors who

controlled parliamentary nominations not only in their own pocket
boroughs but in those corporation boroughs whose seats they bought.
In 1760, according to one informed estimate, approximately 100 landowners, 51 of them peers, influenced, often to the point of control, the
election of more than 190 members of the House of Commons. By the
early nineteenth century their control was even more complete. The
number of influential landowners had grown to 155, many of them
newly elevated to the peerage, and so did the number of seats which
they controlled—307 out of 558, including the Irish and Scottish members. Even among the landlord class, however, there were often sharp
political differences between the landowning aristocracy, who tended
to be Whigs, and the country gentlemen—the squirearchy—who were
often Tories.

This trafficking in seats, known as "borough-mongering," also gave
the government of the day an opportunity to extend its own influence
over both houses of Parliament. "Both the crown and the ministers of the
day, either acting in unison, or, as was frequently the case under George
III, in opposition to one another, bought seats alike of patrons and
constituencies—titles, pensions, or hard cash satisfying the varying wants
of all." Taswell-Langmead, p. 628. Yet however corrupt the system may
have been, it had one partially redeeming virtue. As Lovell points out,
"Ministers of the crown, responsible for the day-to-day administration
of the country . . . had to face the disagreeable fact that their efforts
ultimately depended upon the support of this wayward, perverse, but
fortunately for long periods, corruptible body of men." Lovell, p. 437.

[31] A *rotten borough,* unlike a pocket borough, was one which offered its
seats in Parliament to politicians willing to contribute to local charities
and to such public enterprises as street paving and lighting. The practice was widespread, and it appears not to have aroused much public
outcry except when the bargain struck seemed overly explicit or
extortionate. On occasion a borough would openly offer its seats to the
higher bidder. One, the seat of Oxford University no less, went so far
in 1768 as to demand that its two sitting members pay off the municipal
debt of £5,670 as the price of their reelection. In this case the council
went too far, and the mayor and ten of the aldermen were sent to
Newgate Prison briefly after the matter was reported to the House.
The term now has a quite different meaning especially in the United
States where it refers to those legislative districts which, thanks to
gerrymandering in some form, have a much larger representation than
their population would otherwise warrant. See Lovell, p. 430 and
Taswell-Langmead, p. 629.

[32] *groom of the stole.* See footnote 13.

[33] *It talks about its fine, blue riband like a girl, and shows its new garter
like a child.* An allusion to the Most Noble Order of the Garter, the

most ancient and, among the aristocracy, most coveted of the British chivalric orders. Its members, restricted normally to 26 knights, are entitled to wear the following insignia: a garter of dark blue velvet and gold bearing the motto *Honi soit qui mal y pense* (Evil be to him who thinks evil); a collar of gold from which is suspended the George, an enamelled figure of St. George slaying the dragon; a smaller badge of St. George encircled by an oval garter bearing the motto and worn on the right hip from a dark blue ribbon; and the star, a silver eight-pointed star bearing in its center the red cross of St. George on a white ground, surrounded by the garter and the motto. The garter and collar are worn only on special occasions as are the distinctive mantle, hood, surcoat, and hat.

34 The *certain writer, of some antiquity, [who said], "When I was a child, I thought as a child . . ."* was, of course, St. Paul in his First Letter to the Corinthians, 13:11.

35 *The law of primogenitureship,* as Paine failed to note, was brought to England by the Normans as part of their feudal military system. Until it was abolished in 1926, parents were required to leave all of their real estate to their eldest son to the absolute exclusion of their younger sons and their daughters. The rule and some of the exceptions permitted are discussed in note 52, p. 292. It survives as a rule of law only in the case of royal persons and peers. In continental Europe most countries have abolished the law altogether but Revolutionary France was the first to do so. In America primogeniture was followed in only a few of the colonies, and it was abandoned entirely at the birth of the Republic largely through the efforts of Thomas Jefferson.

36 All *ideas of distributive justice* tend to be corrupted at the very source, because, as Aristotle noted, most men as a rule are bad judges where their own interests are involved. "The oligarchs think that superiority on one point—in their case wealth—means superiority on all"; he wrote, "the democrats believe that equality in one respect—for instance, that of free birth—means equality all around." Neither view is correct, Aristotle insisted, because justice is relative to persons, not to classes. True justice means that those who have contributed to the end of the state should have rights in proportion to their contribution to that end. Aristotle, *Politics,* Bk. III, Ch. 9, 81–84.

37 Baron de la Brède et de *Montesquieu* (1689–1755) was probably the most influential political theorist of his age not only in his native France but in Europe and America as well. In England he was well known for his moderate reformist views and his admiration of the British Constitution. He argued that the laws of each nation should be adapted to its physical environment and to the character of its people, especially their occupation, religion, manners, customs, and maturity. These views seem to have made a strong impression on Burke. Indeed, in

1757, when he was only twenty-eight, he said that Montesquieu was "the greatest genius which has enlightened this age." Guy Chapman, *Edmund Burke: the Practical Imagination* (Cambridge: Harvard University Press, 1967), pp. 21, 142–47. To Paine, on the other hand, Montesquieu was not nearly so towering or heroic a figure. Though he credited Montesquieu with being more "strongly inclined to republican government" than it appeared from his writing, it was for the reason, Paine surmised, that "he had always the Bastille before his eyes when he was speaking of republics and therefore *pretended* not to write for France." Paine appeared to accept Montesquieu's doctrine of separation of powers which later would be incorporated into the American Constitution, but he denied, quite correctly, that it was an essential part of the British Constitution. "To say that the Constitution of England is a *union* of three powers, reciprocally *checking* each other, is farcical," Paine insisted, "either the words have no meaning, or they are flat contradictions." Foner, II, 345, 598–99; I, 7.

38 The *Abbé Raynal* (1713–1796), though trained as a priest, was so strongly critical of the clergy and Europeans for their treatment of the Indians that he was forced to flee France. After several years in exile he returned to France a somewhat chastened man. In 1791 he renounced some of his more radical views in an address which was read before the National Assembly. Throughout the Revolution, he opposed violence and continued to regard the British Constitution as the best government for France. He was known to Paine largely through an historical account of the American Revolution which was first published in English in 1781. Paine took such strong exception to the work that he wrote an extended critique. "Though the Abbé possesses and displays great powers of genius and is a master of style and language, he seems not to pay equal attention to the office of an historian. His facts are coldly and carelessly stated. They neither inform the reader nor interest him. Many of them are erroneous, and most of them are defective and obscure." *Letter to the Abbé Raynal* (1782), II, 221–22.

39 *The Writings of Quesnay, Turgot, and the friends of these authors* established the physiocratic school of political economy. François Quesnay (1694–1774) founded the school through his contributions to the *Encyclopédie,* and Baron de l'Aulne Turgot (1727–1781) first applied its theories in the years that he held high office under Louis XV and Louis XVI. The physiocrats assumed that natural laws govern social relations as well as the physical universe and that government should interfere as little as possible with their operation. In this, their assumptions paralleled those English economists who followed Adam Smith. Unlike their companions across the Channel, however, the physiocrats maintained that land is the ultimate source of all wealth and that production, especially agriculture, rather than commerce, was the foundation of national prosperity. Both Paine and Jefferson were strongly

influenced by the physiocrats. See Paine's *Agrarian Justice* (1796), I, 605–23, and Jefferson's *Notes on Virginia.*

40 *Count Vergennes* was Louis XVI's Minister of Foreign Affairs from 1774 until 1787. Because of his nostility toward England, he supported the American colonies in their struggle, at first secretly but after the treaty of commerce and alliance, openly and effectively. In 1783 he represented France in the Treaty of Versailles which brought the war to an end.

41 *Dr. Franklin* was, of course, Benjamin Franklin, who was better known and more highly regarded abroad than any other American of his time. He had been sent to France by the second Continental Congress to enlist French support for the American Revolution, and he succeeded brilliantly. During an earlier mission to England before war broke out, he had befriended young Paine and, learning that he planned to emigrate to America, gave him a warm and gracious letter of introduction which opened doors which might otherwise have remained shut. Until his death in 1790, Franklin continued to take a kindly and helpful interest in promoting Paine's career.

42 *The then Marquis of Lafayette* (1757–1834) no longer enjoyed the great popularity which greeted him on his return from America in 1781. Although elected to the National Assembly and placed in charge of the National Guard, he gradually fell from favor for his opposition to the Jacobin party and his continued support of the royal family. Nevertheless, when war broke out with Austria in 1792, he was recalled and placed in command of the eastern army. After an abortive invasion of Belgium, then held by Austria, he fled the country rather than answer charges of conspiring against the Revolution. In the meantime Paine had dedicated Part II of *The Rights of Man* to him, but when it appeared in French translation Paine's "dedicatory epistle" had been suppressed with the following grim warning:

> The French can no longer endure dedicatory epistles. A man should write privately to those he esteems: when he publishes a book his thoughts should be offered to the public alone. Paine, that uncorrupted friend of freedom, believed too in the sincerity of Lafayette. So easy is it to deceive men of single-minded purpose! Bred at a distance from courts, that austere American does not seem any more on his guard against the artful ways and speech of courtiers than some Frenchmen who resemble him. (French Translator's Preface, Part II, *The Rights of Man.*) I, 347.

43 *the Augean stable . . . too abominably filthy to be cleansed.* The fifth labor of Hercules was to clean stables in which Augeas had kept thousands of cattle for years without cleaning. This he did by diverting a river and making it flow through the stables.

44 *"Ten years ago," says* [Burke], *"I could have felicitated France on her*

having a government. . . ." Here Burke has been misquoted to say very nearly the reverse of what he clearly intended. What he actually said was this: "Abstractly speaking, government, as well as liberty, is good; yet could I, in common sense, ten years ago, have felicitated France on her enjoyment of a government (for she then had a government) without inquiry what the nature of that government was, or how it was administered?" *Reflections,* p. 8.

45 *"Othello's occupation's gone!"* Othello was a professional soldier, one of the condottieri who sold their services to princes in Italy during the fourteenth and fifteenth centuries. Here Paine is suggesting that with the end of aristocracy there would be no need for professional soldiers and their mercenary troops.

46 *When the French Revolution is compared with that of other countries.* . . . As of the date Paine had finished writing *The Rights of Man,* (February 9, 1792), relatively little blood had been shed. The September, 1792, massacre of political prisoners in Paris had not yet occurred, and the Jacobin Reign of Terror was not to begin until still another year had passed.

47 *The affair of 1745* grew out of the attempt of Bonnie Prince Charles, the Young Pretender, to regain the English throne lost by his exiled father, James II. Raising his father's standard, he advanced toward England at the head of a Scottish army. After initial victories, his army was crushed at Culloden, and he was forced to flee for his life. The aftermath of that famous battle made a strong impression on Paine. As described in T. G. Smollett's *History of England* (London: J. Rivington and I. Fletcher, 1758–59), XI, 239, the Duke of Cumberland and his English troops committed atrocities against the Scots which warrant Paine's description of their conduct as "long, cold-blooded, unabated revenge." According to Smollett, "All the jails in Great Britain, from the capital northward, were filled with those unfortunate captives; and great numbers of them were crowded together in the holds of ships, where they perished in the most deplorable manner, for want of air and exercise. . . . The castles of Glengary and Lochiel were plundered and burned; every house, hut, or habitation met with the same fate without distinction; and all the cattle and provisions were carried off; the men were either shot upon the mountains, like wild beasts, or put to death, in cold blood, without form of trial; the women, after having seen their husbands and fathers murdered, were subjected to brutal violation, and then turned out naked, with their children, to starve on the barren heaths. One whole family was enclosed in a barn, and consumed to ashes. Those ministers of vengeance were so alert in the execution of their office, that in a few days there was neither house, cottage, man, nor beast to be seen within the compass of fifty miles; all was ruin, silence and desolation." In *Crisis* X Paine used the affair, as Smollett

had described it, to impress upon Americans "a sense of the destruction" which might have befallen them "in case Britain had conquered America." I, 195–96.

48 *Doubting Castle and Giant Despair* were two of the many obstacles which Christian encountered in *Pilgrim's Progress* (1678), John Bunyan's allegory of man's difficult journey to God. It is not surprising that Paine should have read the work, because it was widely considered the lay Bible in his day.

49 The *Count d'Artois* (1757–1836) left France shortly thereafter and spent the next six years organizing an armed coalition among the European monarchs, England included, to invade France and crush the Revolution. After that hope was dashed, he lived in England and Scotland until 1814 when the monarchy was restored in France. In 1824 he succeeded his older brother, Louis XVIII, as King of France. His reign as Charles X was cut short by the Revolution of 1830.

50 Many of the *exiles who . . . fled from France* settled in England, where Burke, as Paine notes, did indeed interest himself in their cause. In 1796 he established a school for their children at Penn, only a mile or two from his home at Beaconsfield.

51 *Temple Bar* was the arched gateway which once separated the old city of London from Westminster. Here the royal family and distinguished visitors were received by the lord-mayor and, as Paine notes, here too the heads of traitors were exhibited as an object lesson. In 1878 the gate was removed and relocated elsewhere in greater London.

52 *The execution of* [Robert François] *Damien(s)*, a one-time soldier and servant who stabbed Louis XV in 1757, was notoriously brutal even for that callous age. Although he steadfastly denied that he had any accomplices or any intention to kill the king, he was subjected to the cruelest tortures before and after his trial which he bore with incredible courage.

53 *The burnings and devastations in London in 1780* were the anti-Catholic riots inspired by Lord George Gordon, the eccentric, if not deranged, son of a noble family, who led an excited mob into the House of Commons to demand the repeal of an act of Parliament which lightened the legal discrimination against Catholics. The mob dispersed for a time only to riot intermittently for a week during which many Catholic chapels and dwellings were destroyed, and Newgate Prison burned and its 2,000 prisoners freed. Some 20,000 troops were called in to quell the insurrection and in the ensuing melee some 300 or 400 lost their lives. Though 25 of the rioters were executed, Gordon himself was released, but seven years later he was sent to prison, where he later died, for having libeled British justice and Marie Antoinette.

Elsewhere in *The Rights of Man* Paine calls him a "madman . . . to whom Newgate is rather a bedlam than a prison."

54 *Every man being presumed innocent till he has been convicted* is now more characteristic of Anglo-American criminal justice than of French. Under the inquisitorial method established through the Napoleonic Criminal Code and widely adopted elsewhere, a person may be detained for extended periods and subjected to an intensive interrogation which may not be cut short by his refusal to incriminate himself. Even in the United States it is doubtful whether the presumption of innocence is at all realistic. In any event, it is constitutionally guaranteed only in Rhode Island.

55 *The Court of St. James* was the court of King George III; *Carlton House* was the London residence of his son, the Prince of Wales, later George IV. Here Paine is alluding to the strained relations between the two men because of the Prince's dissolute habits and questionable associates, who included many of the parliamentary opposition to which Burke belonged.

56 *The burnings in Smithfield* were the 300 men and women burned at the stake as heretics during the last 3 years (1555–1558) of the reign of Bloody Mary Tudor.

57 *The edict of Nantes* was the decree issued by Henry IV of France in 1598 granting the French Protestants, the Huguenots, freedom of conscience and permitting them to worship publicly and to hold public office. Less tolerant kings undermined the edict, however, and Louis XIII revoked it altogether. The result was a mass exodus of some 100,000 of France's most able and energetic citizens to England, Holland, Germany, and the New World.

58 *benefit clubs* were an early form of voluntary social insurance in which members regularly paid small fixed sums into a common fund to insure financial assistance in sickness or old age and to provide for their families in the event of death.